BACKYARD POLITICS

Today's Divide
and a Parenting Style to Bring Us Together

BACKYARD POLITICS

Today's Divide
and a Parenting Style to Bring Us Together

CRAIG B. WIENER

Light Messages
Torchflame Books
Durham, NC

Backyard Politics: Today's Divide and a Parenting Style to Bring Us Together
Craig B. Wiener
drcraigwiener@hotmail.com

Published 2022, by Torchflame Books
an Imprint of Light Messages Publishing
www.lightmessages.com
Durham, NC 27713 USA
SAN: 920-9298

Paperback ISBN: 978-1-61153-454-2
E-book ISBN: 978-1-61153-455-9
Library of Congress Control Number: 2022900270

To my sister Roberta,
Steve, Rosemary, and Hank.
In memory of our long walks
and interesting discussions
about our world

CONTENTS

INTRODUCTION

Within free and self-determining societies, individuals differ in their pattern of locating the sources of problems that coincide with human interactions. This divergence of understanding can create divisions that impede agreement on how to resolve problems between races, classes, sexes, and family members. This book attempts to understand the discrepant notions of fairness, blame, and ways to help people that ripple through society by examining the underlying assumptions, interpretations, and expectations associated with two very different political ideologies.

Throughout history, lively contention, and often animosity, about the means to promote the survival, well-being, and advancement of the population inevitably ensues during most political discussions. People wonder how a fair, humane society might resolve competing interests. How might it deal with the disparate fortunes that are inevitable among variously enabled or challenged individuals or groups? Views of the right way to approach these issues can not only vary drastically, but can take on the character of either moral righteousness, in the eyes of their proponents, or of insidious intent, in the eyes of their opponents.

In light of this animosity, this book identifies positive incentives associated with each of our two most popular political factions. There is a good-faith effort to adopt hermeneutics of trust that these ideologies are attempting to advance the well-being of individuals and groups in ways that they think will be most helpful. It assumes that how individuals construe human suffering and what it takes to succeed, relates to tendencies that develop over a lifetime of personal experiences. In response to those exposures, they develop ideas about what is necessary to improve our human condition.

The chapter focusing on families identifies some of the origins of the interactions that we currently see in the political sphere. It is quite intriguing that the struggles of humanity play out in the family, and in the world at large, in similar ways. My hope is that by changing patterns of socialization within the family, in ways that promote mutuality and self-reliance, we can increase the possibility of harmony for the groups and individuals that would otherwise be at odds. Perhaps this will move us in the direction of keeping our society civil, free, and productive, and better prepare us to be contributing members of society.

This book assesses two broadly different approaches to ameliorating society's discontentment, inequalities, and discord. I call the first perspective the outside → in point of view, which generally locates the cause of society's ills in its prominent external factors: its laws, institutions, traditions, power hierarchies, and in its biases and defects that foster oppression for some and not others. In contrast, the second perspective is the inside → out viewpoint, which aims to fortify individuals through skill development, improvements in self-management, and changes in lifestyle and beliefs, so that behavior leads to increased success within a social fabric that may always be less than perfect.

While there is inherent legitimacy to both perspectives, the adoption of one approach over the other often leads to significantly different judgments, recommendations, and conclusions about how society should function. One approach sees rescuing, compensating, and changing expectations and standards to relieve ailments, while the other focuses on developing individual resources to better contend with currently accepted norms, ideals, and regulations. This group is more likely to show a loyalty to, and respect for, social convention. In contrast, the outside → in group prefers to alter the establishment and all who conform to it, as a way to create relief from the harm that it creates.

The disagreement often reduces to whether it is preferable to create well-being by altering the *outside* vs. constructing success by altering the *inside*. The crucial issue is that sometimes people are powerless victims of what inundates, destructs, and overwhelms.

While at other times, they are agents who could contribute to improvements by changing their responses to better align with accepted values, procedures, criteria for success, and customs.

The ever-occurring quandary is that when we operate in the world, it is usually possible to identify variables that encumber us, as well as discern actions that make it possible for us to cope with, and more effectively master, what others want us to do. Perhaps this is why consensus is so elusive, as both the inside and the outside consistently entwine. Moreover, even if a middle ground is sought, it is often difficult to get a consensus on how much internal vs. external change is preferable, given differing views about the acceptability of the environment and the expectations for individuals to accommodate.

Complicating matters further, it is not always possible to derive a compromise. Participants might assert beliefs, values, and policies that are mutually exclusive (e.g., equity vs. equality), and ways to establish knowledge claims might not be negotiable. For example, if one camp gives "lived experiences" that are consistent with their political ideology priority, over the scientific method, what compromise is possible for those who disagree? Either you do or you do not accept the axiom of standpoint epistemology.

Moreover, even when compromise is a possibility, there is usually the necessity to make numerous revisions, as conditions will frequently change and make previous agreements obsolete. New social hierarchies will inevitably occur within each social new arrangement, as some people will excel in the adopted framework, while others will fall behind. This will lead to new disputes and rejection of the current social structures. The higher-ups will want to maintain the regime, while those who struggle will likely clamor that those rules, procedures, and requirements are oppressive. They will want to rebel and highlight the need for fortification and *systemic* change.

As soon as one camp asserts that the *system* makes it *impossible* for their constituents to succeed, disputes spring forth. They claim that their brethren have an *inability* to meet expectations. The assertion of incapacity and the obligation to resolve the external problem is at the heart of the political controversies that follow. One side accepts the assertion of environmental blockage and inundating harm, and emphasizes the necessity to *protect* its *victims* from those enormities. In contrast, the other side asserts that promoting *competence* is a viable alternative. This contingent focuses on nurturing progress within the time-tested existing standards.

The debate usually centers around which factors have the greatest saliency in creating the problem despite the difficulties involved when making that determination. Some will identify details that prohibit and immiserate, while others reacting to the same impasse will discern personal mistakes, shortcomings, and possibilities for adaptation. Frequently, there is a lack of consensus on what, or who, should change, and where to assign blame. These matters have been an ongoing dilemma for humanity throughout the centuries.

To the chagrin of many, empirical claims are unlikely to resolve the predicament. While it is possible to find factual underpinning for each point of view in response to particular problems, there is invariably limited acceptance of any finding. The two polarized camps of thought cling to their convictions by cherry-picking, filtering, slanting, or by over-fitting data. Each side believes that particular data have more or less validity in different circumstances, and frequently engage in motivational reasoning or confirmation bias when studying the various problems.

Each side quotes and seeks data supportive of its assertions, while simultaneously offering differing interpretations of facts for studies with findings that run contrary to their political stance. To prevent contradictory findings from gaining credibility, ideologues may denigrate the character of competing researchers to shut down their investigations or claim that they are "science deniers" because they are raising doubt. They might point out flaws in opposing studies, emphasize their limitations, confounding variables, or cite mitigating and extenuating circumstances as a way to minimize unwanted conclusions and recommendations. They might blame the program's limited scope and funding or the failure to enact the policy correctly. A typical example would be that communism did not fail in Cuba; it was just implemented poorly. Heated disputes continue unabated.

Consequently, while there is a general citing of the books, videos, and journal articles that could support one view over the other, seldom does any finding or claim influence a person enough to shift sides; different points of view are often taken with a grain of salt. Rarely are there insurmountable and consistent findings that make it laughable to maintain a particular interpretation of where to assign accountability.

Often, people insist that their viewpoint remains tenable, and they search until they find a modicum of evidence to substantiate their beliefs. Rarely do they give up their presuppositions about humanity, even when presented with empirical findings that are contradictory. The power of emotional stories, ego, and ideology prevail in the realm of politics. Frequently, facts take a secondary role and seem inept in comparison.

If, however, there is acceptance of the two-category schemata proposed in this book, the first contains the outside → inside proponents who operate as *Protectors*. They see clear victims and sources of distress. Suffering persons become casualties, and a Protector's first impulse is to assume incapacity and the necessity for external revisions that can counterbalance outside hindrances. While there might have been some contribution to the problem on the part of the individual or group, this political camp focuses its energy on providing relief. The presumption is that the outside world caused the problem, and the dilemma requires a rectification of external conditions.

In contrast, for the second contingent, called the *Promoters*, the presumption is that people struggle because life is difficult, and it is each individual's responsibility to acclimate. Sufferers are not, by default, helpless or exempt from accountability. While in some instances their contribution to the problem might be nil, their tenuous situation is still addressed in relation to patterns of survival and the trade-offs that ensue over time in relation to their actions. Even if they did not create the dilemma, they can usually help to resolve it. As stated by the thirteenth-century Persian poet Rumi:

"Yesterday I was clever, so I wanted to change the world. Today I am wise, so I am changing myself." And Promoters agree with this perspective.

However, for those focusing on *protectionism*, individuals cannot progress unless changes from the outside occur first. External modification precedes the expectation for self-governing. The assertion is that individuals cannot advance because they are impaired by outside forces which limit competency that would otherwise take place. Attempts to promote autonomy are meaningless and lack empathy because it is initially necessary to remove external impediments. Strategies that do not proceed in this manner are heartless, and permit needless anguish.

Despite life's vicissitudes, the key issue is whether individuals focus on wanting others to change, or whether they focus on making personal changes to resolve dilemmas at hand; political alignment will vary in this regard. Not surprisingly, this pattern is also evident in psychotherapy, as some clients are preoccupied with what the world, or other people, do *to them or do not do for them*, which indicates a passive-receptive external locus of control, while others attend primarily to changing their own behavior to effect what happens, which indicates an internal locus.

In brief, this framework is heuristic and predictive of the kinds of conflicts that occur between people, groups, and political parties, and we can augur American political attachment by attending to the inside ↔ outside dynamic. Moreover, while people may sometimes recognize the legitimacy of the opposing viewpoint, and find a compromise, the requirement for definitive action in daily life and in politics will often create polarizations. The necessity to make a decision will often require people to take a categorical stance against the opposing perspective.

CHAPTER ONE

THE DIVERGENCE

In comparing Promoters and Protectors, there are differing presumptions about the locus of problems and the way to help. In other words, to what extent is the person's behavior the source of the problem, in comparison to identifying the problem as emanating from outside sources? Depending on the answer to this question, the individual's political stance will vary, and the endorsed elixir will coincide with a particular chosen party that shares the same emphasis. For example, those highlighting outside factors will typically favor price controls, subsidies, minimum wages, and other ameliorative interventions, while those emphasizing internal changes will favor desensitization to overcome anxiety, enhancement of proficiencies, and entrepreneurship in capitalistic endeavors.

To quickly recap, on the Protector side, problems originate from external factors, not from personal limitations, adaptations, or decisions. Promoters, on the other hand, caution that people are too often reluctant to take responsibility for their own actions, even though it is important to do so. They emphasize that people have a tendency to identify outside causes rather than characterize themselves as careless, skill deficient, or mistaken, and they do not want to reinforce that propensity.

Promoters, therefore, are more likely to question the assertion that people are helpless victims, and more likely to see them as misguided, reluctant, or unwilling. They recognize that it is invariably more difficult to take on the burden of having to alter one's own behavior, than to insist that outside forces are at fault. For this reason, they advise self-monitoring, seizing opportunities for self-development, and analysis of personal misstep instead of claiming mistreatment. Promoters acknowledge that people can be escaping, avoiding, and spiraling into laziness and dependency, and they want to shift the focus to working harder and practicing more.

In response, those camped with the Protectors have a powerful remonstration. It is not that wrong decisions, or a particular way of coping, influences competency; individuals are intimidated, brought to their knees, stifled, or kept from achievements by a slew of factors, including the behavior of their parents, the availability of resources, past exploitations, and the presence of people who control and subvert their possibilities for advancement.

In the Protector interpretation of human suffering, people are unconsciously and incessantly yielding to the systemic lines of authority embedded in their language, values, beliefs, and ways of producing knowledge. It is as if a silent and sometimes explicit bully resides within all societal behavior that intoxicates everyone within its reach. These environmental constraints keep those without authority from success, while protecting the others (Boyce, 2020; Foucault and Rabinow, 2010).

This claim gains credibility, in that the more we know about influential factors or "root causes" that affect people, the more tenable it is to see them as influenced by outside circumstances. Historical mistreatments such as slavery and genocide, which have affected both groups and individuals, are often quite compelling and can push explanations in that direction. Since it is usually possible to ferret out what might disrupt and hinder achievement, thoughtful consideration can usually identify sources of environmental influences. It then becomes unreasonable to back away from that emphasis.

Not surprisingly, academics, defense attorneys, and other professionals who are adept at understanding how the world shapes behaviors are quick to endorse a determinist position with environmental focus and a Protector's ideology. They argue that some individuals can be victims of disabilities, chemical imbalances, diagnoses, child-rearing, broken homes, lower intelligence, exposure to delinquent peer groups, climate, dangerous neighborhoods, misfortunes, traumas, social biases, lack of supportive others, and other harmful society patterns. In their view, to assign problems to a lack of personal responsibility ignores the devastating power of these factors.

The important point is that our political debate seems to occur in relation to distinctions between can't/won't and capable/unable. For example, when accounting for the problem of obesity, Protectors will focus on stress caused by an ugly slew of racism, the high cost of healthy eating, the unavailability of fresh vegetables, and perhaps an outside unearned privilege such as heredity. In contrast, Promoters stress the lack of discipline and self-restraint.

Here lies the essential difference between the two polarized views that dominate the polity of our time. Both ways of understanding problems and patterns of interventions have merit in some contexts and situations. Neither is intrinsically better or worse all the time. Clearly, there are occasions when people are powerless victims, and certainly people can benefit from learning and skill development. Often, the problem is discerning the point at which the expectation of personal contribution is reasonable. This seems equivalent to asking, Is the harm from *without* greater than the resources *within?*

When situations are urgent, this assessment is quite easy. For example, when a person is about to drown, it is ludicrous to nurture self-reliance in conjunction with the rescuing. Concerns about secondary or unintended consequences of facilitating a rescue fall by the wayside. In contrast, parents are less likely to advocate doing children's homework for them. In these situations, parents will typically provide a smidgen of help to see if it enables the child to improve. If it does not help, then a different tutoring attempt might occur. However, the object of the intervention is to facilitate the child's skill to complete the work to the teacher's standards, with more independence.

It is interesting to note that the same kind of dilemma occurs at the beginning of life. When a human is born, it is helpless and entirely dependent on outside forces. If the environment is too harsh, the individual cannot survive. If nurturance is not forthcoming, death is a certainty. At this point, the Protectors and Promoters inextricably conjoin. There is no divergence; there is no debate. The infant is not an actor on the outside world; the world impinges upon its inchoate mind. If its basic needs are lacking, it will cry in discomfort and helplessly suffer.

Without instrumentality to change its discomfort, it cannot endure; its caterwauling provides the signal for others to provide a remedy. It is not that the infant has obtained the paired association between a cry and the provision of gratification. The crying is bodily discomfort, and when it is diminished, the crying stops. Much like a reflex, there is no goal pursuit or intention. From the baby's perspective, the relief by others is pure serendipity, and with the next discomfort, the crying recurs.

However, over time, there is a liminal moment when a connection takes place. There becomes a link between behavior and consequence. Repetitious co-occurrences provide the groundwork for learning. Particular behaviors emit under analogous conditions, and certain outcomes occur in higher rates. It is at this point that we say a person is *doing* something, rather than *having* a state such as hunger, pain, or pleasure.

The distinction between unlearned responses (i.e., the crying infant), and having the resources to effect preferred outcomes (i.e., the young child) is at the cusp of where political debate diverges with alacrity. For Promoters, even a prisoner of war can introduce some kind of adaptation despite the fact that the environment is amoral and indefensible (Frankl, et. al, 2015).

In contrast, Protectors believe that some groups of individuals are frequently in a state requiring outside remediation. Similar to the infant, they believe certain societal members lack the agency to bring about particular favored outcomes. These individuals will remain trapped in a catatonic-like state; there is total reliance on outside forces to provide salvation. Promoters, however, are less quick to enable and shield. They wonder if the interventions themselves might be reinforcing the catatonia and impeding the possibility of thriving in an environment that is not as nefarious as Protectors presuppose.

Interestingly enough, the American Economist Thomas Sowell (2007) describes an analogous two-category system in the political realm where each view purports to advance the human condition in a way that is discrepant from the other. The first of these is the "unconstrained vision," which understands human suffering as incident to societal harms and disparities of treatment. Through the capabilities of surrogate decision-makers, this vision expects a freeing of repressed talents and inner goodness, as these gifted experts can create circumstances that are more equitable and just.

He contrasts that perspective with the view that humans will always be imperfect and struggle in a world that has no absolute solutions. This "constrained vision" does not anticipate that any person, or group of people, can derive a utopia. Instead, *individuals* can improve by making adjustments to cope with the unique conditions they face. Through personal incentive and trial and error, they can adapt and survive together within a non-preferential system of rules and processes. Without an excogitated theoretical blueprint, it is possible for the social group to flourish, as people will naturally achieve and cooperate with each other when it is in their self-interest do so.

In an attempt to incorporate Sowell's category system into this current framework, the "unconstrained vision" transforms into *protecting* individuals by invoking third-party initiatives, while the "constrained vision" *promotes* them by facilitating their discretionary authority and learning exposures. Society, in the first view, depends on the expert wisdom of *outside* decision-makers, while in the latter view, it relies on amassing the *inside* decision-making of many individuals.

The template of the Protector/Promoter category system can also be superimposed on the two-category party system in the United States. For example, the Democratic website emphasizes closing the racial gaps in income and wealth, guaranteeing the right to join or form a union, raising wages, ensuring equal pay for women, paid family leave for all, and safeguarding a secure and dignified retirement (Preamble, 2020). These party members also fear White Nationalism, gun violence, systemic racism, and lack of health care (Kruta, 2021)—all topics that emphasize the need for *protection*. In contrast, the Republican Party website emphasizes valuing "the traditions of family, life, religious liberty, and hard work" (Support the GOP's Principles for American Renewal, 2020)—factors that highlight the *promotion* of personal discretion and agency.

At this juncture, however, it is worth noting that individuals calling themselves *classical liberals* might be very cautious about identifying with either Protectors or Promoters. While they want to maintain individual freedoms like the Promoters, they are also amenable to changing the status quo in a way that leans toward the Protectors. Similarly, they want non-aggressive people to live their social and sexual lives as they see fit. They are non-religious, pro-choice, and open to governmental programs, much like the current Protectors.

However, *classical liberals* are not enthusiastic about explaining *all* of society's ills by focusing on identity oppressions, which is now a central theme for social justice activists that seem embedded within the Protector camp. While they accept that race and other personal identities *influence* our social experiences, they do not presume that these factors are always seminal. For them, social behavior does not always revolve around aspects of racial ancestry, and they prefer the ethos, "I am a human," over "I am an identity."

Moreover, they dread the potential of an all-encompassing equity-driven government that controls societal outcomes, which is increasingly enveloping Protector ideology. In their view, a "liberal" and "free" society is the best way to advance the vulnerable in their social milieu. For them, *Liberalism* permits *everyone* to voice concerns and objections. It allows the possibility to change one's beliefs, and it presents a way to determine falsehoods. For these reasons, *classical liberals* have no true home in today's American politics.

Interestingly, the preeminent economist Milton Friedman (1982) claims that the word "liberal" is used differently now, as compared to its past meaning. In his view, traditional liberalism has little to do with the current social justice movement. Yes, they want to *liberally* disintegrate the status quo, but they are not "liberal" in other ways. This is the case, even though many Americans see the social justice advocates within the Democratic Party as liberals.

In fact, some portray the enhanced tribalism of group identity politics as an endeavor to destroy a liberal society, which has always valued the primacy of the individual, the necessity for universal ethical principles, and the importance of free speech (New Discourses, 2020). While liberalism might have emphasized freedom to act in the past, today's social justice liberalism now focuses on the right and freedom to *restrain* and *remove* what offends them. The "new" liberals are essentially boosting some, while blaming and censoring the *harmful* others.

One final note, the outside ↔ inside descriptor utilized in this book does not imply that people will always show a consistent pattern in relation to that dynamic. For example, some people *dependent* in their personal lives might complain that people in general are too reliant on government entitlements. Despite their passive reliance on family and friends, they argue a Promoter point of view for everyone else. Perhaps they show this pattern because they dislike seeing the needy aspects of their own behavior in others. By admonishing dependent behaviors, they shield themselves from criticism.

Moreover, the tendencies of many people might be inconsistent in different situations, with different people, at different points in their lives. They might operate in a dependent and demanding fashion with people who are eager to please them, while indulging others in relationships with different dynamics. For instance, they might be servile when courting a desirable mate, punitive with their children, but extremely doting as a grandparent.

There are a myriad of possibilities when accounting for a particular emphasis on protecting or promoting in different circumstances. Each individual might have a unique history that steers them one way or another at different times, with different problems, with different people, despite a general favoritism for one of the political camps. Moreover, as they learn to understand dilemmas in different ways over the course of their lifetime, their political affinities may change.

The Protector Ideology

For Protectors, the cause of suffering or failure typically resides outside of the individual. They are not against skill building; they are in opposition to making it a necessary concomitant when providing assistance. People need boots before they can pull themselves up by their bootstraps, and they want to first get them the boots. People cannot gain relief by utilizing their own resources to overcome systemic deterrents; solutions must come from abolishing blockades. Only then will individuals naturally flourish to their full potential.

It is interesting to note that luminaries and other individuals attaining success within the established system demonstrate a significant *noblesse oblige* and affinity with protectionism. They often work hard to help, manage, and save others from all of the obstacles and torrents of oppression that society imposes. Despite that these Protectors have attained their status with personal agency, this group believes that changing externals is paramount for those in need. To their credit, perhaps these highly accomplished Protectors feel a moral obligation to use their special stature and influence to support the disadvantaged members of an indifferent and negligent society.

Their allegiance with those who suffer may sometimes relate to pushing back against views thrust upon them in childhood, the necessity to compensate for having personal status that is denied to others, or to the anxiety and guilt that their attainments were undeserved due to their "privilege." However, it could also coincide with a desire to increase moral stature as an altruist, or to an interest in demonstrating their superior intellectual capacity to understand the myriad and subtle criticisms of society. While the empirics are varied, these individuals perpetuate a Protector ideology in the political realm.

Interestingly, a considerable number of these achievers within the Protector camp have also experienced significant hardships and oppressions during their development. They remain sensitive to the plight of those who continue to struggle, and want to help them eradicate what is disrupting them. Often, they have suffered financial hardships, functional or physical problems, or limitations and scarcity of options during their childhoods. They become intent on providing resources to others so that they will not be in a similar powerless situation. While similar affinity toward the needy can occur in relation to later occurring exposures, firsthand childhood experiences can be profound and increase the intensity of these kinds of convictions.

Many of these individuals witnessed the enslavement or mistreatment of one or both parents, and they maintain a desire to keep everyone free from that kind of entrapment. Their experiences of their parent's dysfunctional marriage—which may have included abuse and unreasonable coercions, with limited opportunity to leave—may also spawn a loathing of powerlessness caused by outside forces. They stress the importance of rescuing whoever is low on the power hierarchy.

Consequently, despite their emphasis on independence and skill advancement in their personal lives, these individuals veer sharply toward the Protector camp. Their most pressing concern is to counteract *all* sources of oppression. They become part of the liberation movement, which sees virtually all of human suffering as coming from without. Due to their revulsion of deprived states of being, and disdain for authoritarian constraints emanating from childhood or later in development, they remain empathic with political causes that organize to emancipate as many as possible.

At work, these individuals might be the first to point out administrative flaws and sources of unreasonable behavior enacted by those with power. They maintain the view that authority is creating difficulties similar to what happened previously in their lives, and they do not want to allow those injustices to persist. They use their skills to rescue and protect whoever seems adversely affected by conventional authority.

These individuals may be hesitant to get married, and they are likely to be better prepared for divorce. They might be suspicious, especially when dealing with authority figures who are the same sex as the parent who was overpowering in their childhood family. When these "bosses" (or politicians) become obstructive, they are ready to pounce. Yes, these individuals are competent, but their locus of where societal problems originate reflects an outside→ in orientation.

As you can see, Protectors maintain a tacit presumption of inability to overcome for those with diminished authority, and the necessity to mollify harms that others might see if they only studied the environment with the tenacity that Protectors recommend. If anyone refuses immediate remediation of the suffering, it is equivalent to neglect and abuse. Even if the recipient could make a small change to help mitigate the tribulation, that is not the point of view to advance.

The belief system holds that once we alleviate conditions that hold people back, and accommodate to their preferences and plight, we will finally dissolve inequities. If there are any impingements or limiting factors that impair an individual's opportunity to compete, instant rectification must take place. Only then can we release the individual's true potential. For those with aggrieved status, the world is inordinately oppressive. They become powerless and unable to meet conventional standards.

Protectors invariably balk at the presumption that powerful people can achieve without doing harm to others, or that their advancement will help many people flourish in the long term. They discount the so-called good that owners of capital can offer jobs, or that people without property possession still have the custody of their labor, which they can take with them wherever they go. They point out that people do not always have a place to go, and in these instances, property owners have overwhelming authority.

In their view, owners of resources are inherently oppressors. Their private property gives them "power" over others, and they must be watched and monitored carefully. While the more moderate within this camp might permit the right to hold some possessions, and respect the risks that entrepreneurs take to acquire, maintain, and increase their assets, Protectors are generally wary of capitalistic endeavors. Owners of property can use the advantage of their possessions to control others and to gain more power.

Protectors anticipate equal results, especially between groups, after the removal of the wide variety of oppressions that society creates. While they seem to recognize biological differences between individuals, that consideration has diminished importance. Instead, the view edges toward a "blank-slate" metaphor that sees suffering or lagging as occurring primarily in relation to the differing harms that some identity groups endure more often than others do. If we could demolish those harms, we could approximate true egalitarianism.

Consequently, society's decision-makers must focus their concerns on helping harmed identity groups, even if this means that some people must give up some of their personal well-being. Identifying those who suffer a disadvantage should be at the pinnacle of everyone's concern. People who do not adopt this maxim are morally corrupt and should be excoriated. In some circles, they are not simply mistaken, they are "deplorable" and without a dab of empathy.

Caring for the weak and vulnerable is what it means to be just and civil. Helping the underdog and fostering inclusion in society's available resources distinguishes civilization from the wild. It is our social duty to alleviate and correct what is lacking for those falling behind. Protecting those at a disadvantage is what it means to be human; it is a glorified and virtuous quest. This view requires an honoring of altruism and selflessness for those who have current societal advantage; this will keep people from feeling excluded and exploited from existing structures of power.

Even if *equal results* means endowing some people with the power to hold others back, it is sacred and exemplary to save those who are falling behind. The imagined ideal is that once there is a method that keeps progression even, Camelot is a reachable goal. Few will suffer resentment, envy, deprivation, or malnourishment relative to others after this alchemy creates its effects.

Since there is no equality at the start, Protectors also believe that meritocracy is a sham. We are simply perpetuating the hierarchies that exist when we do not suppress the oppressors. It is unlikely that those at the bottom rungs will succeed; the battle is lost prior to the fight. A race can't be fair if some are starting closer to the finish line. Playing by the same rules will only permit some to flourish, while others struggle, because starting points are not equal.

Moreover, even when enacting a reset, many in this camp believe that there has to be continual adjustments to offset the problem that some people might succeed more than others due to unearned natural talent or luck. A continuous rebalancing must take place to keep the underdogs from falling behind. There must be a constant rebalancing of the scales of justice to maintain the revered equality of outcomes.

Within this mindset, it is important to deconstruct all that came before. The conventions of the past are what formatted the unwanted inequities. With a critical eye, many Protectors work to abolish the culture, previous religions, and history of those in power. Rather than conserve the past and build upon it, a complete deconstruction is a necessity (Gramsci, 2014). Fairness can only spring forth after desecration takes place.

For example, if requiring reliable voter identification obstructs the financially disadvantaged from voting, then that requirement should be removed. Preserving the integrity of the election takes a backseat to protecting their vote. The possibility of helping people meet the requirement to self-identify is pushed aside; *their immediate relief* is the only concern.

Iconoclasm embeds within Protector ideology, and the belief system is implacable for those ascribing to its assertions. They implore others to stop facilitating for those who advance at a faster pace, as it is a moral imperative to limit the strong to prevent their potential to dominate. For Protectors, when there is a powerful enemy, there is a need for maximum protection and extraordinary pushback. This approach seems to be the only way to get others to give up business as usual and accommodate the people who face marginalization within established norms. Someone has to wipe out patterns of behavior that lead to inequity and exclusion, and establishing an almighty governing body is the way to get the ball rolling.

Since Protectors believe that various identities of people at the lower rungs experience victimhood more than others do, there must be a counter maneuver. Even if this means imbuing an authority with ultimate tyrannical power, all oppressive forces against those with victim status have to be ferreted and conquered. Rules restricting people will invariably have to broaden in order to prevent identified skullduggery against the weak. Their goal is to remove all harms, and ironically, many in this flank believe that a *militant bureaucratic force* should be given the authority to make that happen.

For them, it is preferable to elevate a cadre of gifted thinkers who can direct and oversee the social group to compensate for the foibles, irrevocable evils, and limitations of others when they are given the freedom to wreak havoc. These intellectuals will be able to orchestrate a concerto that resolves the injustices of the strong dominating the effete. Somehow, they will know what is best for "the people," and there should be no hesitation to allow these special folks to run the show. Their sanctioned power will supersede those callous individuals who allow and create inequities (Sowell, 1975).

The endorsement of that claim permits ongoing onslaught to extirpate declared oppression and other hardships induced by the dominant culture. All sources of perceived criminality against the fragile should silence; their story is over, and a new one must be told. Since they obtained their power illegitimately through malevolence, inheritance, and unearned privilege or fluke, it is justifiable to take away their ill-gotten bounties by force.

When relieving victimhood is the aim, it does not matter what kind of impact this primary goal has on those who presently hold command. Why permit individuals with power and privilege additional discretionary authority or a means to continue that domination? They have it easy, and can afford to help the needy. If they object to this proclamation, they are too brittle to face the truth.

Like an avalanche, individuals sympathetic with Protector ideology amass into a formidable contingent willing to battle the establishment to bring about desired change. The Protectors marshal numerous sources of power, and they see their fervor to induce change as "progressive," in that it abrogates the jurisdiction of the status quo.

Even if there is no request for help, they are quick to facilitate for those on their victim list. Despite the problem that they might be unwittingly returning us to patterns of civilization where some people (e.g., royalty, clergy, Brahmans, etc.) claim the right to have ascendency over others, they promote this societal arrangement because those who are enlightened by Protector ideology (i.e., the woke) will have the power to remove evil.

While some might worry that this new kettle of power will become the next oppressor, Protectors maintain the hubris that they can insert selfless individuals into authority who will promote rectitude. Yes, they will limit individual freedom, but they are stopping current oppression. Even though (like many people) their actions to vanquish oppressors *appear* to have power, wealth, and revenge as a motive (Murray D., 2020), they temper those concerns by claiming that they will stop retaliating as soon as outcomes equalize.

Only in this way can the society evolve into a benevolent, idyllic place. The brazen morality of those with expert knowledge will be able to conjure a nostrum, which will finally eviscerate social ills. Rather than function to assist society, they will control and uplift society through their powerful insights and fine-tuned calibrations to identify racism, sexism, homophobia, and other identity harms.

In Protector ideology, the elites will work to identify societal impingements, and they will have the *right* to take from others if it can foster improvements in equity. The ideology imbues a ruling class of decision-makers with the power to carry out this plan. The notion of individual competence to adapt and improve through use of personal resources is secondary and can only occur after the removal of standards that impose unwarranted misfortune on some more than others.

People essentially have or do not have privilege. They do not earn success through inner gumption; success befalls them from luck, biology, or identity membership, which leads to unearned gratuities. Even without knowing what will come next, Protectors claim that there is ample justification to wipe out the atrocity of our current state of affairs.

The Promoter Ideology

When operating as a Promoter, the initial action is to inspect whether people have the wherewithal to resolve their dilemma by using their own resources—whether they can construct positive outcomes by changing decisions and amassing new learning. When advocates of this ideology provide assistance, they are building anti-fragility for the recipient systematically, and endorsing behaviors that reduce the requirement for future assistance. The helper works diligently to facilitate the ascendency of effective self-reliance to meet established standards within a rule system that is consistent for everyone.

While those emphasizing external change might continue to find reasons why assistance and outside rectification must continue prior to any expectation of personal agency, a Promoter maintains austerity when giving support. A modicum of help might be provided, but it is rapidly reduced as progress ensues. Aid occurs incrementally, but only enough to avoid languishing, stasis, or regression. They do not want individuals to become dependent on assistance instead of learning to function with less of it.

In their view, relief from others can be counterproductive and unnecessary, especially when remedies impede self-advancement. Even when they recognize the ways in which history shapes behavior, they are intent upon identifying opportunities where options to behave one way or another are available. They do not forget the importance of personal development when offering palliation, and they maintain incentives that motivate achievement.

However, since there is a bias toward developing personal agency, individuals may endure more stress in the short term as they cope with the long haul of self-improvement, in comparison to what they might endure within a Protector approach that emphasizes rescue and immediate relief. Promoters ascribe to the adage, "What doesn't kill you, makes you stronger." Stoicism and self-reliance are prevalent in this view; learning and using reason to overcome is a basic value. While the Protector side errs on the side of safety to guard against momentary suffering, the Promoter mentality errs on the side of taking a chance in the moment for the possibility of a greater future reward.

Promoters encourage people to make adjustments to improve their current and long-term circumstance. They want people to recognize opportunities for adaptation, self-correction, discovery, and invention. They make the world less scary by increasing courage. In this way, individuals develop personal resources, and they increase the likelihood of survival and success, as no environment is completely benign.

They believe that remediation frequently emanates from personal actions. People often have resources to help resolve difficulties, and most often, have something to do with the kinds of experiences they have in life. Rather than sourcing problems externally, the initial focus is identifying endogenous factors that will help to rectify the problem. Instead of harping on what inundates, they focus on what might be reinforcing a person's way to cope and adapt. They do not advise focusing solely on environmental impediments without also considering what a person is doing and what accounts for the *actions* that occur. As stated by Plato, "The man who makes everything that leads to happiness depends upon himself, and not upon other men, has adopted the very best plan for living happily" (BrainyQuote, 2020).

Promoters have some commonality with the group often referred to as conservatives, as they more readily want to retain standards and adapt to them. They also coincide with the group known as classical liberals (and sometimes libertarians), in that they want to *conserve* the *freedoms* of the America Constitution and Bill of Rights. However, while both the Promoters and Protectors are appalled by the racist laws that were evident prior to the civil rights movement, there are many differences between the two camps.

In particular, rather than discard established values, criteria for worth, and ways to determine what is viable and reasonable to believe, they want to preserve and improve upon those accepted ways of promoting survival. They encourage people to have gratitude for what is available, and work hard to reap whatever they can. If individuals "cannot" succeed due to inherent limitations, distress, or historical misfortune, then accommodations are permissible. However, assistance does not mean that individuals receive unearned promotions to even things out.

Promoters emphasize that people facing similar conditions do not end up in the same predicaments. There must be at least *some* personal contribution to what transpires, and they want to respect that possibility. Since these empirics occur, it makes no sense to blame ongoing inequality solely on external factors, and demonize those who succeed. Even if a person's status occurs from happenstance, gifted mental facility, impressive physicality, or ancestral benefit, they do not think that forcefully taking what they have will resolve the problems of those who struggle.

A Promoter claims that it is morally permissible for people to improve their life without feeling guilty, or held back because others are not improving at the same pace. For them, *human rights* are permissions to act, rather than mandated gifts to receive. If people *want* to offer help to others, they have the opportunity to do so. However, their efforts are not designed to catapult someone ahead of others by having them operate under a different set of rules or criteria for promotion.

They acknowledge that you can pull some people forward and hold others back to make outcomes equal, but they wonder why that is a reasonable course of action. They are concerned that preoccupation with equivalence from start to finish is potentially tyrannical and nefarious, in that someone has to coerce "sameness" at all times, at all costs.

Despite the good intentions of the Protectors, Promoters believe that coercive strategies that gift those that are behind, and negate those who are ahead, will not work any better than strategies that prevent the downtrodden from moving forward. For Promoters, the starting point is the axiom "rules for humans" (Pluckrose and Lindsy, 2020). This is the only way to produce a just and noble society over the generations. They believe that liberty for people to advance within this kind of system will lead to greater benefits for *all participants,* in comparison to a system designed and managed to evoke equal outcomes.

In Promoter view, rectifying social hierarchies to promote equity is more likely to do damage rather than good because it can diminish the highest echelons of achievement, and increase animosities and destructive rivalries. Rather than impose the metaphor of "warring tribes," they want to promote an environment of equal laws and processes that evolve as the costs and benefits become apparent over time.

Promoters believe that those on the bottom will progress faster if there are interventions encouraging them ahead, within a shared rule system, rather than introducing helping strategies that could diminish incentives to achieve. They are not denying that inequity occurs; they simply disagree that orchestrating "equal outcomes" is the best and only way to make social improvements. For example, a parent can complete a child's science project in the middle of the night so it is just like the others, but how does this increase the child's motivation to learn and work harder?

Moreover, while removing obstacles that hinder achievement is desirable, equity manipulations that push individuals ahead or hold others back can be a *disservice* to everyone. Yes, the lower performers get immediate relief from their situation, but they are also deprived of the benefits that accrue to them from allowing those in front to role model success, advance their repertoire, and create innovation. This is especially poignant when the society has an urgent need, such as when they await the discovery of a cure for a deadly pandemic, or need to construct a new system of defense against intruders.

Promoters are also emphatic that large sums of money on the top rung do not deprive others from obtaining money. An economy is not a zero-sum game. People can have endless productivity and larger sums of money without putting a cap on what is possible for others (LibertyPen, 2010). While those with fewer resources might feel better when they no longer see opulence that seems unattainable, those emotions do not keep them from achieving. Everyone throughout the world has gotten richer over the decades when individuals have freedoms to achieve, learn from each other, and discover, even if money tends to accumulate at different rates for different people (Sowell, 2012; 2016).

Promoters ask, *Why bring down the achievers?* They have the right to the fruits of their labors, and why dissuade them from working and developing their skills? Moreover, why would anyone work hard and take risks if others are going to take their property and characterize them as pompous and greedy? For that matter, why would anyone work hard when they might obtain a subsidy without the effort? Since achieving is difficult, why give people more reasons to bail out? While decision-makers can "shuffle the shekels," economic floundering seems probable when the goal is *equity*. The outside control is likely to diminish the creation of a society's goods and services.

For these reasons, Promoters work diligently to preserve productivity and personal options. This is what maintains the individual's sovereignty to self-generate. It does not matter whether this is a *right* given by God, or a précis from observations of human flourishing. While they permit the government to arbitrate and protect, they want to maintain the sanctity of autonomous decision-making as much as possible, as that is a necessary condition for resourcefulness, achievement, and survival.

As noted with the example of the child's science project completed by the parent, rectifying the problems without fostering self-development might immediately resolve a hardship, but over time, those interventions are likely to do little good. As soon as the remedy is unavailable, the person is likely to regress to former behavior. Moreover, if the assisted parties demonstrate acceptable competence, then they risk losing the proffered accommodations. Often, that hazard is too overwhelming to face, and skill building diminishes in priority. When individuals receive benefits and remedies from outside sources, self-generated productivity can be threatening rather than advantageous.

Promoters caution that accommodating to failing, and struggling without requiring the simultaneous development of personal autonomy, will likely reinforce more claims of suffering and victimhood. Individuals are *unlikely* to reach the point where they believe that they have received enough from others to recognize that they can make a personal contribution to resolve the problem. This will unfortunately lead to never-ending claims of unfairness, even if other people are not actively causing their problems.

Promoters believe that complaining can be so persuasive that the entire society can be infected with those behaviors. According to Centola (2019), a small contingency of intransient activists can change an entire culture when they reach 25 percent of the population. Likewise, Taleb (2020) points out that groups can "renormalize" a social group by progressively adjusting to the loud voices of inflexible people who clamor for accommodations.

Metaphorically, in their view, the well of grievance is likely to become bottomless. Those protesting the status quo will tend to neglect the pleasures that can accrue from personal development, and accentuate their deprivations instead. Rather than encourage people to look inward to see if personal change is a beneficial alternative, those in need will keep emphasizing the requirement for others to keep sacrificing their preferred status a bit more. There is nothing to reinforce feeling better, as that outcome only lessens the likelihood of more accommodations.

This is reminiscent of what is called "the tragedy of the commons," which means that people will keep seizing an available benefit, even if this to the ultimate detriment of the group. If one person does not grab the resource, then someone else will take it. Eventually, there is nothing left. For example, if businesses obtain bailouts for failed enterprises, then they will enact more risky business decisions. If births to single mothers lead to increased entitlements, then babies out of wedlock will amplify.

For these reasons, Promoters are concerned about a likely competition for societal gratuities. Whoever makes the strongest claims of need and victimhood will get assets funneled in their direction by politicians gaining credence and power from their alignment with each pleading cause. They fear that groups with various declarations of societal oppression, and shared goals of power, will coalesce and galvanize to gain political influence.

Rather than encourage people to work together as a cohesive group, the aggregate of the dispossessed will demand resources and atonements, while those who do not want their resources taken from them will push back. Even though divisiveness is not inherently negative, in that it can lead to higher order unifications, it can introduce problems and potential group destruction if it lingers and devolves into cannibalism.

In any event, while some Protectors insist that the argument for equal outcomes is a "straw man," many in the Promoter camp shake their heads in disbelief; this is exactly what Protectors mean when they assert the importance of "equity." Promoters note that whenever unequal outcomes are found within minority factions, Protectors vehemently protest that power-hungry individuals are *greedily blocking* the marginalized, either unconsciously or overtly, so they can retain their authority. They are invariably the object of scorn and the *cause* of why minorities struggle.

Promoters, however, insist that successful people, in general, are no more or less gluttonous than others, and they wonder about the criteria to determine selfishness. Many are willing to help others, but prior to adjusting a system to make accommodations, they worry about the downstream consequences. They want a thorough assessment of the Protectors' proposals to change society, before deciding that their interventions are the best usage of scarce resources in both the long and short term. They wonder about trade-offs; who might benefit, and who might not. They want to investigate the evidence supporting the recommendations, the cost, and they want to make comparisons to other possible solutions (ZeroFox Given, 2017).

Most importantly, they wonder what kinds of behavioral changes will occur in relation to the recommended rescuing policies that many Protectors advocate. People are not blocks of wood; they will adapt and find ways to cope with a Protector's orchestrations that benefit some, at the expense of others. They do not see the use of authority to *take down* those with resources as an unquestionable advancement that will automatically lead to a better society.

In their view, impositions foisted on some people to ameliorate the difficulties of others is simply a primary consequence, or "leading indicator," but that action might create all kinds of secondary harms and new oppressions that could make matters worse when scrutinized in "Stage Two" (Sowell, 2008). For example, allowing jail release with reduced bail requirements might help individuals with financial limitations, but it could also decrease incentive to appear in court, and increase crime rates.

Even if it appears that funds are available to make the recommended changes, Promoters still want to evaluate the long-term utility of the proposed cures. They might hear name-calling, but their hesitancy to pay up may continue. For them, the primary benefit of diminishing inequities might appeal to many individuals and help elected officials with short-term priorities, but this strategy must be balanced against the subsequent consequences to society as a whole, including whether those receiving the help are gaining skills to produce goods and services to reduce the future requirement for assistance.

As an alternative remedy, many Promoters want assistance to be charitable rather than coerced by a third party. For them, gratitude increases, rather than divisiveness, under non-coercive patterns of give-and-take. They emphasize the importance of socializing people to *want* to help others. They prefer that helping is consistent with the beliefs and values of the giver, rather than have it occur in relation to fear of reprisal from a more powerful legal dictum.

In short, Promoters want to foster benefaction, but they are reluctant to use force in the helping process. They want giving based on individual need rather than group identity, which in their view, is not precise enough to be effective or efficient. And finally, they prefer that assistance is targeted and accurate with minimal risk of enabling dependencies, or other aleatory consequences.

Therefore, while Protectors find it permissible to coerce people to be kind (especially when voluntary kindness seems lacking), Promoters argue that there cannot be kindness if people become hostages to the rule that they *must* be kind. The forceful act is, in and of itself, an act of cruelty. For this reason, they want to *persuade* others to give charitable assistance when help is essential. They want individuals to *initiate* helping behaviors in comparison to *making* them cough up their resources without any say in the matter. They want to nurture generous volitions, and they wonder why individuals objecting to oppression are so quick to coerce those on the other side of the fence.

Incidentally, while some might think that most Promoters will dispassionately allow others to sink or swim without intervention, Promoters believe that this extreme rendition of their character misreads the intent of their political stance. It is not that they want to deny help; empiricism shows that they give frequently to charity (Brooks, 2007). However, they want the people getting the help to show some growth in skill because of the intervention, as they do not want to unwittingly create inertness. They would rather nurture emergent competencies and focus on personal accountability. For example, while they recognize the value of unemployment benefits, they also want to foster a desire to work.

For them, carte blanche passive-receptive assistance is not a recommended strategy. For example, in child-rearing, even if we hold a child's hands while learning to walk, the child must still learn to move each leg in a skillful way in order for success to occur. Benevolence is not enough, despite the possibility that onlookers might accuse the caretaker of not doing enough when observing the child struggling. Rather than reinforce enervation, the caretaker is facilitating the pursuit of proficiency and effectiveness. Promoters want to get the child's legs moving and working better.

At this point, it seems important to distinguish Promoters from the heartless *alt-right,* as some adversaries see an equivalency between the two groups. Perhaps the *Merriam-Webster Dictionary* may help to decide this matter, as that text defines the alt-right as "A right-wing, primarily online political movement or grouping based in the US whose members reject mainstream conservative politics and espouse extremist beliefs and policies typically centered on ideas of White Nationalism." If we adopt this definition, the contrast is clear. The alt-right focuses on the dominance of one racial group over another, while Promoter philosophy upholds *individualism* and legal equalities.

In that sense, Promoter beliefs and the alt-right are completely different animals. Most Promoters are looking to enhance and develop *individuals,* regardless of their intersection of group identities, while the alt-right is looking to stifle and repress those that threaten their *identity power*. Moreover, since the alt-right has no moral authority or political clout in today's post-civil-rights society, it is a red herring. Any Promoter sort espousing those beliefs is likely to be discounted out of the gate.

In light of these claims, it makes little sense to characterize the core of Promoter ideology as clinging to the bigoted system of oppression espoused by the alt-right. Some even assert that John F. Kennedy's views in the 1960's would place him in the mainstream of current conservative ideology (PragerU). While his statement, "Ask not what your country can do for you; ask what you can do for your country," stressed the value of selflessness, it did emphasize the importance of personal contribution. Likewise, he justified his poverty initiatives as a means to reduce dependencies on government services (Sowell, 1995).

Promoters want people to stop seeing them as the "bogeyman." They are simply advocating caution when helping. They are concerned that characterizing political problems as undeniable consequences of culturally imposed victimhood will likely impede the achievement and success of the people they are trying to help, as well as deprive all people of the benefits that accrue from a societal organization that focuses on productivity, freedom of options, discovery, and job opportunity. They believe that the world is a better place with a Steve Jobs and Albert Einstein, and they do not want to block innovations that can help us all.

They fear that a swarming protectionist takeover of society will have far-reaching effects on the populace. As that revolt unfolds, they are concerned that the only way members of the maligned "privileged" groups and businesses will be able to preserve their social standing and economic well-being is to genuflect and take a loyalty oath swearing to honor all assertions of the most extreme

Protector views. They fear that many people will have to signal their "virtue" and moral hegemony as a way to distinguish them from the wretched people who want to conserve a distasteful way of life (Ramaswamy, 2021).

Promoters dread that countless people and businesses will supplicate in this fashion and burnish their reputations by advocating for equity prescriptions. They worry that people will turn away from those who remain quiet and do not separate from the stigma and guilt associated with traditional norms. They worry that people will adopt the belief that they can only be "good" if they oppose a society that is deeply flawed (Steele, 2006).

With great concern, Promoters do not want to go in this direction and immolate a country that they do not define as irredeemable. They anticipate that as the numbers of celebrities, philanthropists, corporate executives, indoctrinated students, and revered pundits and intelligentsia multiply and advance the revolt, there will be more individuals armed to protect and do battle against those wanting to retain conventional standards.

They also anticipate that as the numbers of people wanting special gratuities and entitlements enlarge, there will be even greater clamoring to take resources of other people. They are apprehensive that both battalions of power will proliferate and create a nefarious source of oppression for those in the middle who have sufficient resources, but not an exorbitant amount.

The typical Promoter sees a significant downside to this narrative. As the upper and lower bubbles inflate, the air in the center bubble will squeeze out. They ask, what happens to this middle group? They are not looking for the government to bequeath entitlements that jostle the marketplace, nor are they vying to be part of the centralized sources of power that dole out bureaucratic gifts. They worry that the center bubble will diminish in value and eventually pop.

In this scenario, politicians and bureaucratic officialdom *needing power to do good* will always be entitled to more authority and expansion, as only *they* can solve the problems of the collectives they support. Likewise, those looking for resources will always clamor for more bestowments that only the higher-ups can funnel their way.

The lofty few will retain their status as long as those in need are looking for a savior, and they will always need more money to bolster and justify their supervisory importance to produce desirable effects. For the needy special interest groups, there will always be reasons why funding is a necessity, and more people will jump on board to acquire those offerings. To keep the system afloat, both groups must be in high dudgeon, and they will increase their compensations and power as long as they can avoid legal restrictions.

One final point. Promoters doubt whether life satisfaction will appreciably change in relation to orchestrating the kinds of social justice currently advocated by Protectors. In their view, there might still be significant anguish, even if we reduce identity group sources of resentment, and appease the expression of libidinal desires. They also doubt that money acquisition will matter as much as many people believe, in that levels of happiness might not correlate with income as long as people reach certain minimum threshold.

For Promoters, life for everyone can still be a difficult proposition, as people will always struggle with embedded agony interspersed with moments of pleasure. They believe that the pursuit of equity is an unattainable ideal, and the attempts to facilitate it the way many Protectors are currently advising might create lagging and unintended harms for everyone. While Protectors enact their policies with impunity, Promoters are convinced that those methods could be the end of society as we know it.

Freedom of Speech

A discussion of the problem of freedom of speech is important at this juncture. Concerns related to preserving individual and group survival begin with the issue of free speech. Not surprisingly, freedom of speech is a necessity for those advocating human liberty and a right to existence. Arbitration of differences cannot occur without the license to speak about beliefs, preferences, and values. However, the question remains, is the tolerance of language expression, and the anguish that it might create, worth the benefits that might ensue? If liberty stops when actions harm, who decides harm?

It seems that both political flanks advocate diminishing freedoms of speech at one time or another (i.e., free speech for me, but not for thee). In the recent past, as a way to conserve their way of life, those outside of the Protectors' ideology have attempted to stifle music, dress, sexual behaviors, who to love, advocacy of communism, and criticism of religion. However, concerns about limiting freedoms to express one's preferences and beliefs are currently originating primarily from the Protector group due to their quest to shield the vulnerable and foster a Shangri-La. For example, many Protectors are advocating punishments for failures to use a person's preferred pronouns.

However, present-day proponents of speech freedoms want to maintain the difference between physical violence and emotional distress. In Promoter ideology, speaking words is not equivalent to throwing a punch. People can use the metaphor of being "hurt" by the spoken word, but the *metaphor* should not be lost. They want to distinguish bodily pain from feeling insulted or scorned. Of course, malicious speech—such as falsely claiming a bomb threat, inciting a riot, or making a libelous statement—continue to be non-starters for everyone. But for Promoters, there is tolerance of other forms of speech, as specified in the First Amendment of the United States Constitution.

A Promoter believes the chant, "Sticks and stones can break my bones, but names will never hurt me." Yes, they are willing to be kind and polite and modulate speech according to situation, but they refuse to be *forced* to do so. Moreover, they want to avoid the thorny problem of compelling people to stifle, simply because others complain that they did not like what was said.

This becomes an even greater concern when groups band together and voice the same grievances. It is then that we have mob rule in relation to attitudes, penchants, standards, and societal objectives. The cry of harm becomes a source of power, and free speech proponents do not want to grant permission to this kind of social behavior because it can result in people having to suppress in order to pacify the offended. They wonder who will *not* be offended when prerogative is bestowed to the insulted.

In contrast, those wanting to limit free speech believe that emotional disruption is every bit as devastating and personally destructive as incurring physical pain or damage. In their view, there could be derailment of a person's life if we subject people to insolent verbal behaviors and harassment. They assert that civilized societies should not allow people to intrude and persecute others through verbal means. Much like the problem of defining pornography as, "I know it when I see it," many claim that there are some verbal behaviors that are inappropriate, distasteful, and antithetical to well-being and personal happiness. In their view, concerns about the consequences of diminishing free speech are exaggerated. The intention of their restrictions is reasonable when acknowledging each individual's right to dignity.

Not surprisingly, since Protectors empathize with the victim, they handle the problem of free speech from the perspective of defending individuals that could suffer disruption from perceived verbal onslaughts. Freedom of speech is allowable only when others are not emotionally disrespected. It is important that no one *make* another person feel badly or unsafe. Others must learn caution and become aware of the struggles of adjustment that people confront. They must learn more about respect for others, and adjust to what could be offensive, especially when a person is member of a group with maligned or disadvantaged status. In the Protectors' view, they have suffered enough.

As a way to foster these objectives, they advocate diversity and inclusion trainings. They want people to become knowledgeable about different cultures and identity groups, and understand that variations do not mean inferior status. Since awareness of harming others through verbal channels is a complex and subtle problem, they promote and trust the opinions of individuals who study the problem in depth. By granting these people increased authority, they believe that we can obtain a society that has moral uplifting.

These newly anointed *social justice activists* can inform the purveyors of harshness and subliminal bigotry of their explicit and unconscious verbal sins, and train them to conform to new cultural norms that prohibit those injustices. They alone will decide what can and cannot be tolerated by marginalized people. As long as it is possible for these uniquely informed scholars to *infer* oppression, then there is a forbidding of the behavior.

However, those in opposition to this social movement fear that people will always be at risk to sin. Even with extensive and ongoing indoctrination into the system of inferring racism, sexism, homophobia, and so forth, people will be at risk of offending someone when they speak. To avoid this problem, they might decide to be silent to prevent being the target of calumny. They will dread the tyranny in this arrangement, which can ostracize and cancel a person at the drop of a pin.

While there might be numerous occasions when people agree that certain behaviors are explicitly hateful or truculent, Promoters caution that there are many gray areas, even when people have knowledge about identity group differences. They adopt this view because people, in general, have discrepant histories that may trigger unpredictable reactions to similar stimuli. For example, if a person was sexually molested as a child, seeing a picture of a child molester on the news is likely to evoke a more extreme emotion, as compared to others who do not share that history. Accurately anticipating hyperbolic emotions requires an in-depth understanding of the unique history of each recipient, and that is not always known or apparent to the speaker before words are uttered.

Promoters wonder how anyone can fully control what might be taken as a personal affront to another person. For example, what if the discussion is simply about verifiable facts. Is that discussion off limits because someone does not want to hear the facts? What if the listener is cynically reading into the speaker's motives in a negative fashion? Do we always entertain those inferences? Moreover, why is it always necessary to require the speaker to modulate behavior, when it could be just as reasonable to help listeners desensitize? Couldn't they learn to stop reacting so intensely to what could be minor gaffes or innocent behaviors that are interpreted idiosyncratically?

For these reasons, freedom of speech defenders find virtue in an approach that helps to build resilience rather than cater to fragility—the latter of which is becoming prominent in today's American culture. For them, lack of concordance with social justice activist's *interpretations* of harmful speech does not mean that people are *enacting* their ever-expanding list of harmful oppressions. Simply because justice activists assert wrongdoing, does not make it true, although they operate as if it is incontestable when defending their position.

Those who question these assertions also wonder if the claim of "microaggression" is itself an example of an "unconscious bias." That is, might the accusation that a person is inducing a vortex of harm (when other interpretations might be feasible), be just another instance of imposing unwarranted discomfort upon an innocent person? How often do social justice activists look at the scourge of their own implicit "bias" and imposition of "power" when pointing their fingers at these supposed perpetrators? Are they simply project-ing what they are doing onto others, showing partiality toward those with victim status, and stereotyping everyone else?

A proponent of free speech might illustrate this problem by noting a scenario that finds a Black male having problems with his credit card in a convenience store. In this narrative, a young Caucasian female overhears an interaction at the cash register and offers the advice that the man could call the credit card company to find out what is wrong. Unbeknownst to the female, the man leaves the store wondering if the woman thinks that Black people are stupid. While his interpretation could be accurate, perhaps it is also a reflection of his "implicit bias" pertaining to Caucasians (i.e., Whites think Blacks are inferior). However, what if the female wanted to help, and offered the only solution that she knows? It is conceivable that her intent was merely to facilitate well-being, without the slightest conviction that Blacks are dimwitted. Do we believe that rendition, or his interpretation of the event?

While Protectors will align with the interpretation of the oppressed minority, Promoters might question that tendency. Rather than claim furtive unconscious bias enacted by a White person (who must be racist), Promoters find it reasonable to pursue the possibility that the recipient of this communication is assessing the interaction and making *inferences* about the other individual's motives. It is not that the person *communicated* an insensitive or disrespectful message; it is how the respondent *interpreted* the speech and made suppositions about its meanings.

At times, there can be a wide discrepancy between what the speaker associates with the communication, and what the listener construes and comprehends. In the credit card scenario, we have no idea whether the individual's race had anything to do with the kind of help offered (i.e., she might have given the same advice to a Caucasian). However, due to ethnological considerations between Blacks and Whites, and the presumption that power imbalances should be rectified, Protectors declare that the Black man's views must have precedence. Interpretations by marginalized group members should have priority in "racist" societies, according to that doctrine.

Promoters, in contrast, do not want to subscribe to that edict. For them, while it is easy to obtain a consensus that some speech is vile, often there is significant ambiguity during communication exchanges. It may not always be reasonable to lambaste the speaker when these kinds of problems arise. Subtle misreading of tone might change the meaning of an utterance, and when reporting to others about a communication exchange, those misunderstandings can magnify and proliferate, even though a crime was never committed.

A similar problem occurs when people become self-conscious and think that another person is "staring" at them. While this could be true, it is also possible that these individuals are anxious about their own acceptability and blaming others for their discomfort. As Milton so elegantly stated, "The mind is its own place, and in itself, can make a heaven of hell, a hell of heaven" (John Milton Quotes).

For these kinds of reasons, promoters of free speech believe that censoring speech can lead to serious problems that require thoughtful consideration. If social justice advocates, and many others, can attempt to wield power by utilizing censorship to promote their agenda, then their growing numbers and vociferous complaints can shut out any verbal behavior that interferes with their objectives. They simply have to deem speech as hateful, and it can be stifled. Their requirements for emotional safety and the preservation of their beliefs trump the freedom of others to express their point of view. In some ways, this is reminiscent of what happened in the "witch trials," where disagreeable actions led others to impute evil and gain the justification to incinerate.

Unfortunately, the matter is unlikely settled by imposing permanent criteria, as *acceptable behavior* is not a fixed assessment. It is a reflection of a malleable ever-changing norm that varies within subgroups, with different people, and in different circumstances. For example, sex prior to marriage was taboo in the recent past, but seldom admonished in the present for many subgroups, and rarely do people follow the rules of etiquette and dress that were sacred just a short time ago.

Consequently, while we might change our culture to outlaw particular instances of speech that are deemed harmful by those with enough power to gain ascendency, we are not eliminating power dynamics or uncovering truths. We are simply shifting power to whoever holds beliefs that are granted preference and authority.

For Protectors, since only enlightened social justice activists can thoroughly access embedded identity harms, they have the prerogative to "problematize" the behavior of others. They alone have the unique wherewithal and credentials to accurately search out racism, sexism, homophobia, and xenophobia. They are permitted to deconstruct the traditional and impose their ideology, and they have license to apply particular labels to behaviors they find disconcerting. Through targeted propaganda, they are entitled to enact a great deal of oppression in order to eradicate it.

Promoters, however, are not happy about that solution. They worry about the consequences of outlawing particular acts of speech. They are concerned about who decides the criteria, and what happens if only a select few mandate the criteria. In their view, if we hand over dictatorship to this newly anointed class of harm scholars, we cannot ask questions or oppose them. To do so would supposedly be *proof* of an unwillingness to divest from those who marginalize others with their structure of power that has permitted majority oppression (PragerU, 2021). However, they fear that without the possibility of debate, and the weighing of pros and cons, we simply have a new political faction determining "the system."

Promoters find this solution to be unacceptable. They do not want advocates of speech censorship to have the authority to force people to submit to their views. They fear that if this takeover comes to fruition, it is not that people will comfortably agree; it is that there is no allowance for them to disagree. In that regard, proponents of speech liberty wonder why this is superior to any other social order that purportedly has unreasonable power to control behavior.

The Quest for Power

Contentious political beliefs seem inevitable. The assignment of blame during human interactions is interpretive. Much like a jury decision of guilt or innocence within the confines of the legal instructions given by a judge. The notion of personal responsibility, the assessment of harm, and capacity to act differently can be argued ad infinitum. Even when data seems supportive of one view over the other, people can assign different weights to the variables, and argue about the relevance or importance of including some data and not others. Consensus might be difficult to reach, even when using scientific principles. The problem is often not about the data per se; it is often about the interpretation and usage of data.

Often, individuals marinate in an echo chamber, listening only to people and "experts" aligned with their views, and turning their backs on anyone who disagrees. Likewise, when people from the opposite political group commit misdeeds, the culprit is emboldened in disgrace, pressured to give up social position, and rarely forgiven. In contrast, crimes and misdemeanors perpetuated by members of political affiliates are often overlooked or minimized.

Behaviors that are clearly instances of racial animus when directed at the opposing group, are permissible and tolerated when invoked by cohorts who are imbued with special same-team status. Those falling within the circumambient net of a person's political viewpoint are defended, and justification is found for their actions. This bias protects politicians, teachers, rioters, and movie stars, as each has unmitigated liberty to express themselves when supporting their favored cause. Even when their group leaders and their families become wealthy from possible corruption, their allies overlook those potential sins as long as it constitutes helping them forge an overthrow of the demonized other.

Meanwhile, individuals dissenting from the orthodoxy of their minority group are expunged. They are pejoratively diminished as "inauthentic," in possession of "false consciousness," or looking to gain the favor of those in power (e.g., Uncle Toms). The opposition claims that they have been brainwashed by a system that must be warping their judgment, as they *should* feel oppressed in the social structure that envelopes them. If success occurs for them, it is only because they are complicit with the bigotry of the society, and out of touch with the oppressive factors that befall the essentialism of their racial group (New Discourses, 2021).

In this way, all the failures and hardships of marginalized identities become irrefutable proof that society is corrupt against them. They protect, massage, and coddle the ideology, and with enough investigation, they find a way to establish that outside forces are constantly harming. Since there is legitimacy within their view, in that America allowed legalized racism, people get on board with the belief, which can unfortunately eventuate into a totalitarian political movement cloaked in civil rights advocacy (Sun, 2020).

The perceived iniquity created by the opposing group justifies intense, escalating, and quick retaliation against the enemy in power. Often, those responses are more virulent and heinous than the precipitating actions and traditional patterns that purportedly created the uprising. The belief is that the other side outright deserves it (i.e., they did it to us, so we will do it to them). The goal is to wipe them from the face of the earth, and anything that happens to them is their own fault. Despite the great probability that these responses increase negative stereotypes on both sides, they seem warranted for those who feel beaten down and exploited. In the name of "the cause," it is permissible to use power to overcome power.

Unfortunately, while many ignore, excuse, or justify these behaviors when they are accordant with their objectives, they are still denigrating and labeling outsiders as a hated inferior group without internal individuality or variation. The mission is essentially a repetition of bigotry and authoritarian control, but the asymmetry of logic is pushed aside. At its core, there is *intolerance* for anyone objecting to destroy the "intolerant" who reside within the extant culture (Wolff, et. al, 1970).

While the zealots aligned with the weaker, more vulnerable group attempt to get around this problem by claiming that it is not possible for *people without power to be bigots*, this claim makes little sense to those falling prey to the rebellion. For them, putting many innocent people on the chopping block because of the behavior of some historical affiliates (i.e., guilt by association), or because they disagree with the tenets and resolutions of the opposing camp, is not an advancement of human dignity.

Moreover, they assert that within this prescribed definition of bigotry, groups claiming mistreatment can essentially do whatever they want to combat their enemies. For example, we saw this when the Nazi Party "fought back" with extreme cruelty against Jewish economic success prior to their attaining formal authority in the German Government. However, within this Protector system, at what point do we hold people accountable for their unconscionable acts?

Given these kinds of concerns, the following questions come to mind: Is it better for there to be equality of outcomes so that no one begrudges, even if that effort inhibits some people from achieving? Do we always presume injustice and oppression when we observe varying rates of success, and what does it mean to be fair? Do claims of victimhood and "lived experiences" always have preferential status, and do individuals making these claims give up their rectitude as soon as they gain societal prominence? Do we know for sure that the quixotic theme of equity will lead to less oppression than traditional "liberal" social norms? If help is given, should it be voluntary, and what if concern for others, without legal force, does not resolve the problem? Are some outcome inequalities acceptable? And if so, why some and not others?

CHAPTER TWO

THE POVERTY PROBLEM

Since we live in groups, there is competition for resources and a struggle to establish preferences. We need each other for various fulfillments, but we also produce threats to each other. How might we organize our interactions to maximize the possibility of obtaining what we want, and minimizing what we don't want? To the extent that doing things one-way advances the ends of some, but not others, how do we decide on the rules of the game when those rules might limit the success of some, but not others? What limitations might we impose to prevent harms, and at the same time, not obstruct so that individuals might still retain the freedom of their preferences, and the possibility to advance and survive?

Fairness

Generally, it is enticing to say that it is fair to play a game by the same rules. However, even at this stage of the discussion, there is controversy. For example, when playing a sport with a child, some might contest that it is preferable to change the rules so that the child has some opportunity for success. By proceeding in this fashion, the child might be encouraged to keep playing and not give up in futility. It then becomes a misnomer to claim *equal opportunity;* the child does not have the same ability to operate within the rules for success to occur. In fact, the child's situation is not comparable at all to those with more advanced skills.

Protectors emphasize this problem and find it essential to compensate those who lag behind. They become adamant about this when helping marginalized groups, as they believe that other people have caused their performance difficulties (Rawls, 1999). They remind us that this procedure occurs throughout society, as we often provide individuals with a handicap to manufacture a competitive game. With ongoing intervention, the playing field can be kept level, and everyone will be able to experience equanimity.

For those who question this approach, leveling the playing field might produce some initial relief to those who might otherwise fail, but Promoters prefer competitions that allow merit to be unleashed without a harness as a general procedure. People might then have the incentive to become virtuosos. After all, if success is guaranteed, why would people work hard to overcome defeat? If fairness means always staying even, why would anyone want to participate in a predetermined competitive activity (Free To Choose Network, 2015).

Consequently, Promoters want qualifying criteria to be consistent for all people, and they know that people will only get involved in activities when there is a relationship between skill and success. They prefer this mindset, even though many Protectors consider the requirement to adapt to a dominant rule-based system as an instance of oppression and bigotry. Promoters, however, wonder why people would want to become proficient if their success is discounted.

For these reasons, Promoters advise keeping the rules of the game consistent. They have no guilt observing varying degrees of achievement across people. They know that unless someone fixes a game to promote a particular outcome, there will always be winners and losers in all games, as people have different talents, skills, and motivations. For them, manipulating outcomes, where some benefit at the expense of others, is a worse option than letting a game proceed under consistent rules. They are not bothered by variations that occur at the starting or the finishing line; it only matters that individuals deal with the world within the same parameters and constraints, and demonstrate individual growth in whatever way they can.

As you can see, one side focuses on preventing failure, while the other recognizes the benefits of success. Protectors prefers trophy for everyone to promote equity, while Promoters see the advantages that accrue from allowing winning and excellence to come to the fore. Protectors blame problems on the adoption of particular rules that favor some over others, while the Promoters argue that giving advantages to people who lag, by handcuffing those who do not, is also a form of favoritism. It is simply a matter of changing where the handcuffs attach. For them, two wrongs don't make a right, and the repackaging does not make an improvement.

So what does this have to do with poverty? While there is consensus that some people have biological and environmental advantages that are conducive to monetary success, Promoters argue that it makes little sense to coercively divest them of their prosperity because others have needs and a dearth of what it takes to accumulate wealth. In their view, rather than redistribute resources through legal governmental force, which may increase the expectation for the beneficiaries to *receive*, they want to promote wealth creation by maintaining each individual's incentive to *achieve*.

They also argue that depending on circumstances, society as a whole might benefit from funneling resources in different directions at different times. For example, when there is prosperity, it is easier and reasonable to put more resources into advancing the bottom rungs. While in times of crisis (e.g., a war, pandemic, etc.), it might be better for everyone in the group to channel resources into discovery and innovation that only highly trained people can perform.

Promoters also question the presumption that the poverty is invariably due to harms caused by dominant groups. While this is sometimes the case, they see this as an empirical matter that should be investigated. If they find episodic unjustified harm directed toward the innocent, they want it to stop. However, they want facts to substantiate the charges; it is not a matter of declaring its presence a priori simply because people are complaining. While unreasonable treatment occurs, it does not mean that all unwanted outcomes are always attributable to that factor alone, all the time.

Moreover, Promoters wonder why people who dislike subjugation would want to dismantle a society that is predicated on promoting *freedom over coercion* for all citizens. In their view, if we accept the claim that it is inevitable that people are always indoctrinated into cultural rule systems that impose restrictions of some sort, why not adopt the least coercive type.

Crenshaw's (2019) proposal to reorganize society illustrates this problem quite well. She argues to assess people in relation to their "intersectionality" of marginalized traits, and proposes a novel social power grid that gives socially harmed people priority and more credibility so that others will accommodate to their preferences. She identifies traits associated with vulnerability and harm, and people with more of these traits are granted increased power and authority because life has been more unfair to them (and their ancestors), as compared to others.

However, the following questions seem relevant at this point. Are Protectors who want to deconstruct society in this fashion, offering a power structure that is less confining, or oppressive? Are their efforts to disable those with prominent achievement going to lead to fairer society? Or will those interventions simply enable a different agenda to gain ascendency, which allows new groups of identities to oppress those who had previously been successful?

For Promoters, rather than eliminate social hierarchies, the reorganization is simply giving new identity groups social authority to advance their preferences without making it clear how this will be fairer or less oppressive. It also goes unnoticed that the method tacitly uses estimates of group averages to determine how much credit or debit people receive for each identity trait. This can be problematic, in that the standard deviations of harm incurred for any specific trait may be inordinately large. For example, even with numerous marginalized traits, an individual might incur severe oppression, or none at all, depending on particular life experiences.

So how might we decide whether Crenshaw's proposal is reasonable or fair? If some Protectors believe that asking for dispositive evidence is itself an act of bigotry (i.e., using science to oppress), how can respondents ascertain the value of her thesis? If we do not "agree" to use the scientific method, what alternative will help us decide what to believe? And in what way will that substitute be an improvement? If what breeds success in a society (e.g., expanded time horizon, scholarship, punctuality, etc.) is unfair to groups who do not as frequently enact those behaviors (Davidson, 2020), what behaviors do we value instead, and who decides? In short, why take stock in one power structure over another?

Group Victimizations and Government Solutions

There is an important difference between social science and mathematics, and the study of natural elements. In social science, we do *not have identity of category.* For both mathematics and chemistry, all numbers and chemicals will always retain their basic properties. We can rely on this fact and know that each number or chemical will relate to other numbers and chemicals in the exact same way, at all times.

However, in social science, we can study the poor, males, females, immigrants, video game players, depressives, and the disabled, but individuals within each category may differ, despite the one characteristic that places them in a particular group. They might respond differently to situations, and interventions to influence the aggregate may have different effects on the various members within the category.

In relation to poverty, we can parse individuals into a specific category, such as "people with low income," although the various individuals within the collective may have many characteristics and histories that are not shared. Given this intragroup variability, there might be many different reasons that account for group membership. In contrast, all differences between copper and iron are attributable to the *singular* fact that they are different elements.

Due to the occurrence of intragroup variability, there can be significant problems with false negatives and false positives when making general statements about the characteristics of designated groups. There remains an error rate. Some people belonging to the group may not show the characteristics that generally apply to the group. While some people *not* in the group may blatantly display many of the same behaviors associated with the comparison group.

With that in mind, Protectors and Promoters diverge regarding how they handle the problem of group differences when addressing the problem of poverty. Protectors typically reduce analysis to the level of group affiliation; all individuals in the category unify much like the pattern of assuming that all number fives are the same. Members comprising the group become objects acted upon by outside sources, and there is overlooking of differing histories, talents, and preferences of the different people in the group.

While the "margins" of the groups can reduce for specific analysis when it might be advantageous to promote a particular argument, differences within the group are airbrushed. When Protectors use this approach to address poverty, all individuals lacking money incur an "essential" identity. It is presumed that enough people in the group will benefit sufficiently to make the intervention worthwhile, and thus render the problem of intragroup variability inconsequential.

This way of conceptualizing the problem is not surprising. Protectors want to advance the status of a struggling collective, with as much authority as possible. Regardless of differences within the faction, remediation can then focus solely on group advancement, without concern about the lesser important within-group differences. They can identify a blanket harm that is disintegrating the group's well-being, and marshal the entire group for maximum push back. With a bigger barrel, more resources can be mobilized to rectify problems. Help usually occurs faster, even if some individuals in the group barely need, or might not benefit in meaningful ways, from the prescribed interventions. For example, a program might give sums of money to prevent homelessness, but individuals on drugs might not use the money for that purpose.

For Protectors, actions and decisions made by individuals have little to no bearing on the problem. Since *outside* forces are the cause of poverty, changing outside variables are the only considerations. While some group members might not know it, they still could benefit from the prescribed interventions. Everyone within the category is welcome to jump on board and take advantage of what is offered.

As in all collectivist ideologies, detailed parsing of who needs what becomes unwieldy. Potential waste and inefficiencies are pushed to the back burner, and as many people as possible are gathered into the catchment. The incentive is to magnify the numbers that qualify, and assign *blame* to *external* forces, in a quest to provide compensation to all the putative victims.

Moreover, even when acknowledging that individual behavior leads to poverty, including the ways in which people handle and spend money, Protectors explain those behaviors by identifying external factors that induce the troublesome actions more often for people belonging to particular identity groups. As always, it is outside forces that cause the decimation of their behaviors. The belief is that they would have more success if society were different. So by widening the definition of who is poor, without regard to how or why they are poor, Protectors claim more leverage to cry foul and seek societal change.

Since Protectors want to incite social activism to address poverty, they also find it reasonable to conflate economic struggling with the persistence and permanency of identity bigotry. This maneuver mobilizes the power of tribal alliance to promote their political ideal of changing social hierarchies and creating equity. They justify their efforts to push the lower income brackets ahead by harnessing the guilt of those who have adequate resources. They propound the idea that the financially secure obtained their wealth from the crimes of past and ongoing identity sins.

The belief that people with power cause all kinds of suffering for vulnerable people gets injected into the accepted narrative of society by the insistent efforts of the Protector camp. For them, it is the hyper-agency of the dominant-identity group that invariably causes poverty whenever it is observed. Those systemic, clandestine, and ubiquitous biases attack those who do not belong to the dominant power group, and this invariably impedes their financial advancement.

In opposition, Promoters are more likely to maintain the sanctity of individual differences, even when making statements about poverty. They remain preoccupied with finding explanations that are increasingly precise. They are not satisfied with the imprecision of group designation. They work to identify subcategories within a group that better explain the outcomes of the larger, more encompassing collective. Since it is always possible to find increasingly smaller subcategories, their task is neither quick nor easy, but they want remediation to demonstrate usefulness with minimum waste.

For that reason alone, they are more likely to study individuals, and limit the study of groups. This might help to explain why the Protectors make statements about *group identity* and associated group problems, while Promoters remain preoccupied with the sui generis nature of individuals. They focus on the distinctiveness of each person, and the particular behaviors each individual *enacts* that corresponds with the adverse outcomes under scrutiny.

For Promoters, it is worthwhile to intervene with utmost precision despite the increased problem that this approach will be cumbersome. They note that in-depth analyses will typically nullify dominant culture bigotry as the cause of economic disparities between groups (Bloggingheads.tv, 2020). They present accounts that relate to particular behaviors, and decisions that occur more frequently within certain groups, and they note that people in dominant groups are poor when they behave in similar ways to minority group members who are also poor.

They remain steadfast that relegating people to nebulous identity groups with diverse patterns of behavior, and blaming all problems on dominant culture bigotry to determine who will receive assistance, is a deficient and ineffective way to resolve resource deficiencies. To reinforce this view, they cite a recent government report on race and ethnic disparities that *did not find* "institutional racism" in relation to policing and crime, employment, health, or education (Triggermometry, 2021).

They understand that past societal injustices and present circumstances exert influences on current behaviors, but they want to unravel the unique histories of each individual, with the hope of reinforcing alternative responses in the situations that each individual encounters. They want to help individuals *learn* to do behaviors that increase their probability of succeeding. If there are unyielding barriers for "types" of people, they acknowledge the importance of addressing those concerns.

Promoters also want to avoid the imperative that affluent people *must* give up what they have, because in reality, they did not really *earn* anything. That is, the belief that people only have, or do not have, *privilege* (i.e., lucky genes, lucky environment, bigotry, pilfering, etc.), and the collateral view that they should not complain when we take what is *unearned* in order to promote a redistribution. While they recognize that sometimes success occurs in relation to gifted advantages or past injustice, they reject the premise that nothing is earned. They believe that people can still achieve, even if they qualify as privileged, as achievement and privilege are not mutually exclusive.

While Protector beliefs seem aligned with the philosophical perspective called *determinism* (i.e., we operate more like robots that depend solely on input), Promoters do not want to negate the construct that people (particularly, dominant-identity group people) can *earn* an accomplishment. In their view, the concepts of *earning* and *privilege* are useful to distinguish, as this enables us to differentiate between *enacting* behaviors that require working and learning from instances where people *receive* gratuities without effort or action.

The political debate often revolves around the distinction between an achievement and a gift, and it remains important within Promoter ideology, even if there is an existential argument that claims no one truly "earns" anything. Moreover, even within a "determinist" belief system, what justifies *coercively taking* what people have, simply because other people assert that those individuals did not earn it? When indignantly behaving in that manner, the usurping individuals are also taking money without earning it, and Promoters wonder how that represents an improvement.

Promoters are also unwilling to label successful people as just another environmental hazard that *inflicts* poverty. They believe that people can produce achievements without causing harm, and often their acquisitions and accomplishments are beneficial to others. For example, is job creation a harmful act? Are people oppressed when others demonstrate mastery, innovation, and make their discoveries available to others?

Given the possibility that successful people can help others, Promoters believe that the "Robin Hood" solution is unlikely to be the wisest option, both practically and morally. Adam Smith, for example, asserts that a society needs the wealthy in order to have enough surpluses to give to the poor. In his view, the aim is to have an adequate number of people relieving distress through philanthropic endeavors; it is counterproductive to make the rich a villain class (School of Life, 2014). For him, there is a need for excess in order to help those who struggle, as you cannot assist the poor by making everyone poor.

Moreover, bashing the rich can be problematic in many ways. For example, reducing the tax rate on the wealthy has actually resulted in the government bringing in even *more* money on numerous occasions—an outcome that makes more resources available to those in need (Mitchell, 2019). Given that empiricism, it makes sense to tread carefully when bleeding the rich, as running faucets can run dry and make everyone thirsty.

Promoters believe that people, in general, will benefit when businesses make money in a competitive market economy. When that happens, more jobs are created throughout the system, and there are more options for alternative employment. When businesses mushroom, competition for workers leads to increased wages, and everyone inherits improvement in resources and living standards, including greater opportunities for business ownership (Hazlitt, 2014).

In this view, opportunity prevails over entitlement, as the poor often get richer with lesser centralized regulation, which ironically is put in place to rescue and help them by taking money from the wealthy (Sowell, 2011). In fact, on the parameters that are important to Protectors (e.g., income inequality, poverty, unemployment, etc.), outcomes are better across numerous countries when individuals are making more economic decisions, as compared to government-controlled economic dictates (Liberty Pen, 2017).

For Promoters, while it might be reasonable for 90 percent of the people to help 10 percent of people in distress, it is morally different for a group of people to take money from those at the top and give it to those at the bottom as way to orchestrate a particular vision of fairness. In their view, advocating for a minimal standard of living is morally different from requiring a standard of sameness. For that reason, Promoters wonder why the oppressions needed to produce equity are ethically permissible or better than a system of equal rules for everyone (Free To Choose Network, 2016, B1238).

Nature or Nurture

To quickly recap, Protectors emphasize that sums of money grow in relation to privileged experiences that occur while living in the world. Those occurrences create undeserved accumulating advantages for some groups, relative to others. In their view, even when a person shows grit, that quality results from the blessings of outside forces that help the individual's group learn that behavior.

In contrast, minority groups do not have the kismet of favorable occurrences. They experience deprivation, in comparison to the *gifts* of favored environments that befall to majority-identity groups. For Protectors, if we want to induce financial success for all identity groups, we must manipulate society in ways that keep dominant groups from depriving minority groups the opportunity to earn money. This maneuver alone should be sufficient to bring all marginalized identities out of poverty.

However, let us take a closer look at the debate that is at the heart of the seemingly inevitable problem that group poverty hierarchies exist. More specifically, are society's power structures forcing poverty on some groups? And to what extent are some people, or groups, more innately equipped to operate effectively within a particular system, and then able to socialize each other in ways that enhance the behaviors that produce financial success.

The nature-nurture controversy has been with us for a long time. Since "intelligence" (and its numerous meanings) has some relevance in determining success in a vast number of endeavors throughout technically advanced societies, exploring the controversy surrounding this seminal, well-studied trait seems relevant for both Protectors and Promoters. For example, Herrnstein and Murray (1994) cite data showing that genetics play a role in intelligence scoring for individuals, and according to "Spearman's Hypothesis"

(Rushton and Jensen, 2005), there may be genetic influences when observing differences between ancestral groups as well.

These kinds of claims then ignite the question whether innate biological sources have a dampening effect on environmental interventions designed to induce success for activities that depend on high levels of intelligence. Moreover, to the extent that people with similar identity characteristics (including intelligence) mate with each other, various biological and behavioral differences can persist and remain discrete between groups.

Dunkel, et al. (2019), for example, reports that people of Jewish descent, when compared to two other ethnic groups, have higher intelligence that is, in part, due to polygenetic factors. The implication of the study is that within-group breeding leads to between-group differences in genetics and intelligence. While many other factors such as acculturation are at play, biological determinists allude to these kinds of data to undergird the contention that biology is a variable to consider when explaining individual and group variations in intelligence.

Lending more support to this view, advocates of genetic effects also note that identical twins are more alike in intelligence, as compared to typical siblings. They note that adopted children are more similar to their biological relatives than to their adopted relatives, and identical twins reared apart are more alike than siblings reared together. All of these findings implicate inherited biology as a notable source that affects the stratification of human behavior, and that data brings into question the swaying power of environmental causality.

Adding fuel to the fire, with the possibility of studying genetic material directly, geneticists are now identifying specific aspects of DNA that are contributing to the disparities that occur in our cognitive functioning. For example, according to Plomin and Stumm (2018), variance in intelligence scoring is 50 percent due to genetic variations, and the other half due to environmental variations. In their genome-wide meta-analyses, they identify twenty-four genomic loci linked to variations in intelligence scoring. Their data alone identifies 20 percent of the 50 percent of the genetic contribution to intelligence.

Also consistent with the view that intelligence is *not* under complete environmental control, Deary (2014) notes that intelligence scoring shows *stability* over the course of a person's lifetime. Even though future attempts to alter intelligence scoring might show more possibilities for alteration, many lament that the trait is not showing the pliability they hoped to see happen (The Archangle911, 2017). Again, the implication is that factors occurring independently from environmental experiences (i.e., innate contributions) seem to influence intelligence scoring in meaningful ways.

In brief, while many bright people fail, and other factors such as conscientiousness and innumerable environmental variations influence success, the factor of measured intelligence and its possible relationship to genetics retains value for many social scientists. Even though high intelligence is not a prerequisite for many well-paid jobs, many hold the belief that it is a variable to consider when looking at the layering of wage earning in professions where the trait has relevance.

Of course, the caveat is that intelligence will not matter at all if we prevent certain people from having a chance to compete. Genetic researchers pointing to group differences are also quick to point out that group data is merely averages, and say nothing about the individuals within these groups, as many individuals in the lower scoring groups will exceed the scoring of those in the higher groups. They emphasize that studies between ancestral groups say nothing about what social policies to enact, and they do not negate the importance of treating people as unique entities with equal moral worth and possibilities to learn. The studies also do not tell us how to help people, why ancestral groups might show particular characteristics of behavior and biology, or what might happen if we alter their environments.

Despite these tempering comments, Protectors vehemently object to any claim that suggests genetic advantage when discussing ancestral groups. They often confront individuals with accusations of bigotry when showing an interest in this topic. They also cite findings that demonstrate the malleability of intelligence, and they note that there can be significant alterations in intelligence scoring that can occur well into adolescence (Ramsdan, 2012).

With fervor, they insist that we must never forget that some identity groups suffer more environmental harms and deprivations, as compared to other groups. They cite data showing that racial groups scoring well on intelligences tests in some learning environments, will score poorly on the same tests when they are living in destitute circumstances (Hoover Institution, 2015). These kinds of empirics demonstrate that differences in performance between ancestral groups are not rigid or fixed, and that outcomes are highly dependent on the many factors that nurture the assessed skills.

They emphasize that when people make claims about intelligence and ancestral groups, that data only reflects the particular kinds of cognitive proficiencies (and underlying biology) that have developed over large or short spans of time due to differential patterns of living in the world. They note that environmental circumstances over the course of many generations typically influence the kind of incentives, skills, and associated knowledge that are important for individuals to retain and learn. The development of behavior and biology contours in relation to these ongoing and ever-changing requirements.

In this view, intellectual proficiencies, such as attaining knowledge through conjecture and refutation, are likely to develop as those skills become increasingly necessary as part of ongoing life experiences. Even if these changes occur more slowly than many prefer, they evolve consistently for both groups and individuals from one generation to the next, in relation to the requirements of day-to-day life (Flynn, 1984; 1987; 1999; 2009). Environmental proponents anticipate that modernity, improvements in nutrition, and common living circumstances will influence the ways in which ancestral groups perform on intelligence tests, and change underlying biological correlates as well.

They emphasize that current intellectual lagging does not mean that we have to stand ideally by or give up in futility. For example, there are numerous studies showing that increased positive attention from parents, language exchange, and adequate schooling can have a tremendous impact on a child's well-being, cognitive functioning, and later flourishing (Amato and Fowler, 2002; Hoover Institution, 2018). Findings like these remind us that there is an opportunity to influence intellectual adeptness. And usually, the earlier this takes, place the better.

The example of the disorder called phenylketonuria (PKU), illustrates the extreme potency of early environmental intervention. While individuals with PKU will develop mental deficiency when eating in typical ways, if their diets alter to be phenylalanine-free, they develop normatively. In this case, the condition is entirely genetic, yet *completely* resolved by environmental change. Moreover, in that genes turn on and off in relation to environmental exposures (i.e., epigenetic effects), not only do aspects of an individual's molecular biology alter in relation to lifetime experiences, but later generations can be impacted as well.

Environmentalists also note that biological adaptations within the brain can be remarkable, and occur relatively quickly in relation to how a person lives in the world. For example, the brains of cab drivers (Maguire et al., 2000) and musicians (Gaser and Schlaug, 2003) become different due to exercising one part of the brain more extensively than what takes place under usual circumstances.

Studies like these remind us that neuroplasticity exists (Draganski, et. al, 2004), and that living in the world can influence the architecture of the brain in significant ways. While people might drive cabs and play music when they can rapidly learn the required prerequisites, the co-occurrence of their *biology and environment* develops their brains in particular ways, and Protectors appreciate these kinds of findings when battling biological determinists.

Proponents of non-genetic influences also point out that some environments might be better for some genetic constitutions, and worse for others. For example, Simons (2011) notes that individuals with a particular gene segment were the most aggressive in the most adverse social environments, but the least aggressive in the least adverse social environments. Given these kinds of findings, we might not be aware how much change we can create apriori from one person to the next, even with the same genetic starting point.

Applying this to poverty, those who are poor now, might not be poverty-stricken when given an opportunity to have a different upbringing. Namely, learning exposures that might help them build the skills and biological machinery needed for success for particular activities. This argument is important, given the lack of intellectual stimulation some people are experiencing in their current situations.

Even twin studies are not as ironclad as biological determinists claim, as there are many uncontrolled environmental factors (Joseph, 2015). For example, while differences between identical twins are related to environmental exposures, it remains unknown how much of their similarities might also relate to the similarity of their environments. Since identical twins usually grow and develop in environments that are more similar than what occurs with typical siblings, they might also be alike because their environments are closer to being identical, and this includes the fine details of their interactions with others. Again, we do not know how different they might become if we expose them to *substantially* different learning environments.

However, and just as reasonable, a person emphasizing biology might argue that (except for identical twins), genetic starting points are always varied. Those starting points represent thousands of years of biological evolution within the environments of the individual's ancestors. Even though we assume equal motivation and design environments to maximize success for each person (much like what happens in professional sports), we are unlikely to obtain identical outcomes, as some people may continue to excel more often than others do. While there are always many factors in play, it is difficult to exclude innate biology as a variable that influences some of the disparities we observe as people operate in their available milieus.

So what does all of this mean, since it seems as if both the environmentalists and biologists bring something valuable to the table? Surely, development is not predetermined at conception; much can happen as individuals live in the world. Clearly, it is possible that different learning exposures will introduce significant changes in both biology and behavior. Scientists are aware that it makes little sense to think that endogenous components can designate an individual's fate at birth, especially when nothing defective shows in the person's genetic coding. However, and just as reasonable, geneticists can posit that innate factors are influential in the stratification of behavior, especially when environments are not overwhelming destructive or unusual. How might we resolve these differing points of emphasis?

With both perspectives in mind, instead of separating biology and environment, what if there is a blending of the two frameworks? What if we conceptualize the environment and biology as inextricably conjoined? What if both subtle and not subtle changes in one or the other can alter what happens in appreciable ways? What if the dichotomy is like a duet or dance, where outcomes depend on the intertwining of each participant's actions, where small changes might have big effects, and vice versa?

Perhaps the following is reasonable: Since people are not inert lumps of clay, environments will not have the same effect on everyone, and different results will occur, depending on the environments we introduce. While genetic coding is not an unremitting force that dooms a person to a particular fate, there is still the problem that biology exerts influence. However, and despite being limited by the currently available mixtures of environments and biology at our fingertips, we can still continue to find ways to enhance the performance of each person, despite the likelihood that differences will appear as biology and environment foxtrot through life together (i.e., inside ↔ outside).

One final note seems important: High intelligence does not have to be the only way to secure a satisfying and economically stable life. As long as a society maintains and cherishes moral standards and employment possibilities that are attainable for most people across the cognitive spectrum, life can still be a positive experience. Under these conditions, people might still financially succeed, gain respect, and attain interpersonal happiness, with or without advanced cognitive skills. (Herrnstein and Murray, 1994; Saint Vincent College, 2019).

Income Inequality

Protectors argue that poverty-stricken individuals will reject their society if they feel it *prevents* their flourishing, and they believe that income inequality is proof that society oppresses. However, Promoters claim that income inequality, even when moderately extensive, is not a confirmation of tyranny. For them, measures of inequality between income "brackets" are snapshots in time; they do not represent an individual's permanent placement in an unchanging poverty status. Promoters emphasize that studying category groups, or brackets, leads to different inferences and explanations, compared with the information gleaned from studying individuals.

In Promoter ideology, as long as individuals have the freedom to move up and down, which is true in America (Sowell, 2015), the problem is not malignant. While people generally gauge their well-being and personal adequacy in relation to other people, it does not mean they are stuck, or that they are being wronged by those doing better, even though people gravitate to those conclusions.

Consistent with the Promoter assertion to study individuals, often, older people with more work experience are in higher brackets. House sellers, beneficiaries of sporadic capital gains, and a small number of recipients of large inheritances might quickly gain entrance into the highest income quadrants for short periods of time. However, while people might see "the rich" as a stagnant privileged bunch, only 3 percent of millionaires in the United States inherited over a million dollars, according to The National Study of Millionaires (Ramsey Solutions Research, 2019).

Indeed, many of these individuals have spent most of their lives in the lower rungs, and data shows that they are likely to fall from grace very quickly as well. One only has to note that the vast majority of people in the United States in the bottom quadrant do not remain in that sector. Most at the top got there from a dint of hard systematic work, innovation, and years of saving and climbing (Sowell, 2016). For many people, incomes are more often transient rather than permanent.

Additionally, prior to indicting an economy as inhumane, it is important to assess the standard of living for those "below" the poverty threshold, and assess whether economic resources in all quadrants are consistently on the rise. Those measures might differ markedly from one country to another. For example, poverty levels in America might be closer to the middle standard of living, or higher when compared to many other countries, including Russia (Sowell, 2016; Brittle p.13, 2009).

Thus, prior to deconstructing a society and repudiating its way of life, Promoters want Protectors to look at that data. Moreover, they point out that yearly measured income may change rapidly, giving the impression that a person is "poor," when assessed for a particular year. However, that evaluation may not correspond even remotely to the individual's wealth status (Sowell, 2016)

While Protectors assert that income inequality is obscene, in Promoter ideology, *income mobility* is a more reasonable way to look at the opportunities available for individuals within a given economic system. For example, according to the Brookings Institute, only 2 percent of people remain in poverty, and 75 percent join the middle class in the United States, if they graduate from high school, work full time, get married, and then have children after the age of twenty-one (Haskins, 2013).

Given those findings, it seems beneficial for interventions to help people achieve these early life goals, especially if the objective is to facilitate an *equalization of opportunity* in society. That a person's zip code correlates with future income does not negate the possibility that individuals can still make behavior changes like those suggested by the Brookings Institute. This approach may well alter the "neighborhood effects" that currently create obstacles.

However, Protectors point out that this is not easy to do. People must first learn the behaviors that are necessary for there to be the *probability* of graduating high school, delaying marriage, and consistently holding a job. And prior to that, they must learn many other behaviors. This developmental problem can take us back to the beginning of one's life, and this is the primary reason for a Protector's desire to have full control. True *equality of opportunity* can only occur by orchestrating *equity* from birth, onward.

Succinctly put, the probabilities for success will not be equal unless people encounter a beneficial opportunity with exactly the same rates of learning, tastes, talents, motivations, and accomplishments. For example, a college might allow all children in the surrounding impoverished neighborhood to attend their school "free of charge," as long as they can qualify for admission. However, despite this "opportunity," many fail to attend the college because they have not achieved enough to meet the specified criteria. Only the most prepared and interested move forward and obtain the benefits of the "special privilege." The only "equal opportunity" was that money became a nonfactor, and the rules were the same for all students (Free To Choose Network, 2016; B1238). As noted, while Promoters are satisfied with this latter view of fairness, Protectors are not. They want to find ways to equalize the progression of achievements, even if this means slowing some people down.

Despite this difference, if the task is to find a way to help *individuals'* progress so that they can take advantage of the *privileges* that are available, then this entails gauging participants' current level of functioning, and intervening in ways that help them learn. While it is relatively easy to design rules and processes that apply *equally* to all people, it can be difficult to get individuals with unique problems and talents to improve their standing, let alone keep them moving at an equal pace.

Rarely is it possible to equalize each person's learning prowess and earlier achievements so that potentially enhancing situations will have the exact same effects on everyone. The problem of *equality of opportunity* seems complex and multifaceted. The progress emphasized by Promoters, and the equalization emphasized by Protectors, are both difficult goals to achieve. People are not clones of each other, so outside circumstances can never be truly equal from one person to the next.

Yes, we can try to create *equality of opportunity* by continuously attenuating achievements to keep everyone at the exact same level of functioning, but this could significantly impair the vast majority. Moreover, if are limiting the freedoms and learning opportunities of those who could advance, innovate, and discover, will those in poverty be any better off under this new social arrangement? According to Friedman (1982), the answer is no, as poverty will reduce more effectively in relation to making economic pies bigger, rather than changing the size of the slices in the pie (Sowell, 2012).

In sum, while Protectors talk about people not having access to privileges, as if external provisions are all that matters to enhance a person's prospects, it also seems that *giving privileges* may not lead to advancement unless the person also has the necessary wherewithal to utilize the privilege in ways that create progression. Privileges might be provided, but this remedy is unlikely to produce any kind of advancement unless the intervention also considers the competence and response patterns of the individuals they are helping. For this reason, it is important to develop the precursor behaviors that are necessary for available opportunities and privileges to yield the desired results. Otherwise, the donations are unlikely to be useful. This problem is aptly illustrated in the previous example of high school students who could not attend a cost-free college.

Education: The Remedy for Poverty

It is a long-held belief that education is the panacea for poverty. What better way to resolve a lack of capital than to increase a person's resources to contribute in social exchanges, with increased knowledge and skill. Both political camps advocate education and recognize *know-how* as a way to enhance wealth accumulation. However, the viewpoints differ in the ways they prefer to foster that result.

Protectors advocate that K–12 education be squarely in the hands of the federal government. They postulate that families and local governments cannot provide adequate educational services. The more we identify people with skill deficits, delays, and defects, the more assets we must make available to a curative bureaucratic agency, which will use its acumen to provide the appropriate remedial concoctions.

Since those possessing disabilities, enduring oppressions, and experiencing scant resources are the most handicapped, the presumption is that a *protective* overseer will best safeguard their interests. A powerful central authority must covet educational funds and prioritize those funds to the needy. The weak and vulnerable must be protected and advanced within this ideology.

Importantly, the insistence on centralized decision-making leads many Protectors to oppose *school choice*, which enables parents to select a public or private school of their preference (sometimes with the use of vouchers). Teachers' unions also combat this solution, as they do not want to give up their discretionary power and employment protections. Both conjoin as a force to oppose any policy that might diminish their control.

The union pledges votes in exchange for monopoly protection, while the government maintains its authority to orchestrate their point of view. As is often the case, large contingencies (e.g., big tech, social media, unions, etc.) symbiotically jump in bed with legal authorities to propound each other's objectives (Hillsdale College, 2020), and as long as the teachers remain complicit with the government, they reign supreme.

The problem of school choice, however, continues to be hotly contested. Protectors fear that school choice and the establishment of charter schools will likely give more advantage to those who are already winning the competitive race, and leave vulnerable students behind with fewer resources. They worry that charter schools will reject students requiring extra resources, and relegate these students to inferior schools. The voucher system is too similar to a financial market solution, and for Protectors, this is a recipe for allowing the strong to dominate the fragile.

They also have concerns that parents lacking resources will not be able to make wise decisions for their children. Without overriding advisement, this could perpetuate the inequities of the status quo. By keeping decision-making sequestered within a comprehensive governmental agency that can monitor the vulnerable and uninformed, they can foster a reorganization of the unjust school system which occurs when there is inadequate oversight.

Moreover, for Protectors, keeping education under the auspices of a powerful agency gives unmatched discretionary control over shaping values, beliefs, and knowledge. By preventing the siphoning of students away from central control, they can maintain better surveillance of discipline, attitudes, curriculum content, teacher behavior, and threats to equity. The entrenched bureaucracies, like most officialdom, will then have the power to construct a system that is stable and comprehensive, and they cite numerous studies that question the efficacy of "school choice" programs as a way to justify their actions (Charter Schools, 2020).

In contrast, Promoters argue to restore the authority of parents to make decisions about their children's education. They want to subsidize the consumers of education, not the producers, and they see the *family* (not an appointed agency) as the cornerstone of society. They believe in parents' ability to guide and protect, and see parental ineptitude as the exception rather than the rule. Promoters believe that parents are in the best position to advocate for their child. They are most likely to identify the child needs and find a match for their values and preferences. If they have difficulty making decisions, they can voluntarily access available consultation.

While Protectors are concerned that parents will not adequately handle the responsibility of school choice, Promoters claim that they are likely to do better than our current system of denying them a choice, as standardized scores are plummeting, especially for those in poverty (Sowell, 2018). Moreover, in response to studies that question the efficacy of charter schools, Promoters emphasize that those studies do not typically compare similar student populations. They note that charter schools generally educate students from minority groups with lower achievement and limited financial resources. In their view, it is important to find out how these kinds of students perform in both traditional and charter schools when assessing effectiveness (Sowell, 2020).

In Promoter ideology, when schools can free themselves from the counterproductive teacher union rules, and have more control over the firing and hiring process, pedagogical improvements and learning enhancements will ensue. Public schools can remain in business, but they will have to compete with other schools instead of having a monopoly over families without the resources to attend non-assigned schools.

While middle-class families have always had the resources to pick a school for their child, the utilization of public funds for "school choice" allows *all* families the freedom to select a school destination. They are not siphoning money away from public school students; taxpayer money simply follows the child. Promoters point out that this is a reasonable and productive way to equalize opportunity across a society.

By increasing the number of educational options, there is added opportunity to better match students with curriculum and school milieu. Students with extra needs can receive adjusted resource allocation, just like what occurs in the traditional system, and a market economy will develop.

Handing "school choice" to the parent means that schools must *compete* for student enrollment. Rather than assume the outflow of students, public schools can adapt to retain students by finding a way to keep up. This encourages all schools to improve services and specialize in ways that attract students with differing requirements and preferences.

In this "free choice" system, Promoters want parents to have access to *data-driven* assessments to determine which schools improve learning for particular children. Through the examination of *outcome* data, parents can make informed decisions about the schools to attend, and those to avoid. Schools not producing good results will attract fewer students, and many will have to close or improve, just like what occurs within any market economy. Moreover, and as a way to enhance their viability, Promoters also believe that *taxpayers* should have a say in the use of vacant spaces in school buildings, rather than allow the frequent practice of allowing public school officials and government bureaucrats to control these spaces to stifle competition (Sowell, 2020).

While outcomes need an ongoing randomized assessment where every child has the opportunity to pick a matched school, there is already supportive data for charter schools, especially in urban areas. For example, according to The National Charter School Resource Center (2015), low-income minority students with low achievement showed advantages across five studies in their math and reading scores, compared to their "unlucky lottery" counterparts. Moreover, in a New York City study, charter school students housed in the same buildings as traditionally educated students outperformed those children to a greater magnitude than the achievement differences between Whites and Blacks (Sowell, 2020).

While benefits might differ from one selected school to the next, "school choice" remains a viable option for those who want a freer market in education, and many minority families advocate for more educational options. They emphasize the need for this alternative in the inner cities, despite the fact that minority group leaders have played politics and not endorsed this approach (Academy of Achievement, 2017). Promoters insist that students of marginalized families require good education without regard to the ethnic makeup of the class. They point out that bureaucrats typically send their children to private schools, and they claim that all social strata should be able to do the same.

Another benefit of school alternatives and competition is that by dispersing educational power and introducing options, if there are educational mistakes, they will be less pervasive and more magnified. That is, if people have only one school option, what happens if that system has unanticipated flaws? Rather than adverse consequences affecting only a subset of the population, there could be harmful effects disrupting the whole society.

For these reasons, Promoters abhor the trend to embed political ideology into common core school curriculums for credentialing and/or governmental funding (e.g., The 1619 Project). They believe that as this movement continues to gain traction, and it imposes restrictions on private schools as well, it will mitigate the benefits of "school choice," and inadvertently create an intellectual straitjacket throughout the nation. If there is a singular interpretation of data and events, and one approach to discipline, conformity with those views will metastasize, and education will become synonymous with brainwashing (Taylor and Bloom, 1988; Mac Donald, 2019; Taylor Gatto, 2017; PragerU, 2021).

Once the indoctrinated venture into journalism, the judicial branch, cinema, academia, private corporations, government bureaucracies, and every form of digital media, they will become the singular voice throughout the nation. As these flames ignite, it will not matter if parents have an opportunity to pick a school; the schools will be alike in the most crucial ways. Since youths are attending school until their late teens or longer, and many are starting school at age three, the academic system will have the authority to "monopolize the mind," and they will be able to enact their mass mandate with little consideration of the long-term consequences seriatim.

Capitalism: Panacea or Poison

Here lies a core difference between the two political views. Promoters believe that people must have the freedom to advance their well-being and learn from their mistakes. They believe that *other* people usually do *not* have the necessary information to make optimal decisions about what people should or should not do to manage their unique affairs.

In contrast, Protectors believe that some people have the acumen to make better economic outcomes occur for society as a whole. These uniquely trained experts can be more effective in shielding people from their shortcomings, and they can rectify situations with more facility when errors occur in the society.

As has been the case quite often, both points of view have merit. Often, people understand the idiosyncratic conditions under which they operate, better than outside observers do. And frequently, third-party decision-makers have insights that could lead to increased fulfillment and success for particular individuals and for groups. This is generally the case with parents and children, and people show differing proficiencies with all kinds of subject matter, which makes consulting experts a reasonable endeavor.

However, when viewing society as a whole, Promoters believe that self-management, when spread throughout the population, will generally outperform a select few, even if they are exceptionally gifted and wise. In their view, when exchanging goods and services in a market economy, people maintain the prerogative to make monetary decisions, set prices, react to success and failure, and choose goods and services; they have *ownership* of their financial decisions. When they perceive benefit, they make voluntary exchanges. As they learn from consequences, their actions and decisions emend. As with the learning of any skill, if they want assistance, it remains a voluntary option.

In this view, the plethora of individually instigated economic decisions will result in a coherent well-oiled machine that can operate more effectively than any individual or group of lionized experts can plan or design. Shortages and surpluses are less likely, as mistakes of planning will not magnify when decision-making spreads amongst many participates with insights into their unique circumstance. Promoters believe that the give-and-take in a market economy can avoid "the knowledge problem" of central planning, in that it draws upon millions of self-interested minds.

The productivity of this kind of consequential knowledge is likely to be more impressive than what takes place with "surrogate decision-makers" (even with computer models). For advocates of a market economy, it is literally impossible for "experts" to account for all the subtleties of each individual's unique situation, so their decision-making is likely to be markedly inaccurate and wasteful (Hayek, 2015). As Friedman points out, we should always direct our efforts toward decreasing government control and spending, which is typically only half as efficient as what occurs with private sector activities (BasicEconomics, 2021).

While politicians often bloviate about giving power to *the people*, Promoters insist that capitalism is the best economic system for that to happen. When individuals manage economic decisions, there is personal choice rather than directives from above, and this promotes ingenuity and creativity, as people only get rich when they find a way to please others who also retain their options and preferences. The wonderful consequence is that society as a whole benefits in the process. Promoters ascribe to the belief that no one values other people's money as well as they value their own, and they anticipate more frugality, more perspicacious decision-making, and ultimately more society wealth when people interact with each other in an economy that retains individual discretionary authority.

For them, the more we displace economic power to centralized bureaucracies and the decision-making of non-elected managers and directors, the less jurisdiction people have over their existence. Passing one's life decisions to someone else is unlikely to be as precise, effective, efficient, or humane, unless there are extenuating circumstances or personal incompetence that requires a displacement of personal freedoms. The key difference is that Protectors identify many more justifying conditions to adopt that tactic, in comparison to Promoters.

Of course, allowing people more discretionary options requires a shared morality and value system, as purloining and swindling would require so much litigation that the format would not be efficient enough to offset a population of charlatans and miscreants. While common decency and trust are important in any society, those virtues are even more essential when a government has limited power to restrict and direct behavior. In a free society, people must exude and reinforce those ideals so that honesty, integrity, and reliability become contagious, as people must be willing to take economic risks with individuals of varying degrees of familiarity.

However, in response, Protectors assert that free enterprise operating unabatedly is a recipe that allows predators to run amok. Similar to a sporting event where rules are equally applied, the burly hulks will be able to trample their opponents. Since success begets success, and vice versa, the only way to protect the hapless is to monitor the accumulation of resources that only some can obtain, and redistribute those possessions to level things off. In that money accumulates at the top due to the nature of a capitalistic economy (Piketty, 2014), monitoring has to keep the extremes from becoming both psychologically and economically cruel.

Protectors emphasize that in any group, there will always be people with limited possibilities, regardless of the system. There has to be a requirement to protect these people, and charity often comes up short. Since they presume that capitalistic interaction is predatory, a protective governing body must assume the task of caring for vulnerable individuals. Promoters might give lip service to a social safety net, but Protectors claim that they spend little time and energy making sure it operates with adequate coverage and mercy.

In contrast, while everyone agrees that there should be a way to care for the needy, Promoters see no problem with the rich getting richer. In their view, if the presence of rich people adversely impacts poverty, why is it that America has many more billionaires than other countries, yet the poverty levels that are very low (Hoover Institutions, 2018)? That data indicates that the poor do not remain poor because other people have money. Everyone can become richer at the same time, even if some go faster.

Promoters also point out that when some people have sufficient funds, they can hire others and give those individuals access to money. Employees can then obtain money without assuming the risks of investment. Entrepreneurs have the opportunity to earn without a salary cap, but they also go out on the limb and lose more. Wage earners might achieve less, but they risk less, and they benefit from having a job invented by someone else.

If the workers are dissatisfied with the terms of employment, they can take their *labor assets* elsewhere. They are not powerless; all parties involved have negotiating power. For example, while a company has a *physical plant*, which leads to monetary capital as long as the owner runs the company well, workers have *labor power*, which also yields monetary capital. The workers might have limited options for employment, but they can shut down production, band together, and insist on better salaries. Power can flow in both directions.

The arrangement is a voluntary contract, and lasts only as long as the involved parties have satisfaction. Each party has comparable incentive to make the relationship work; it can be troublesome to find new economic possibilities for everyone involved. For Promoters, capitalism thrives in an environment of cooperation, not when one person plunders or takes advantage of another. As long as participants have available options, the system operates on mutual benefit. Charity is included in the system to help anyone who needs uplifting, but crafting the entire system to alleviate the most desperate circumstances is essentially designing the entire system for the exception rather than the rule.

However, as a Protector sees it, this scenario makes little sense. When some people have more resources than others do, the wealthier have a perpetual advantage that is unlikely overcome. Some people will keep winning, and some will have only a slight possibility of grasping a livelihood. The winners will generally want to conserve the rules, since they prosper under those regulations. While the losers will typically struggle to change the system, and advocate redistributing inequities to settle the waters.

For Protectors, the idea that people engage in voluntary agreements is comical. Individuals lacking in funds are the unfortunate souls with little bargaining power during the parley to establish wages. Sometimes they must accept the terms of employment, or starve. And since owners have wealth, they have more haggling options. Yes, the employee is better off with a job, but satisfaction in the "voluntary arrangement" seems precariously tilted. Those with weaker standing might remain perpetually mired.

Promoters, however, are not convinced. While they recognize that it is sometimes necessary to introduce a governmental solution due to the shortcomings of volunteerism, they want that kind of solution to be a last-ditch effort to relieve distress. In their view, third-party maneuvers often have many unintended consequences, such as reinforcing people to cloak their earnings or show less interest in making money, as the absence of monetary possession springs forth additional aid and protects against other people taking possessions. While everyone pulling back might feel victorious, it is a false triumph, as the economy is less robust for everyone.

Moreover, for those at the bottom, the reliance on the aid requires them to remain destitute. They must live in perpetuity within the confines of how the society demarcates poverty (Harvey and Conyers, 2016). While climbing the employment ladder might eventually pan out better than relying on fixed government subsidies, they must ignore this possibility. They must instead marry the largess of the government, which can legally divorce them as soon as they succeed. The unfortunate consequence is that they cannot work, save, or have a legally binding relationship. This problem is so extreme that in eight of the most generous states in the United

States, a person would have to earn twenty-five dollars an hour to outperform the social safety net in those locations (PragerU, 2014).

How many people are in a position to risk leaving that arrangement? Unless they have assurance that they can outperform their granted entitlements by working, they will not change their orientation to remain dependent on fixed entitlements. Since people are generally cautious with economic decisions when there is future uncertainty, it is not surprising that people usually take the safer option (Hutchins, 1979; Friedman, 2015).

Of course, remaining on welfare also deprives these individuals of the kinds of benefits that occur when people experience accomplishments that have value to themselves and others. Basic income is great when the choice is starvation, but programs that necessitate languishing in a needy state may not yield much happiness. While the objective is to help, there may be an inadvertent creation of a hammock rather than a temporary safety net, which can be personally depleting rather than an enhancement one's existence. Others can lavish goods and services upon those in need, but personal accomplishments recognized by others, such as becoming a lawyer, veterinary assistant, or house painter, are more likely to create long-term well-being.

As a way to resolve this problem, Promoters prefer assistance programs that maintain incentives to keep working, such as "topping off" the earnings of low-income individuals. For example, they might advocate a "negative income tax" program that gives more control to the individual. These kinds of programs presume that most people in poverty can operate effectively without a monitoring system that introduces bureaucratic inefficiencies and accusations that recipients are not behaving correctly. These programs respect the importance of having individuals maintain economic control over their lives, and recognize that personal betterment is essential, even when assistance is given (Buckley, Jr., 2017).

This brings up the crux of the political debate. Promoters think that people make *voluntary* decisions in capitalistic economies, while Protectors think that this is a mirage. They believe that power differentials and coercion are always occurring, and it is preposterous to think that people are *choosing,* or acting *voluntarily,* during capitalistic encounters.

In response, Promoters insist that the concept of *volunteerism* only means that people do not suffer incarceration and/or brute force when declining an economic arrangement. While some might think that this distinction is trivial, especially when people are destitute, Promoters claim that the difference is meaningful. When there is legal freedom to enter or leave a transaction, the individual can decide whether it is better to say *yes* or *no.*

In Promoter ideology, this option is better than having no option at all, which is the case in a government command economy. In that sense, Promoters believe that a capitalist system protects the individual's right to maintain *discretionary* preference better than any other economic arrangement, despite that no one has *complete* freedom from the limitations of their circumstance, the laws of the land, or any other constraints.

Yes, Promoters recognize that in a capitalistic system, large corporations, for example, can wield power over other businesses by compiling and disseminating negative information about their competitors in order to brainwash the public and deracinate them. However, for them, even with these attempts to bully, individuals can still *voluntarily* push back as long as there are enough people discontent with the actions and products of the plutocrats at the top. Even if smaller businesses have to charge higher prices (like sellers of organic foods), if enough people jump on board, there is still *opportunity* for survival, and the possibility of forming new business endeavors, as long as the *government* does not safeguard the plutocrats by enacting restrictive laws.

A similar debate occurs when our two camps argue about the power dynamics of "ownership" during capitalistic exchanges. While Protectors assert that owners and their right to exclude invariably impose oppression, Promoters do not believe that an employer, or owner of capital, relative to being an *employee,* is always superior. For example, they point out the tightening of options when owning a house, as compared to renting, and they note that owners of restaurants often kowtow to their cherished chefs. In these situations, participants are on equal footing, as both have incentives to keep each other happy. If they do not meet those requirements, each could suffer in the process.

For Promoters, the issue is not *ownership* per se; it is dealing with the options available to each party engaged in a particular capitalistic exchange. Sometimes it might appear that employers have the upper hand, but this is not always the case. Life is generally not as restrictive as the zero-sum game of Monopoly, where property owners invariably win. Depending on the circumstance, legal restrictions, alternatives, and perceived value of the resources possessed by each participant, the power dynamics can vary.

There is one final point to make regarding capitalism vs. state control. While government programs get money in the pockets of needy people immediately, Promoters worry that these programs decrease an interest in giving charity. The receiver gets monetary help from a nebulous source, and no longer recognizes that the earner is making a sacrifice. It appears as if money grows on trees, and the obligation to be grateful or pay back the offering loses importance.

Unfortunately, the taxpayer no longer feels appreciated, and they may stop wanting to be generous. Moreover, why should they be charitable if the government is providing what the poor need? Over time, there is less reinforcement for people to take voluntary actions to care for others, and the induced psychology creates a greater dependency on government interventions.

As a result, in our current system, people can campaign for centralized programs, but instead of having the people who endorse the policy pay the bill, the cost imposes on all the taxpayers. Those who advocate for the program assume that an amorphous entity called the government will automatically fulfill their interest in providing assistance. However, for many people, giving is no longer associated with being magnanimous. Instead, it pairs with indifference, or perhaps coercion, when the individual believes that the policy is counterproductive.

Rather than bequeathing a gift with hard-earned dollars, people may grow numb to the automatic deductions in their paychecks.

Others might feel as if they are enduring a theft in the form of a tax, and some might bemoan the fact that federal bureaucrats are printing fiat money, and then presenting themselves as saviors who endow their needy constituents with gifts that require nothing in return. It is therefore not surprising that some claim that the welfare state has essentially destroyed private charity due to operating in this fashion (Buckley, Jr., 2017).

Just as concerning, the status of *requiring* help leads to *expecting* help without the moral obligation to give back and participate in resolving the problem. People indoctrinate into the belief that they *deserve* it because the receiving is legal and mandatory. Promoters dislike this outcome, and instead want to retain personal initiative and responsibility between the giver and the receiver. They want to mitigate the possibility of diminishing common decency on both sides of the equation.

Dispersions of Power

To reset the argument, Promoters believe that if people need extra help, they can get it, initially, from other family members and charity groups. If *willing* sources are insufficient, they can look to government agencies that make it compulsory for people to earmark money for the purpose of helping and protecting.

Although, for Promoters, when seeking mandatory assistance, it is best to access the most decentralized sources first (i.e., local, state, and then federal government). The belief is that by keeping aid close to home, the abetment is likely to be less wasteful, and more precisely tailored to meet the specific needs of the problem. In contrast, the Protector group desires a singular authority to provide remediation, as blanket control means more *safety* and more coverage for the needy. A larger agency is better equipped to rescue, and its pervasive power can more effectively eradicate all the wrongs in the world.

Promoters are skeptical of that perspective. They claim that Protectors never want to let a good crisis go to waste. They admonish them for manufacturing urgency, chaos, and fear as a way to shift control to centralized sources, which justify their ambition for top-down control, even if they allow for local administration of their policies. After all, many seem to agree that greater power can outperform local and private activity when there is the necessity for quick all-encompassing remediation (e.g., natural disasters, war, lethal health threats, etc.).

In crisis situations, the expectation for people to sustain on their own often diminishes, as the greater resources of the government seem needed to address the urgency. Moreover, when there is excessive upheaval similar to our recent pandemic, social media and academic gurus gain importance, as everyone wants to hear the reasons for the calamity, and the recommended expert solutions. Dependencies and deference to the almighty experts and politicians will increase, as a metaphorical all-knowing parent is desperately needed.

However, while Protectors often find reasons to take radical action and usurp control of society, Promoters are more likely to see societal problems as circumscribed and effectively resolved with far less bureaucratic action. They grow suspicious and wonder whether Protectors are secretly pleased that upheaval is occurring. They know that with the wave of turmoil, many will submit to a usurping of authoritarian power. The helpless populace will welcome a needed savior, and Promoters lament the unfolding of these kinds of events.

In response, Protectors wrinkle their brow. They claim that it is spurious to frame their behavior as a manipulation to gain control. They deny that they are exaggerating external harms, and maintain the belief that government management is needed to address problems, which are more tragic and extensive than what the Promoters admit. They maintain that unless there is a powerful watchful eye that can dissolve the inherent societal and economic oppressions occurring in our social group, those currently in power will keep accumulating funds, marginalizing others, and allowing floundering and tragedy to persist.

For those espousing protectionism, there is no fear of increased centralized power as long as it is doing the biddings of equity, which lays the foundation for acceptable *social justice*. As a way to gain influence, Protectors work diligently to persuade the masses by taking over all the available megaphones in social media and entertainment. Through infiltration, they gain control of law, religion, education, and family.

With that impressive influence, they progressively deconstruct the dominant culture (Horowitz, 2021). Even if this leads to destructive rioting, the end justifies the means, as they anticipate the appearance of a significantly improved umwelt that bears a resemblance to their fantasy that all humans will have comparable life enjoyment and security.

Outsiders, however, wonder whether it makes sense to characterize Protector officialdom as redeemers that function without avarice. Promoters remain suspicious that the people running government agencies will be susceptible to the same covetous motives as those that are currently in authority. In their opinion, as we increase their bureaucratic power, we might all become their servants, rather than recipients of their benefaction. A Promoter believes that government officials will want to retain their influence and power, just like everyone else.

Moreover, from a Promoter's perspective, non-governmental sources are *more likely* to gain monopolistic power when the government is influential enough to orchestrate the marketplace in significant ways, and they do not want to give the government more power to accommodate some interests, at the expense of others. Since people are generally eager to gain an upper hand, those vying for governmental appeasement have powerful incentives to work in tandem with government officials. Often, they can get politicians to change laws or divert funding their way by promising contributions. Politicians then alter regulations, licensing requirements, contract awards, and tax codes in ways that are favorable to the special interest groups.

Often, only well-endowed entities are able to influence, withstand, and benefit from the bureaucratic maneuvers that proliferate. For example, the government might be willing to maintain laws that protect large media companies from liability as long as they maintain efforts to censor information that speaks poorly of the bureaucrats in charge (Ramaswamy, 2021). For these reasons, Promoters assert that marketplace unfairness is less likely to occur if we restrict the expanding power of the government.

They believe that when government is limited, it is easier to keep power concentrations from occurring, in that collusion, and ultimately the neglect of the public good, is less likely when government has constraints in its ability to influence the marketplace (PragerU, 2016). For instance, what would happen to competition if the government gave a subsidy to only one food supermarket, and not any others? According to Milton Friedman, monopolies of all kinds form almost exclusively through governmental intrusions that support and benefit certain entities, at the expense of others, including when there are limitations on competition from international trade (Free To Choose Network, 2016; LibertyPen, 2020).

Not surprisingly, Promoters like Milton Friedman advocate for policies that stop governmental actions, which *provide* for monopoly formation rather than focus on antitrust legislation, which in his view, will not get to the heart of the matter (BasicEconomics, 2021). Promoters ascribe to the aphorism, "Power corrupts, and absolute power corrupts absolutely," and they note that one only has to look to history to observe the litany of heinous atrocities perpetrated by rulers and oligarchs with centralized social and economic power.

Without hesitation, Promoters dislike the pattern of big government serving the interests of the most powerful organizations and businesses who can give them something in return, and they are not surprised to find the largest companies, unions, and institutions typically advocating for a Protector's agenda. They know that powerful groups will make political contributions to support candidates and mobilize voters, and then receive payback with policies that benefit their market dominance. In these ways and more, businesses, unions, and governments become handmaidens for each other.

In the case of public unions, the relationship with government is notably incestuous, as government officials represent the taxpayers in negotiations with the union, and simultaneously take money from the unions to enhance their campaigns to represent the taxpayers.

Moreover, the diminishment of a union member's freedom becomes even more extreme when employees are *required* to join the union. When that happens, their union dues could easily end up financing candidates that they do not want to support, yet they have no recourse to resist.

In light of these observations, people often ask, "Who has the upper hand in influencing voting in America—factions within the government, private businesses, corporate media, or the intelligentsia?" This is a difficult question to answer, as power is sinuous and multidirectional. For example, with fair elections, each network structure depends on public reaction to perpetuate its authority, and this is not always easy, especially when people are concerned about a policy's impact on children. On the other hand, businesses, organizations, the media, and the intelligentsia can influence public opinion, and each of these entities can synergistically unite with the government, and other nodes of power, to forward their special interests.

However, when certain views within the government gain ascendency, there can be a wielding of a unique sword; there can be the imposition of legal authority. With the stroke of the pen, a government dictum can promote or cancel projects, such as a significant oil pipeline employing thousands of people. It can confiscate property through eminent domain, regulate and control research funding, impose additional taxes, enact surveillance, and make accusations and arrests. (Fox News, 2021; Shapiro, 2021). When voices in this network gain imperium, overtly or clandestinely, others quickly recognize that they can remain viable only if they tow the party line.

Although, where the scales tip depends on the circumstance, and in each instance, it is important to decipher who benefits and who has the wherewithal to advance their cause. For example, when President Trump was in power, the media pushed back, and it had sufficient allies with other nodes of power, including sources within the government to roadblock what he wanted to do.

Nevertheless, and regardless of its source, Promoters are against the concentration of power. Yes, they are apprehensive about *corporatism* and the expansion of large special interest groups that can conspire with governmental decision-making, but they are especially fearful of the *power* that government has to incarcerate dissenters and close down options completely (Hawley, 2021). When governments grow in size and authority, it seems that susceptible entities are at risk to lose many freedoms. Their economic, political, and discretionary alternatives can shrink appreciably in relation to the ability of the government to legally silence.

For this reason, Promoters want to ameliorate government supremacy, as this helps each person maintain at least a modicum of choice. Their vote in the private economy always counts, and they can often find enclaves that more closely match personal preferences, even if bureaucrats or the majority prefer something else. They can enact their inclinations with their *individual feet* as long as it is legally permissible to do so.

For Promoters, submitting to a government-directed economy is always the option of last resort, and they claim that it brings with it many problems not immediately identified. In their view, while the initial benefits of governmental actions are *concentrated* and easy to discern, the downstream negative side effects happen later, and are typically more diffuse and difficult to causally trace. For example, while stimulus packages, bailouts, rent control, and money printing to cancel debt provide some immediate benefit, those magnanimous acts may lead to unintended consequences that are to everyone's detriment in the future (PragerU, 2015; Heresy Financial, 2021).

Promoters dislike that third-party social engineers such as John Maynard Keynes (2009), who often side-step the long-term economic consequences of their ideas, have a dominant voice when advising politically popular rescuing procedures that are wrong or implemented incorrectly. While their recommendations seem quite enticing on face value, in retrospect, they often fall short. For example, Sowell claims that even the Federal Reserve failed in its raison d'être to control inflation, to prevent deflation, and to stop bank failures (Hoover Institution, 2015; Sowell, 2008). Moreover, many believe it was its failure, not capitalism, that spurred the Great Depression (Free To Choose Network, 2015).

In Promoter ethos, the government has utility *only* to the extent that it enables a market economy by establishing a rule-governed format. Government is *merely* responsible to do what the free markets *cannot do*. For instance, it can help to maintain law, order, and policy to prevent unreasonable coercions and infringements on other people's freedoms. It can preserve the peace and provide for national defense. It can adjudicate disputes and enforce voluntary contracts. It can define the meaning of property rights and provide the means for modifying them. It can provide a monetary framework and foster competitive markets, which entails helping to overcome technical monopolies. Finally, it can address "neighborhood affects" (e.g., pollution), which can harm uninvolved parties (Hatcher, 2013).

Therefore, Promoters are *willing* to give government the power to protect life, liberty, and property, and to function as a referee. However, they are content only with those duties, and they are not in favor of expanding governmental power beyond those limits. Since bureaucracies have incentives to keep finding reasons to spend and manipulate the economy to justify their existence, they want to keep government as small as possible. They believe that government incentives make their activities ever-expanding, and reductions in personal freedoms are simultaneously inevitable. Rather than increase the government's power to *compensate* for failures to produce equity ideals, they would like to see government eliminate factors that *inhibit* economic productivity.

Whenever feasible, Promoters prefer to let individuals resolve their economic problems amongst themselves. They would rather see the principles of supply and demand play out, and to have people whittle compensation by engaging in exchanges of goods and services that they find mutually beneficial, instead of having a governing body determine the ways to allocate resources. In this believe system, governmental distributions of money, or *providing* people with a growing array of government jobs, is not the best way to develop a prosperous well-functioning society.

They anticipate that in a market economy with limited governmental involvement, there is less likelihood of power becoming concentrated in any sector. Even if certain companies become large, one only has to remember the cliché, "The bigger they are, the harder they fall" (IBM, Sears, etc.). Without a competent business model (and no governmental bailout), even the largest companies can plummet from grace (Free To Choose Network, 2016).

Moreover, often it is *more difficult* for larger companies to maintain efficiency, as smaller size can help a company stay nimble. Behemoth companies have to keep earning their size by providing more benefit than cost. As noted by the Economist Walter Williams, conglomerates must offer great service to consumers in order to survive in a market economy (PragerU, 2015). Since there can be "economies of scale and diseconomies of scale," size alone does not guarantee insurmountable power to control a market sector (Sowell, 2015). Even Facebook and Uber were once fledgling entities that overcame companies with extensive market share.

For those who claim that smaller businesses cannot flourish in the marketplace because larger companies "buy them out" as a way to maintain market control, market advocates want to study the problem in detail, prior to seeing the acquisitions as an egregious problem. While it is true that many "start-up" businesses get squashed by bullying tactics, some are bought out because this is what they wanted to see happen. The buyout was essentially a low-risk option, and a preference from the outset. In this scenario, everyone in the group became richer from the sale. The transaction was equivalent to allowing people to offload aspects of business onto those specializing in market areas that were beyond their purview.

Consequently, Promoters do not *necessarily* see the buying of small businesses by larger businesses as a victim scenario or a failure of competitive capitalism. However, they want to retain business rivalry, which can disappear quickly when government or private organizations get into cahoots with each other, or when government commissars envelop the economic system and expurgate all competing forces that are not simpatico with their political agenda. When that happens, it is even worse than private attempts to censor, as then, no one outside of government dictate will have the freedom to enact their desires.

By keeping marketplace options available, many problems resolve on their own. For example, if individuals dislike a company's acquisition policies, or other concerning actions (e.g., cartels), they can induce antitrust legislation, boycott, or find alternatives in order to diminish the authority of the strong-armed entities. Moreover, while the power of a cartel might sometimes seem insurmountable, it can also break apart on their own when competition from a variety of sources oozes into their arrangements (Sowell, 2015). Like most of us, they are likely to pursue their best options and follow the money. For Promoters, the infusion of competition, in any number of ways, is what keeps advantages accruing to all social strata.

However, even when it is permissible for new entities to enter the market and compete against those with inordinate power, it might sometimes be close to impossible to overcome the barricades of the entrenched. For example, when private Internet service platforms collude and have control over the "public square," and simultaneously conjoin with other nodes of power, including the government, then consumer boycotting may be the most viable option. While legal action remains a possibility, it assumes that there is a modicum of bureaucratic interest in preserving market competition and consumer freedom. And in some political climates, that might be hard to find.

In sum, market competition is a Promoter's Holy Grail. They prefer this to various forms of concentrated power that can inundate and overwhelm a society. Promoters caution that any move in that direction will yield a coinciding decrease in personal freedom, which may lead to more detrimental outcomes in the long term. However, in comparison to enduring and eliminating the hardships that occur with civilian misbehavior, a government takeover is invidious, and potentially even more oppressive. It can be the most formidable monopoly.

Promoters note that while collusion and hidden law breaking create a lack of competition, fighting those kinds of problems is preferable to letting the government orchestrate a tyranny. Inordinate sources of power from all other sources can be kept at bay more easily by finding ways to incite competition. Promoters believe that the best way to fight poverty is to increase options to find a job, create a job, and have choice in what to believe and what to buy.

Market Restrictions

Without compunction, Protectors advocate central decision-making to protect the public good. This includes imposing restrictions on business practices in order to protect the weak against those in power. For example, they want to monitor decisions pertaining to hiring, employee mistreatment, and minimum wages, and they advocate vigilant oversight to protect unsuspecting people from deficient products and other harmful business activities. For them, a chief agency is the most effective way to resolve these problems.

In contrast, Promoters generally argue that a marketplace will factor out misdeeds with reasonable efficiency, and with lesser reductions in freedom. For example, when people find out about unacceptable practices, they can shun the establishment, look for substitutes, sue for damages, or promote competitive businesses to displace the wrongdoers. The fear of reprisal will get others to be careful in their practices and take more precautions with decisions and safety risks that could have repercussions on their pocketbooks.

Promoters believe that companies can financially enhance themselves by attending to health and safety, if that is culturally valued. For example, people often buy Volvos for that specific reason, and subscribe to *consumer reports* to get the latest updates on safety and quality. Promoters wonder whether most of the security that governmental oversight tries to achieve might be better accomplished in this fashion, as companies *compete* to increase profits by advancing their image of "doing good." They anticipate that the private sector will usually outperform government bureaucracies when unleashed.

However, the problem has additional complexity. While people generally agree that people should suffer prosecution when knowingly enacting harmful behaviors, often people find out about harm *after the fact,* even when trying to be cautious, and their mistakes can affect vast numbers of innocent people. To address this matter, Protectors advocate federal agencies to oversee business output that could create significant danger in order to gain an *extra* step of safety assurance to prevent disaster. While private sector companies can and do perform product certifications with their reputations on the line, Protectors opt for government oversight, with the presumption that it is a more reliable source to factor out marketplace debacles.

In response, Promoters point out that government surveillance is also fallible. For example, Ralph Nader claimed that Chevrolet Corvairs were unsafe to drive, although further study revealed that Corvairs were no more dangerous than other cars (Wikipedia Contributors, 2018). They note that "experts" allowed the release of various opiate drugs into the marketplace, and they blundered terribly when requiring the use of fire retardant chemicals on children's pajamas that turned out to be carcinogenic (LibertyPen, 2010).

In their view, governmental processes have their own foibles. They worry that its stamp of approval can function as a liability *shield* instead of fostering further investigation. They point out that the benefits of the sanctioning process must outweigh the adverse effects of its delays, costs, and misjudgments. They are concerned that the processes can impede innovation and protect and increase profits for those who are established. Moreover, corruption can and does occur within the sanctioning agencies (Sowell, 2015). Unfortunately, with fewer people in control, problems can magnify, and Promoters are skeptical about the reliability of the processes that monitor the interworking of these broad-scale agencies.

Additionally, since the agency assessors must identify danger potentialities and make recommendations that could affect many vulnerable people, their evaluation of the pros and cons of what is best to do may differ substantially from what many other people might tolerate or prefer. Since their concentrated cost of allowing harm to seep through is greater than the dispersed lesser evident harms, risk aversion may prevail, and they might often orient to create initial safety where the only limiting principle is legal permissibility. Since they are an all-encompassing legal agency, their rule affects many people who have no other option other than to comply (Stossel, 2021).

In this scenario, the downstream effects of blanket proclamations may create a variety of unexamined serious secondary harms. Everyone might be safer in a particular way, but in doing so, other risks and complications might increase as well (Sowell, 2008). For example, while some people benefited from the government mandated COVID-19 sheltering decisions, others suffered harms that might have avoided had they been able to make personalized safety assessments.

Seldom, though, is there inquiry into the kinds of *diffuse* problems that government *monopoly* agencies create in relation to their biases, licensing laws, and numerous other criteria for safety. Despite being a difficult matter to pursue—especially since weighing the benefits and harms of their decisions might be subtle and difficult to ascertain over longer spans of time, for different groups and individuals—this continues to be an important concern.

However, Protectors do not seem motivated to delve into the conditions under which government absolutism might be an inferior approach in comparison to allowing the private sector, or more local sources, a greater voice in consumer advocacy and safety. Yes, governmental intervention has helped in many instances with recalls of defective products, dangerous drugs, unhealthy foods, and other health concerns. But it is an empirical question whether more self-advocacy, community oversight, and market dynamics for some or many people in a variety of situations could produce preferable safety outcomes, despite the trend to expand governmental control (Friedman and Friedman, 1990).

As expected, our two political camps also handle the problem of *workplace discrimination* in their usual divergent ways. Protectors desire a watchdog bureaucracy to ferret out minority-identity bigotry, while Promoters want limited government interference as the first selection on the menu. They believe that no matter how much discrimination exists, businesses will do what is best for their bottom line. They will hire minority group members if that decision promotes their economic viability. When left alone with neutral laws that prevent employee mistreatment, the problem will iron itself out.

Promoters are also concerned that oversight showing bias in favor of some identities may lead to more problems than solutions. For instance, if employers must have a certain number of minority employees, or confront prima fascie allegations of racial discrimination, they might hire under-qualified minority individuals to avoid expensive legal challenges. They worry that the slanted legal intrusions essentially create disruptions that could impinge on business prosperity and the cost of products for everyone. Moreover, others might move away from minority communities to sidestep the problem altogether (Archive, 2019; Sowell, 2012). The granted "special rights" makes the cost of hiring these individuals prohibitive (Sowell, 1996).

Predictably, our two camps also differ in their advocacy of minimum wage laws. While the debate continues, and Protectors argue that it will immediately help many struggling workers earn a living wage, Promoters are concerned about other kinds of consequences. For example, prices might rise to cover extra expenses, and automation becomes more enticing. Owners might reduce the number of jobs and change the allocation of hours to mitigate benefits (Yu et al., 2021). Businesses might close or curtail customer services, and this might be frequent with small businesses that cannot withstand the extra costs.

Many businesses will have to cut lower-paying jobs in an effort to economize, and they are likely to have more applicants for the remaining positions. This situation could be especially harmful for people with limited employment history, and for individuals most likely to encounter bigotry (The Rubin Report, 2018). Moreover, there might be hesitation to hire minorities with questionable qualifications, simply to avoid the sticky problem of not being able to terminate the arrangement for fear of a bigotry accusation. Unintentionally, divisiveness and attentiveness to race as a discriminating factor could well increase.

For these reasons, Promoters want to make it easier for employers to hire by allowing them to set their own wages and allow workers to gain experience and skill. This approach permits individuals to progress in the workforce rather than stagnate in unemployment. Promoters find it unconscionable that government officials can take away the right of others to negotiate an opportunity for employment, simply because they do not approve of the negotiated terms. Moreover, while minimum wage advocates are attempting to foster "a living wage," most entry-level workers have *other* means of support; they do not need the job to remain solvent. More often, the wage laws simply create fewer job opportunities for the least skilled individuals (Sowell, 2015).

While Protectors believe they are rescuing these workers from destitute poverty and exploitation (which can be the case), some workers might be willing to work for less and gain skills. Individuals in many lines of work might relish the opportunity to get "their foot in the door," and minimum wage requirements can create obstacles, especially for those who are in need and eager to work. For example, according to Sowell (2012; Hoover, 2012), Blacks in America had lower rates of unemployment compared to Whites in 1930, which was the last year before there was a federal minimum wage law.

On these grounds, Promoters advocate for fewer regulatory efforts controlled solely by government agencies. They believe that oversight is often more effective when allowed to come from a variety of sources. They see many opportunities for people to prosper when not encumbered by interferences from outsiders who do not know enough about the kinds of feedback emanating from their local and unique situations.

Health Care

For Promoters, the benefits of a market system are evident even in the domain of health care. While Protectors assert that medical care is a "human right," and advocate for "universal" coverage, Promoters push back against the ideology that a *service* or *commodity* provided by others is a "right," as defined by our legal system (Peikoff, 1998). Additionally, Promoters differentiate concerns pertaining to medical insurance, medical care, and self-care, as each category has its own concerns and priorities (Economics in the Media, 2015).

Generally, Promoters address problems related to illness and gaining access to medical assistance, in the same way that they recognize the importance of a society not letting anyone starve. They would rather nurture a system that advances benevolence instead of forcing people to care about others. Rather than shift decision-making to a central government, they prefer a system where individuals maintain authority over protecting their own lives. Similar to automobile insurance, they want people to have the opportunity to select the kinds of policies that suit them best, and while it is important to persuade people to enact healthy lifestyles, they do not want to coerce people to do self-care.

It seems that both groups acknowledge that a humane and decent society should work toward the goal of making medical care accessible to everyone. However, Protectors want to make this possible through pivotal governmental allocation, while Promoters would like to retain market resolutions and charity to address the need for innovation, coverage, accessibility, provider cost, patient affordability, and quality. By doing so, they hope to reduce burdens placed on the taxpayers (PragerU, 2017; Scotty, 2018; Freedom Speaks, 2017).

Both recognize that each variable is important to consider, although they also understand that the variables often shift in opposite directions when people try different ways to ameliorate health care problems. That is, when one parameter goes up, others might go down. For example, when fostering *coverage* through government-controlled universal care, it is likely that *costs* will double, as incentives to economize diminish, and *accessibility of higher-level services* and *innovation* might dip as well (Academy of Achievement, 2017)

Given these constraints, Promoters (as usual) look for the best *trade-offs,* knowing that there is no perfect solution when addressing life's inevitable problems. However, both political camps recognize the requirement to diminish monopolies within the health care industry, such as the price gouging that occurs with drug patents (Open Society Foundations, 2020; Think Big, 2020), and both realize the necessity for people with limited resources and preexisting conditions to have access to medical treatment.

The important difference is that Protectors are more at ease with government expenditure and its consequences to facilitate health for all. They are comfortable allowing bureaucrats to orchestrate a system that operates under the rubric of equity morality. In their view, this kind of system is the best way to provide *coverage for all,* as well as (in theory) diminish preferential treatment that dominant groups and individuals can impose upon the vulnerable.

In contrast, Promoters would like health-related resources generated within a competitive price system. They would like to fill the gaps with benevolent contributions, and they want individuals, providers, and numerous insurance companies to retain a voice in the domain of promoting and protecting health. While they recognize that it is commendable to improve our current system, they emphasize that self-care, personal financial contribution, the maintenance of an individual's incentive to economize, voluntary giving, and market competition have addressed many health care needs and costs over the decades. They want to enhance that trend rather than detract from it.

However, the downside is that in a market system, it becomes necessary to socialize people to live in health-conscious ways, and to maintain health care insurance coverage as much as possible so that there are fewer people taking advantage of the *goodwill* of those providing subsidies. Although, as noted throughout this book, a lack of concern for self and others is a problem in all social arrangements, and it does not apply only to the issue of health care.

Immigration

A society can be a closed-door group that isolates from the rest of the world, although groups that are detached from others have been notoriously poor (Sowell, 2016). However, group solidarity, consistency of traditions, ways to generate agreements, and shared beliefs and values are likely to increase when groups are insular. Additionally, they side-step the problem of multiculturalism, which sometimes requires a society to assimilate people with discordant preferences and lack of know-how to prosper in the host country.

Despite these concerns, many Protectors advocate increasing immigration without limits or laws. They believe that if people from other groups desire to enter, they are doing so because they presume that their life will improve. To the extent that a Protector is prone to rescue and shield, they welcome and accept all immigrants with open arms.

Rather than balk, they insist that these individuals will increase the genetic pool, which could strengthen resistance to illness and perhaps lead to more idealized human forms. Weaknesses inherent in the traditions of the recipient group will mollify as well, and the group will become more adaptive and able to withstand the crises and difficulties that inevitably come from our disaster-laden world.

If they consider limitations on immigration at all, they downplay any drawbacks for the recipient group. Their mission is to save as many people as possible and enrich the group with variety. Their purview is a global ideal, and not a national subset. Even if the immigration is outside of legal bounds, there is an imperative to accept the person and create a net of safety.

For Protectors, if the receiver group has surplus and it values asylum, it is premature and unconscionable for that group to set limits on immigration. The tipping point, if harm is created, is so far into the future it makes no sense to consider at this time the possible long-term consequences of overriding a civilization with new members.

In this approach, those with propinquity will have an advantage. But the most pressing concern is to provide services that ease immediate hardship for the incomers. Some even make the case that the United States will benefit from increasing its population to one billion in order to compete on the future world stage (Yglesias, 2020).

Protectors also claim that even if incoming people have lesser skill, they are more likely to work at jobs not preferred by the inhabitants, such as what often happens in America. Moreover, many of these incomers have historically shown better work performance compared to the workers currently available to do the existing entry-level jobs. This benefit is in everyone's best interest, and it may also help to maintain lower prices.

Overall, rather than entertain a possible downside of large numbers of people rapidly entering the group, a Protector believes that new members will create variations that will strengthen the citizenry. The influx of people with differing backgrounds will provide the recipient group with new solutions to problems.

One only has to remember the proliferation of "think tanks," and the procedure of "free association," to grasp the benefit of allowing novelty to come to the fore. The new arrivals will enrich life by increasing diversity in customs and behavior that had not previously occurred. Multiculturalism will be the bromide that the group must take in, and hesitation to swallow is xenophobic.

The possibility that the new entrees will introduce novel ways to live in the world enthralls a Protector, especially if they help to diminish the power of the prevailing and bigoted Anglo-Saxon culture. Since they believe that there is excessive majority-induced racism in Western societies, there is likely to be improvement with the influx of new traditions. The barrage of incomers will create enough social force to bring about a quicker overhaul of what they do not like. Moreover, since they believe that the technologically advanced countries have caused significant environmental havoc throughout the world, they argue that it is a moral imperative to allow these casualties the freedom to escape from their degraded living situations, which modernity had a hand in creating.

In total, since Protectors are *not* enamored with the status quo, they are far less concerned with new people coming in to disintegrate old cultural patterns. Eventually, with enough penetration from abroad, they are confident that the new groups will align with their politics and aid in their quest to obtain power and political supremacy. In their view, the best way to defeat the incumbents is to outnumber them. They want to create something new, and in that sense, they want to oust the old.

In contrast, Promoters are cautious in their approach to immigration. Since they are less intent on accommodating to newcomers at the possible expense of citizens, they prefer to measure the trade-offs when considering whether to allow a person into the group. They also recognize that if the country cannot effectively assimilate all of the people who want to enter the country, it is necessary to have a system that legalizes who gains admittance. In their view, the flow of immigration must be monitored, and this means that violators must have legal consequences.

While Promoters recognize the importance of maintaining a sufficient birth rate, their first inclination is to investigate the reasons for the decline. *Empirics* will show whether immigration is the only way to resolve that problem. For example, they might explore whether helping parents find ways to work and take care of children might be an important first step, as well as explore other reasons for young adults to show an aversion to having children.

Promoters also want to consider whether the incomers will add to the group or create danger, harm, or a lag. They want to evaluate whether an immigrant's skills will benefit the citizenry or require them to provide support, which may stress the social safety net for others. They wonder whether a rapid influx without defined limits will impose burdens on communities to educate, house, and provide medical care, which could overwhelm the local residents and the society in general.

While they acknowledge that many non-citizens will work at jobs that others do not want, Promoters are also concerned that excessive immigration will keep wages excessively low (PragerU, 2018). Moreover, they want to investigate whether second-generation immigrants will be as forthcoming to work at these jobs. Yes, some might gain skills that enable employment advancement, but work ethic might subside for many others. As touched on previously, this problem occurs frequently when societies have a large number of government entitlements, and burgeoning resentments toward the majority culture (Sowell, 2008).

Overall, the following questions come to mind. While immigrants might accept employment that others are more likely to shun, what if there were fewer migrants? What would happen if we address and remediate the factors influencing work refusal or poor work ethic for the native population? If there were more restrictions on immigration, would respect for resident workers and wages rise to the point where job rejection would occur less often? Might owners automate more rapidly due to the dearth of cheap labor, and could this lead to the development of safer, more acceptable kinds of employment over time?

When there is no selection process, Promoters are concerned that there could be overwhelming numbers of workers entering into an economy when modern technology is rapidly eliminating the kinds of jobs that these individuals are skilled to do. Might excessive immigration of people without the knowledge and proficiency necessary for success in America, simply exacerbate complaints about income disparities and poverty?

Without question, Promoters are skeptical of unfettered immigration. When countries consider welfare and medical care "human rights," they are concerned about the increased responsibilities thrust onto the group when accepting new entrants. Decision-makers might want to save the incomers, but others will have to pay the bill for both the short and long term. In this regard, many Promoters have expressed the view that they would favor "open borders" if the entitlement movement imposed some limits. If that were the case, there would be little downside to a free immigration policy (Free To Choose Network, 2016).

In short, Promoters are unwilling to presume that the variety of identities entering the country will be an unmitigated advantage. While differing perspectives and diversities of passion can be aesthetically wonderful, and often helpful during problem-solving, in that new ways of adaptation and looking at problems can be enlightening, they do not assume that diversity is always an inherent plus. They ask, *What if the person's beliefs, civics, and values are in opposition, or distant, to the group at large? Would this kind of immigration overwhelm it and diminish public trust?*

Rather than assimilate and adopt the citizen group's way of living, the colonizing group could potentially disassemble and ultimately unravel it, especially if the numbers coming in are extensive and overpowering the system (The Federalist Editors, 2019). Instead of the saying, "When in Rome do as the Romans do," the outcome will be that the Romans to end up without their former way of existence.

Certainly, this outcome is more probable when large numbers of immigrants gain enough authority to influence politics soon after migrating, and prior to mastering the legacy patterns of indigenous living. Unfortunately, no one is presenting data that might help to determine what kinds of limits (if any) are necessary to impose on the incursion of foreigners who are entering.

Promoters wonder if there is a point where the host country ceases to maintain its integrity and its ability to protect and care for both incomers and current citizens. Since they know that the host country cannot save everyone in the world, they think about whether it is better to spend resources to increase human flourishing in the immigrant's homeland. Those exploring this matter also wonder whether we are robbing these countries of their human capital, even though we think we are helping. Moreover, considerable numbers of illegal immigrants end up being exploited by cartels and human trafficking. And in that regard, how much good are we doing?

Promoters believe that societies are held together by a shared way of living in the world, where there are standards for institutions, ways to resolve disputes, and common values related to the importance of industriousness, religion, education, marriage, and family. They wonder about the extent to which the individuals coming in will add to the "coming apart" that is already occurring in the United States, and diminish the group's prowess to innovate, discover, and excel (Murray C., 2012). Something has to hold the group together, which perpetuates a common good and a shared sense of civility, and Promoters are concerned that unfettered immigration will exacerbate the unraveling that is already occurring (Wax, 2017).

Rather than disassemble our society, Promoters would like to see people working for a common goal, such as a multicultural commitment to the promotion of a national identity. Under these conditions, they anticipate that affinity for others is likely to increase, much like what happens on sports teams questing for a championship. They also believe that if a nation allows all citizens to vote, it is essential that the populace understand the country's principles in order to achieve its long-term objectives. They want citizens to make sound decisions about who to elect in order to help carry out those ideals, and it is not clear how quickly a country can educate and assimilate people so that they can fulfill those duties and help to maintain the country's fundamentals.

While Promoters acknowledge that most people are able to learn patterns consistent with American legacy patterns, they remain concerned that when immigration is too rapid, it will make this kind of learning difficult, and perhaps hinder its probability. This is not an argument against people retaining their cultural patterns that are not disruptive to the core values of the homeland country, as those variations pose no danger and can be beneficial to the immigrants and inhabitants. It is simply a cautionary perspective that advocates maintaining a way of life that many immigrants are drawn to, and could benefit from preserving.

For Promoters, if the objective to accommodate to every nuance of preference, and ways of settling disputes, for every culture that enters the homeland group, and not even try to encourage receptivity to a national identity, what is the linking bond that keeps the society coherent? For example, is it reasonable for the United States to show diffidence toward the practice of Shariah law, or permit the circumcision of young females?

Of course, if the objective is to decimate the culture, then there is less emphasis on getting immigrant accommodations to occur. Many disruptions become a welcomed gifting, and most previously revered patterns of behavior are simply unwanted instances of dominant-group bigotry that require destruction. The new voting bloc essentially helps with culture shattering.

However, rather than hope for destruction, Promoters would rather preserve a way of life, and they also question whether the trend toward multiculturalism is always in the best interest of the incomers. While they recognize that the new arrivals can remain insular and develop economic accomplishments within their own self-contained economic activities (Sowell, 2012), immigrants may also derive benefits when they learn the language and the behaviors that are compatible with the laws, concepts of fairness, and other customs of the indigenous group that have allowed them to be successful. While some might consider any requirement to adapt as a "supremacist" ideology, Promoters focus on the probability that assimilation will be advantageous for immigrants, rather than dismiss it as another form of "racial oppression."

Attempting to alter an immigrant's behavior might seem culturally insensitive, but Promoters believe that it can also increase the prospering of the entrants in the new society. They want the recipient group to understand the importance of cultural differences, and perhaps ameliorate language transition with lingua franca, but they do not want to make significant changes that might disrupt the flourishing that is already occurring. Since many people migrate to America because they desire that way of life, it makes no sense for the recipient group to give up its modus operandi; those basics are the reasons for the immigration in the first place.

With that in mind, Promoters are concerned about the ease with which immigrants can transition into the larger group. They wonder whether the individuals have the kind of expertise, talents, and patterns of behavior that will synchronize with others and allow them to comfortably assimilate. Since the United States employs admission standards for most institutions, they find it reasonable to impose some kind of filtering process for immigration, even if it is only to monitor the flow of numbers.

Consequently, Promoters find it important to balance the welcoming of new arrivals with the social cost of assimilation. They believe that if the numbers admitted to a country are not restricted in some fashion, the process of successful integration is unlikely, and the cost to others might be formidable. They wonder about the meaning of the word *citizenship*, if obligation or a sense of duty to others is not bidirectional. That is, we can talk about what a country is giving to the immigrant, but what is it expecting from those who enter?

Once again, for Promoters, there is rejection of passive receptivity, and a preference for mutual contribution. Rather than focus solely on providing help to immigrants, they want to consider problems with absorption, and the tacit *downstream effects* that could take place. They find it important to weigh the benefits that occur for the migrant, against the impact that the entrée will have on the larger group. While this equation can be ephemeral—as many factors can influence the decision, including the status of the larger group, and the urgency of individuals to flee their homeland—they find it essential to ascertain a middle ground.

Finally, there is one looming concern. If those in power continue to advocate for an equity ideal, the entire discussion about diversity resulting from immigration is moot. If political authorities shun departures from what they command, adding individuals with diverse characteristics, ideas, and backgrounds will eventually lead to increased homogenization of decision-making and opinion, regardless of their different physical appearances and previous ways of living.

CHAPTER THREE

RACISM UNLEASHED

As humans, we have evolved not only in families, but also in larger groups. Tribal alliance affords extra protection from outside harms, and cooperation within the group (much like within families) permits access to a greater array of resources. When distinct groups cooperate with each other, even more possibilities come to fruition. But the likelihood of conflict is typically greater between groups than within groups, in that their decisions, preferences, ways of life, histories, and incentives may not be compatible. We often refer to these differences as *culture*.

When there is incongruity between subgroups within a larger group, the integrity of the overarching group can be threatened. This can become so extreme that what embraces group members can no longer maintain group cohesion. Destruction of the group is possible when in-group conflict becomes greater than the benefits of working in harmony.

As the uproar of identity politics starts to ascend, the balkanization between the warring tribes becomes glaringly visible. While subgroups might compete and cooperate within a society in helpful and benign ways, there can be conflict as well. Power imbalance and resultant harm may become evident, and it becomes necessary to resolve this problem.

Preliminary Concerns

When racial minorities suffer *legalized* oppression in relation to majority institutions, the maligned groups might combine forces to defend themselves. In their eyes, the protectionist message rings true, and they are likely to argue for rule changes to foster advancement for their group. Given that some people in America had shameful acceptance of slavery and other forms of sanctioned racism, it is not surprising that many people align with Protector ideology.

Generally, when a struggling minority defines its circumstance as oppressed by the status quo, it becomes focused on stopping those harms (Cooper, 2019). Nationalism is rejected, as in their view, the country has benefited from bigotry against them. Their singular objective is to counterbalance the mistreatments that persist, and the intensity of their efforts revolves around inducing changes in the current state of affairs. Both the victims of oppression, and people sympathetic to their cause, form an alliance to fight conventional norms of behavior.

The uprising quest for emancipation and *Social Justice* is born. Tearing it all down (not improving it) is the first order of business. Accusations that the society is built on racial discrimination are heard loud and clear. The mission is to destroy the corruption in morality that has been at the heart of the United States (The Heritage Foundation, 2017).

With growing intensity, the Protector camp is endorsing this cause and asserting that there is an ample basis for vengefulness. Some are advocating to "defund the police," as a symbolic effort to undo all incumbent authority. If people are *unwilling* to cancel the culture, fragment its contents, counterbalance wrongs by pushing victimized groups forward, and reset social hierarchies, then they are accomplices to the panoply of historical and ever-present forms of racial bigotry that still exist. In their view, since the system continues to yield unequal results for particular racial minorities, it must be maintaining its original sin, and therefore, failure to act is enabling continual injustice (Zinn, 1980; Hannah-Jones, 2021).

For Protectors, only the people operating within a victim group can accurately know what it is like to be the recipient of racism or marginalization. Their opinions of their "lived experiences" gain preferential status. Policies recommended by outsiders, especially those *not advocating* passive-receptive compensations such as reparations, must be silenced. Those individuals cannot possibility know the needs that must be gratified to erase the past traumas.

In this view, it is likely that individuals balking at these assertions are simply protecting their *privilege*. The best policy is to ignore them, treat them with caution, or have them censored. As a way to rectify past wrongs, there should be extensive hiring, sponsoring, and anointing of individuals who have firsthand knowledge of the life struggles of marginalized groups.

This is why it is essential to elect officials *within* the aggrieved group to represent their causes in government affairs. Only leaders and teachers inside the group can provide adequate role models for optimum guidance to occur. Instead of endorsing a cultural standard, such as judging people by the content of their character and not by the color of their skin, the battle cry is to "lean in," double down, and fight with the sword of identity politics.

While the shift to use race as a criterion of employment may defy Title VII of the Civil Rights Act, many businesses seem to be following this course in order to be consistent with the progressivism of our times. They purge remnants of guilt for being part of the "bigoted" establishment, and justify remaining capitalists by forwarding the advancement of marginalized people. In this way, they become "good people," and they avoid the negative publicity that occurs when individuals defy the "progressive" message.

In contrast, Promoters bring forth the argument that reductions to racial problems can, and do, come from people who have not directly experienced bigotry. For them, the motto, "You don't have to have cancer to treat cancer," applies. They do not think it is necessary to destroy the culture, and they emphasize that many people have worked hard to rid the country of legalized racism. Moreover, they point out that only a subset of people and politicians endorsed that doctrine when it was sanctioned (D'Souza, 2021).

Even from the outset, many worked hard to correct bigoted mistakes and hypocrisies in order for the country to reach its idealized goal of "equality before the law." They note that while there was initial *inheritance* of laws permitting slavery, in disloyalty to its ideals, as well as problems transitioning slaves into free society, significant bloodshed has occurred to eliminate that worldwide debauchery well before most other nations (PragerU, 2017).

In their view, those who characterize America as inherently racist are promulgating lies (Grabar, 2019), and this includes the recently acclaimed 1619 Project (PragerU, 2020). Promoters believe that these critics are libeling a society that is, in its founding principles, quite exceptional in fostering benign and tolerant treatment of fellow humans, despite its initial "birth defect" of allowing slavery and not declaring its elimination until the Emancipation Proclamation in 1863.

This does not mean that Promoters are so naïve that they believe there is no bigotry in America's racially diverse society. They realize that in-group preference is a likely psychological phenomenon whenever groups differ in their behaviors and decision-making. However, Promoters want to preserve a current way of life and keep improving upon it without taking drastic counterproductive measures. They do not want to obliterate "the good," simply because it is not perfect.

For them, Western civilization is not the font of all evils, especially when compared with the storied histories of other cultures and empires. While they recognize that in-group preference might make multiculturalism difficult, they do not see this as an insurmountable problem. In contrast to Protectors, they do not believe that people invariably learn better when instructed by someone who mirrors a similar identity. They claim that there are no pervasive empirics supporting that assertion (Program on Constitutional Government at Harvard, 2018).

In their view, even if there is some initial lessening of anxiety when students and teachers are from the same ilk, how important is that early reaction in comparison to the interactions that play out over time? For instance, do the instructors show ongoing respect and competency? Moreover, one only has to note that the Success Academy Charter Schools in New York City achieved superlative results with a Caucasian founder and a staff of White teachers instructing a population of Black and Hispanic students (Sowell, 2020).

Promoters also question the recent trend in the economic mainstream to elevate race over traditional employment credentials. Once again, they point out that there is no empirical basis supporting the claim that institutions or businesses produce better outcomes when they hire particular racial assortments in their employee population (Razo Bravo, 2020). Of course, if people boycott organizations that do not abide by a mandate for diversity, then business would, in fact, suffer in relation to the coercion of that political agenda. But that has nothing to do with the assertion that racial mixtures produce better outcomes.

Overall, Promoters do not believe that the race (or any other immutable characteristic) of the person who makes an idea or performs a task will matter as much as what Protectors proclaim. Moreover, if we apply a *universal* principle to the Protector rendition of how people learn, we would not hire a qualified Black teacher if the class contained primarily White students. In this circumstance, the teacher could not possibly know how to teach students of a different color endowed with so much privilege, and students would have trouble learning as well.

Therefore, while some advance empirics showing the benefits of racial diversity in a classroom (The Century Foundation, 2019), Promoters doubt that group outcomes will invariably enhance by introducing diversities of race or cultural blends, just as creating a diversity of personalities may not give individuals more meaningful group experiences in mental health units. They remain skeptical that having people from a wide ambit of economic backgrounds, skill levels, ethnicities, genders, or sexual preferences will always lead to predictable outcomes in the classroom, for all students, or in any other setting (Thomas Sowell Channel, 2021).

Despite that many people (including some Supreme Court justices) endorsed the view that classroom diversity has inherent advantages, this issue is far from settled. Those who question this presumption recognize that successful outcomes might relate to many subtle factors including the kinds of diversity mixtures, the particular goals of the group, the particular conditions that are extant, and the unique people in the groups.

For example, in the case of busing students, did the coerced diversity result in positive effects for all, most, or even some students? According to Thomas Sowell, those diversity initiatives did not result in any general educational advances. He adds that racially segregated education is not inherently inferior, and points out that numerous Black and Hispanic charter schools have performed at very high levels in numerous cities. Likewise, the all-Black Dunbar School (on a very limited budget) was exemplary, and produced many Black scholars for decades prior to the disruptive forces imposed by political ideologues (Sowell, 2006; 2019; 2020).

In addition to these concerns, Promoters also object to the assertion that every occupational group within the society must have the same racial composition as the population at large, or it is practicing bigotry. They do not presume that the racial composition of an occupation is a litmus test for racial injustice, as disparate outcomes do not provide information about whether racial fairness did or did not occur.

For them, the occurrence of diversity of color in the given realm of achievement is not prima facie strength or an indictment of an institution or society, as they do not see disparate outcomes as a bigotry clue. Since it is *normative* for ethnic groups to differ in achievements, skills, and preferences throughout the world, they believe that there is no reason to presume racial prejudice unless there is *evidence* to the contrary (BasicEconomics, 1981).

As you can see, Promoters are unhappy about making the diversity issue the panacea for society. They ask, *In what way is orchestrating different proportions of different identities serving the goals of any group, business, or institution?* For example, in the academy, it might be to transmit and build upon a history of knowledge within reasoned, courteous, and free discussion that puts ideas under scientific scrutiny. They wonder whether the identity selections and topic censorships that are so prevalent in these institutions are helping to accelerate those objectives.

While private organizations may select whom they want to hire and include, as long as they are not violating federal civil rights law, promoting *a diversity of identity* agenda may take the organization far afield from their raison d'être. This quest might also penalize many individuals who have worked hard to meet the meritocratic criteria of the establishment. It gives administrators the license to advance their political bias, simply by saying that particular individuals were less "amiable" or preferable for community objectives (Blogging-heads.tv, 2020).

Do the people supporting these organizations and businesses know about what is currently happening? Do shareholders or alumni know how their money is invested? Might this be an important civil rights issue?

In general, while the inclusion of various identity types, socioeconomic strata, and racial mixtures might enhance novelty, increase the number of perspectives, or yield social pleasure in various ways, Promoters believe that selecting for quality of performance might actually enhance more achievements and a greater number of usable ideas. For them, creating a concoction of diversity does not necessarily equate with raising the quality of any particular outcome. After all, this is an empirical matter, not a self-evident truth, and a Protector agenda may have all kinds of repercussions on organizations and society that are not currently assessed (Mac Donald, 2018). However, if the aim is to overturn the status quo, then possible disruptions are not a concern.

Insidious Racism

When considering the viability of a race within a larger group, it is important to examine the ways in which patterns of behavior in the minority group sync with the dominant group, particularly if the minority group wants to intermingle. It is also crucial to understand whether explicit laws or subtle patterns of behavior within the majority group might be negatively affecting people with minority status. While the majority might not think that they are being harmful, it is important to do a careful investigation.

As expected, Protectors focus on systemic bias, or the ways in which majority-group behaviors and laws exacerbate achievement difficulties for the minority. In their view, these factors are the cause of the difficulties that envelop the minority, and eradication of those events must occur. In contrast, Promoters examine the minority's current patterns of behavior. If others harm them, they want it stopped. However, instead of seeing adaptation to the majority group as oppressive, they see this approach as potentially helpful.

Moreover, rather than presume nefarious intent from the majority, Promoters seek alternative explanations when accounting for social hierarchies. They are even willing to consider the possibility that *helping* policies enacted for *benevolent* reasons may have backfired and created substantial uncalculated negative results. They do not want others to see their attempts to *assist* as another instance of bigotry.

For example, they point out that the deficient skills of many Blacks were improving at a faster rate soon after slavery, and prior to the implementation of our current welfare system (Hoover Institution, 2019; Hillsdale College, 2015). They adhere to the belief that harmful racist environs may not be the main culprits at this time, and they do not want to ignore data that points us in a different direction.

Promoters want to avoid grossly overestimating the power of prejudice when explaining the social stratification of various races and other marginalized identities. They refuse to accept the view that identity harm is always the *primary* explanation for the achievement and life satisfaction differences between racial groups. For example, if more successful jazz musicians are Black, this does not mean that they attain this status because they are adept at suppressing White players.

They also reject the view that society organizes in relation to fixed-status identity groups, where particular groups are either oppressors or victims. They believe that this explanation lacks coherence. For example, Jews have clearly been victims of unvarnished racism, which often takes place when minorities function as economic middlemen (Sowell, 2006). But some will characterize this group as supremacists who perpetrate harm against other minority groups. In some circles, Jews are not only occupying stolen land, but they are also successful capitalists who control of large quantities of financial resources that relegate others to poverty. These factors alone provide enough grounds for many to show a viral hatred against them (Brokin, 2010).

However, given these opposing characterizations, are Jews oppressors, or are they the oppressed when ranking their position on the hierarchy grid? Since they are not prioritized, Promoters wonder why successful minorities such as Jews, Asians, and others who endure significant racial discrimination can remain low on the Protector's totem pole. Despite the bigotry directed toward them, Protectors seem disinterested in providing them safety from racial harms.

The presumption seems to be that the prowess of these groups is likely depriving others of their assets, and in that sense, they are "White adjacent" minority oppressors, even though they may suffer racial discrimination. Consequently, if they do not pledge devotion to the social justice agenda, they have little value within the Protector camp, regardless of the amount of racism they bear.

For these reasons, Promoters assert that Protectors are *not* primarily concerned with bigotry; they seem more focused on promoting a political agenda, which they imagine will produce a more idealized society. They believe that Protectors might be cloaking that objective with the justification that they are eradicating bigotry harms, which tends to mobilize more empathy and political interest.

Moreover, even if a struggling minority group has cultural practices that are inconsistent with Protector ideology, they might still gain entrance into the Protector fraternity if they can buttress their political cause. For example, Protectors typically align with Muslim groups, even though those groups do not ascribe to feminism. But the alliance helps the resistance toward White culture, which is often a more important endeavor.

Promoters bring these contradictions to light, and wonder whether identity politics, as currently practiced, is an honest depiction of what they are doing. That is, are they racial discrimination warriors and saviors of individuals suffering from racial harms? Or are they activists questing to organize society as they see fit?

While there may not be a definitive answer to this question, both political camps agree to the imperative to wipe out blatant laws advocating the unequal treatment of individuals based on race, other immutable characteristics, and harmless sexual preferences. However, the two sides diverge when accounting for ongoing disparities in quality of life between races. Promoters focus on changing the actions of the individuals in the groups, while Protectors focus on what other people are doing to the individuals in the groups.

Protectors claim that there are still many forms of racism in modern societies; it is important not to be lulled to sleep. In their view, underachieving minorities still experience adversities caused by bigoted incumbents. While certain laws might seem to apply to all individuals, majority group cultural patterns still exist, and they are subtlety creating harms upon vulnerable groups. These patterns are not explicit like slavery laws, but they are influential, and they affect some racial groups more others.

Protectors believe that certain racial identities struggle because of an unspoken and *insidious* bigotry that emanates from the dominant group, and they will not be swayed. This is always the case, and the blatant mistreatment of racial minorities in the past creates the *truth nugget* for this assertion. Protectors claim that patterns of majority group actions stealthily and unconsciously maintain acts of prejudice, control, and subjugation. They hold that even when powerful groups are unaware of their *bias*, they continue to design laws and enact behaviors that safeguard and perpetuate their societal dominance. They call this "unconscious bias," and it purportedly happens even at the early stage of evaluating an applicant's resume for a job (Kang, et. al. 2016).

However, in rebuttal, Promoters point out that careful scrutiny of that kind of data frequently illuminates an alternative explanation that does not relate to bigotry. For example, when looking at the aforementioned job resume findings with a discerning lens, racial preferences are not consistent (Elejalde-Ruiz, 2016). They also emphasize that there are *socioeconomic factors* that correlate with the kinds of names on the applications that are influencing the decisions. In their view, racism is not the culprit that accounts for the assessment discrepancies. Those doing the evaluations were sorting according to economic class, regardless of race, as a way to predict job success (Chen, 2018).

In response, Protectors have many concerns when they hear these kinds of alternative interpretations of data. They are skeptical of empiricism that leads others to doubt the presence of implicit bias. They remind us that the usage of science can be simply another way for people in power to impose on the vulnerable, and close the door on their concerns.

Although, in an attempt to defend scientific procedure, Promoters ask, *Why is it necessary to presume that science is bad or oppressive, simply because one racial group uses and excels in this way of producing knowledge? Might we instead help other groups learn about the advantages of systematic inquiry, the value of due process, and the use of evidence to formulate conclusions? Might the scientific method compare favorably in relation to other ways of producing knowledge, such as relying on religious beliefs, mythologies, or anecdotal accounts and personal narratives?*

Yes, science can create social power, but it can also help to identify the crux of a problem and help to eradicate it. However, and without wincing, Protectors frequently ignore science when it seems to be imposing on the vulnerable. In their belief system, there is always an *implicit* tendency throughout society that impairs the progress of minority groups, and this includes how people create knowledge, and how facts are used. They are wary of any social pattern that seems to diminish the advocacy of struggling minorities, and they maintain this view, even after the elimination of unjust laws. They would rather ensnare acts of bigotry as those acts that *casually* occur throughout day-to-day living, as determined by "woke" scholars who are capable of seeing the true nature of these unrecognized injustices (Pluckrose and Lindsay, 2020).

This assertion, interestingly enough, seems remarkably consistent with the views espoused by Sigmund Freud over one hundred years ago (Freud and Strachey, 1965). Within that framework, it is possible for people to have motives that reside outside of their awareness.

Only keenly educated observers (i.e., psychoanalytically trained psychiatrists) can unravel the mysteries of these hidden motives, which are invariably more nefarious than what the enactors of the behaviors are willing to admit.

Analogously, Protectors assert that people have been oppressing others for so long, they are no longer aware of their aberrant behavior. They should alternatively recognize that their past and present actions are the cause of many unsavory behaviors that are presently occurring within marginalized groups. Everyone should remember that the true menace is racial persecution, which continues to impair the well-being of these groups. It is not that racism is gone; it is that people are oblivious to their villainy and the consequences of their past crimes.

Protectors remind us that it makes sense to keep looking for racial harms, because sequela currently exist from previous acts of legal racial wrongdoing. They point out that there are likely to be current problems associated with the behavioral changes and coping strategies that took place to deal with the restrictions on freedoms imposed on certain racial groups.

Even though the legal sanction of racism seen in past decades is gone, the effects of past discriminatory policies and the culture of the antebellum South are still weighing heavily on many segments of Black minority population (Sowell, 2006). As noted by Shelby Steele, ongoing problems associated with manumission account for a considerable amount of their underdevelopment and failure to progress in the dominant culture (Hoover Institution, 2018).

Even though both camps agree with this analysis, the debate is not settled. The camps continue to recommend different ways to address the problem. While Protectors want to replace what was taken from people who were harmed from bigotry, Promoters emphasize that a cure may not always be a matter of reversing past mistakes; undoing strategies may not automatically make people whole. The method of compensating for past wrongs through gift giving and easements may not be the best or only way to help the harmed individuals.

If helping strategies unwittingly inhibit working, and simultaneously do not aid in producing behavioral changes that allow economically disadvantaged people to compete on equal footing with others, Promoters are concerned that we are condoning dependency and conditioning these individuals to rely on special external accommodations ad infinitum. A Promoter wonders how this is reparative in any meaningful way. After the gifts deteriorate, so do the individuals, who still do not know how to create their own wealth.

While this argument is compelling, Protectors are not persuaded. They continue to emphasize the occurrence of ongoing racial harms, which if eradicated, *would* produce acceptable healing. While Promoters harp on skill development and adequate schooling as a way to instigate improvements, Protectors assert that emphasizing those kinds of variables is simply bellicose *victim-blaming,* and further evidence of a cauldron of racism.

In their ideology, we must always look to racism as the all-purpose creator and reason for the persistence of struggles for marginalized minority groups; it is always present and always influential. The extenuating and ongoing effects of racial (and other identity) injustices essentially instill disinterest in education, law breaking, and economic failures. All roads lead to that Rome.

It is therefore unreasonable to expect new learning to make a substantial difference under these conditions; David cannot eradicate Goliath without a total undoing of the majority culture. While some might argue that many groups start out far behind, incur social hardship, and eventually catch up, many Protectors discount that data. They attribute the success of these groups to lesser amounts of historical bigotry, and fewer experiences of bigotry undertones that still exist for some identities.

Since Blacks in America endured slavery, Jim Crow laws, and other explicit and implicit racial harms, Protectors believe that their situation is exceptional. For this group, we should avoid any insinuation of personal accountability for their economic and social difficulties. We should instead continue to eliminate continuing maltreatments, including those that are unconscious, as the first order of business. It is simply unconscionable to require systemically harmed individuals to learn and make changes as a first order of business. We should instead gauge what we took from them and give it back.

Protectors claim that until we eliminate our subtle and not so subtle acts of racism, our national character continues to be unjust. We should be condemned until reparations equalize the quality of life between the previously enslaved racial group and the group that perpetrated the egregious sin. Observations of inequalities of achievement between these groups, as well as their lesser representation in higher status activities, should ignite inquiry into the possibility that the aggrieved group is still being debilitated by sources of majority power.

If minorities, for instance, show underrepresentation in university physics departments, then it must be because of hidden racism. It is not that racial groups differ in their preferences for achievement and learning exposures without the involvement of racial animas. Likewise, if they have deficiencies in health outcomes, it is not that endogenous characteristics or non-coerced lifestyle preferences affect those results.

The assertion is that past and current pernicious sources are causing those outcomes and creating obstacles. While, for a variety of reasons, these accusations do not occur in minority-dominated sports, they do occur when minority groups struggle. For example, while no one blinks an eye when both Black- and White-owned banks show similar patterns of disparate racial outcomes when giving bank loans, *racism* is the default explanation whenever outcomes show that Blacks are lagging behind Whites (Sowell, 2019).

Not surprisingly, Promoters focus on the many notable problems with this way of thinking. For example, despite the supposed power of the White majority to oppress, Asians are more successful than Whites at obtaining bank loans and surviving employment cutbacks, and they show higher standardized test scores and school achievement than Whites on a consistent basis (Sowell, 2011; 2012). Promoters cite that kind of data to underscore the *possibility* that racial disparities can and do occur independently from majority group incentives to promote themselves over others.

In this regard, Sowell (2015) points out that what emerges in *systemic economic outcomes* relates to a multitude of cause-and-effect interactions, which can be very different from the intentions of the individuals participating in the system. That is, a person might have a purpose in mind, but what transpires will also depend on what others do, and a myriad of other variables. Likewise, Dawkins (2015) asserts that "evolution" occurs within massive numbers of cause-and-effect interactions without a preconceived plan or knowledge of genetics.

When applying this conception to racial disparities, it means that no one has to be *intending* racial harm (either consciously or unconsciously) for differences to appear. To illustrate, did ardent supporters for higher minimum wages *intend* for Black entry-level workers to have more unemployment, when that is what occurred? As the saying goes, life can often disregard even the best of intensions.

Moreover, rather than understand the persistence of bigoted *beliefs* as having an insurmountable and ongoing negative impact on vulnerable people, Promoters claim that this factor is less important than many presume. For example, it is currently advantageous for the academy, Big Tech, and others to discriminate against White males in order to include *more* underrepresented identities.

Whether or not they have bigoted beliefs against White males, they are free to make these discriminations, and ultimately enhance their "brand," even though they are *acting* with racial bias. In this example, *not* exhibiting preferential treatment for various races and identities is a tremendous social and economic systemic risk, so they have no compunction *acting* in a racially bias manner. In other words, s*ocial and economic consequences* seem to determine actions and decisions; silent *beliefs* do not seem as consequential.

Moreover, if we assume that an undercurrent of in-group preference will often occur because people typically favor what is familiar and similar to them, then there might often be a partiality for people showing common identities. As the saying goes, "Birds of a feather flock together," and this tendency also occurs for people *within* an identity group, as they will also self-sort (Frazier, 1997). Nevertheless, while this propensity might exist as part of the human condition, it may not be the dominant force in determining myriad real-world *acts* of bigotry, if those preferences have unacceptable costs.

We might then conclude that the power of *bigoted beliefs* pales in comparison to looking at the real-world outcomes that occur when *behaving* in bigoted ways, which others may evaluate as positive or negative, depending on the circumstance and the identities of the individuals involved. The problem is not whether people have or do not have bigoted beliefs; it is that people sometimes *act* to diminish certain racial groups and identities when it is in their best interest to do so, and they do not act in those ways, when it is counterproductive.

The pocketbook and social reaction will determine the occurrence of *bigoted behaviors.* For example, owners of NBA teams might or might not have the same racial beliefs as they did in 1950, when Blacks were first allowed to play in the league, but they currently employ Blacks at high rates in order to win games (Sowell, 2021).

Protectors will likely respond to these assertions by saying that people are still behaving in unacceptable bigoted ways in many other organizations, professions, and activities. They will insist that people's actions are still creating faint, but notable, harms. We just have to look for them with more intensity in those domains in which they are still affecting outcomes.

While this might be true, Promoters claim that this is an empirical matter, and they wonder whether there are currently too many negative social and economic consequences in mainstream endeavors for ongoing bigoted *actions* to be an overwhelming scourge. They doubt whether teachers, academic institutions, or Big Tech, who are fountainheads for anti-racist causes, are going to be so racist (consciously or unconsciously) within their organizations to create tangible disruptions for minorities. Instead, Promoters note that these groups are bending over backward to promote a diversity agenda. They remain steadfast that there are viable alternative explanations for disparate racial outcomes other than bigotry. And they retain this view, even when evaluating our current legal system.

Racism and the Law

While Promoters recognize that there *were* laws designed to *explicitly* oppress some racial groups, they are unwilling to deduce that current laws written in a racially neutral fashion have the *unconscious intent* to maintain racial bigotry, simply because outcomes continue to be racially imbalanced. They are vehemently against *fast-forwarding* what happened in the past as a way to explain what is occurring now, and reject the claim that those practices are still frequent and common. In their view, we must be careful not to create *phantom racism* with a specious argument.

For Promoters, disparity of arrests, prosecutions, and incarceration rates do not necessarily expose racial bigotry. In their view, if particular crimes occur more frequently than expected, compared to population percentages, the associations could occur because particular racial groups are committing particular crimes at relatively high-frequency rates (Mac Donald, 2016). For example, while data shows that Blacks get longer sentencing than Caucasians for similar crimes (Demographic Differences in Sentencing, 2018), when disaggregating that finding, about 80 percent of sentencing disparity relates to the seriousness of the crimes and criminal histories of the perpetrators (Starr and Rehavi, 2012). Moreover, variables such as inner-city location, access to quality of legal help, and differences in plea bargaining seem to explain the preponderance of differences in length of sentencing more effectively than racial bigotry (Ball et al., 2011; Chen, 2018).

However, these empirics do not change the views of most Protectors. For them, each one of these variables becomes a *consequence* of racism. The enemy is not misbehavior; it is prejudice. Protectors remain firm in their belief that disparate outcomes indicate the lingering and ongoing effects of racial bigotry, and others cannot persuade them to adopt any other explanation.

For example, while different rates of school suspensions for different races might relate to frequency or the intensity of misconduct, Protectors advocate laws that *prohibit* discipline that might lead to differing rates of suspensions between racial groups. They believe there is ample reason not to penalize minority students for their "wrongdoing." To do so is equivalent to denying the social harms that caused their behaviors. They refer to this as "blaming the victim," and they would rather show increased tolerance for the students so as not to create even more harm to them. In essence, the crimes were not their fault.

This trend continues despite the possibility that the aforementioned law might actually help numerous minority students. Pupils of all races might learn better when not disrupted by other students who misbehave in the classroom. The law might be prosecuting more individuals within a particular minority bloc, but it does not mean that the law is *detrimental* to that minority, when considering all the non-offenders in the group.

Echoing this sentiment, Mac Donald (Hoover Institution, 2018) points out that the recent trends to impose double standards on school discipline to correct disparate group impact is undermining achievement for struggling minorities, and widening the racial divide. In this view, prior to denigrating any social policy as summarily harmful, it makes sense to do a thorough analysis in relation to the consequences on a wide range of individuals, over an expanded time frame, before trashing the legal enactment (Flanders and Goodnow, 2017). This approach might be particularly helpful for *most people* in a particular minority group, even if more of their members are punished for their actions.

Consequently, Promoters remain committed to retain laws, even when disparate-group impact occurs. As long as the law is not cruel, applies to everyone, and the benefits seem to outweigh the harms, it has utility. They recognize that some groups might be more likely to suffer the negative effects of the law, but that does not mean the law has malicious intent. They are willing to help individuals who break the law learn to abide by its limits, and study possible legal changes so that the law is not counterproductive. However, they remain unwavering in their efforts to keep punitive consequences, even if there is a simultaneous effort to rehabilitate by finding the so-called root causes of crime.

While Promoters recognize the problem that some races are experiencing difficult circumstances and misfortune at higher rates, there is still the necessity to change unwanted behaviors. Of course, we can send mental health workers into the schools and attempt to modify the recalcitrance through psychotherapeutic intervention. However, even if this helps to some extent, Promoters believe that it is still important to impose laws that have a track record of empirically reducing crime rates (Sowell, 2012).

For Promoters, having a law is a way to dissuade people from future unacceptable acts, regardless of the historical events leading up to the crime. Promoters want laws that influence learning and subsequent behaviors, and they believe that consequences for breaking laws helps people modify ensuing behavior, as well as provide redress to victims. In their view, it is not kind to the perpetrator who is not corrected, and it is neglectful of all the other people affected by the crime.

Again, if there is suspicion of bigotry, this is an empirical matter that should be dealt with earnestly and supported by the facts that evolve from a thorough investigation. However, Promoters recognize that there is still the necessity to improve tactics of discipline, and they are willing to rewrite laws and penalties for various crimes that could needlessly ruin a person's future. This approach is simply questioning the impulse to see bigotry as a first and only hypothesis to account for all racial disparities in our legal system, including lethal force by the police (Mac Donald, 2017; Fryer, 2019; Alpha News, 2020).

Moreover, Promoters insist that even if certain instances within a legal system qualify as racist, it does not mean that the *entire* system is bigoted. Using exaggerations and the fallacy of composition to prove a point can only exacerbate misunderstandings and incite people. With the power of the media to disseminate and highlight troubling incidents, it is not surprising that singular events become emblematic for uprisings. When people believe that disparate outcomes and unseemly events mean pervasive racial bigotry, it becomes close to impossible to refute any explanation that does not conform to that point of view.

Racial Disparities: Causes, and Solutions

Clearly, polemics are at a standstill. Protectors vehemently believe there is a silent toxin that continues to saturate society, much like it did in the past, even if people do not know it. Individuals failing to recognize this are complicit with racism, and in that sense, they are morally corrupt (Kendi, 2019). Put differently, if they do not ascribe to his orthodoxy, they are racists. However, that proclamation does not sit well in the Promoter camp. They wonder why it is not possible to disagree with Kendi without suffering debasement, and they dislike the coercion embedded in his belief system. (Intercollegiate Studies Institute, 2020).

While extremist Protectors implore others to denounce their "privilege" and find ways to ease the burdens they impose on the marginalized, as advised by Kendi, Promoters remain focused on altering patterns of functioning that are occurring within a racial group—whether or not the behaviors are caused or influenced by past and present-day racial sins. These patterns of actions are important to address and change, regardless of their etiology. Their focus is on moving forward, and they believe that searching for hidden racism may accomplish little in the long term.

Interestingly enough, and consistent with the view that racism is not always the most important variable to pursue, Sowell (1994; 2006; 2016) claims that variations in landscape, climate, isolation from others, technology, and cultural patterns will typically account for significant differences in economic achievement between different groups, races, and countries. Even when groups have no contact with each other, it is the rule, rather than exception, that the skills, patterns of knowledge, and the achievements of groups will differ in significant ways. All of that data *contradicts* the view that disparities between different groups must relate to harms that one group imposes upon another.

Other data consistent with this conclusion are evident when immigrant groups with similar appearance to a struggling indigenous group quickly outperform the established group. While this result could relate to "the selectivity of migration" (i.e., moving correlates with talent and ambition), and that they did not endure long-standing legal discriminations, it does suggest that *skin color* alone or minority status may not impede upward mobility. Even if we presume the ongoing presence of discriminatory practices, these groups are able to flourish in the same country where similarly looking people continue to struggle.

This pattern has been evident for many West Indian migrants (especially the females), who succeed in America despite their racial status and physical resemblance to other struggling minorities (Model, 2008). Likewise, a similar pattern of success (that often surpasses their previous standard of living) is evident for Nigerians and other African populations of immigrants, and it occurs for Indians, Pakistanis, Filipinos, Taiwanese, Lebanese, Sri Lankans, Chinese, and Iranians who outperform White Americans on a regular basis (Data Driven Conclusions, 2020). Moreover, Asians continue to flourish despite the overt systemic discriminatory policies of some elite colleges who are making it more difficult for them to gain admission to their schools (Churchill, 2020).

Promoters wonder how any of these outcomes are consistent with explanations focusing solely on racial harms and the insurmountable nature of ongoing racial bigotry. They also wonder why White Appalachians are one of the poorest demographics in the country, if they possess the sought-after "White privilege." While some might claim that this group is not taking advantage of their special social prize, what data is evident to support that claim? In what way do they neglect their societal *gifts,* as compared with other racial groups operating in destitute conditions?

For these kinds of reasons, Promoters want to investigate other ways to account for disparate outcomes. Those inquiries might be more helpful in comparison to fixating on the racism dynamic. For example, if there are more Jewish doctors than what is anticipated from the group's percentage in the population (Templar and Tangan, 2014), does it mean that medical schools are basing admission on the ascertainment of Jewish heritage. Very likely, there are many other reasons that could explain the higher percentage rates for this group's involvement in the medical field.

Thus, the question remains: To what extent is a group's current hardship attributable to unwarranted and harmful treatment instigated by the majority culture in the past or present? While Promoters recognize that Blacks in America are suffering from harms perpetrated against them, they also want to explore the possibility that some, or much, of their current difficulties relate to factors that have little to do with past legal injustices, ongoing systemic bias, or unconscious bias.

As previously mentioned, Promoters speculate that the origins of present-day observed inequality attributed to acts of bigotry against Blacks and other minority groups might even include the *unintended* consequences of acts ostensibly designed to *alleviate* their suffering. This inference is tenable particularly when studies show that the upward trends in economic and social well-being were rising faster prior to the appeasing social interventions, which many call the "cradle to grave" mentality. That data shows that community civility, family breakup, income advancement, and educational skills all became worse after the Great Society policies and welfare mindset came into play (Tanner, 1995).

While these policies came to the forefront to *help* relieve suffering, flourishing did not increase; *intentions* did not result in better systemic outcomes. Blacks victimized by legalized bigotry seemed to function better in many respects with less permissible freedoms and more racial prejudice, in comparison to societal trends that perpetuated more dependency (Independent Institute, 2014). For example, even in the late 1800's, in a period much closer to the end of legalized slavery, there were Black high schools outperforming White high schools in Washington, DC (Sowell, 2019). That kind of data led some to ask, *What is it about progressive policies that invariability lead to regressive results* (The Rubin Report, 2020)?

Clearly, Protectors and Promoters alike agree that the post-civil-rights era is *morally superior*, and many individuals might be better off *materially* due to the gifted entitlements. However, the created subculture arising from the kinds of attempts to repair damages seems to be a step backward for long-term upward mobility. This is especially the case in relation to losses in personal responsibility and family disintegration, which has had an extremely detrimental impact on males who might otherwise benefit from having a positive male role model within the home.

Giving more credence to this interpretation, Thomas Sowell notes the same constellation of subculture deterioration is evident in England, with Caucasians dependent on entitlements (Guest Editorial, 2015). The problem is not restricted to only one racial subgroup and its unique history.

Consequently, while people might agree about the likelihood of past racial sins exerting influence on what is happening now, as history always has an effect, current negative outcomes may also relate to helping policies that are making problems worse, and influencing community decision-making in deleterious ways. Given the complexity of the problem, it is difficult to calculate how much of a group or individual's current lagging is due to the original sin of slavery, racially bias laws, explicit mistreatments, unconscious bigoted acts, or related to other factors, which may well include the kinds of help offered that worked contrary to predictions. The adage, "The road to hell is paved with good intentions," comes to mind.

In any event, if Blacks showed more rapid improvement closer to the time of slavery, as compared to what happened after the civil rights movement, why attribute the current lagging primarily to the occurrence of slavery (Sowell, 2021; 2011)? Moreover, since it is common for groups of color to come to America, with or without necessary skills, and in one generation, escape poverty, it is conceivable that long-term submerging into our welfare system is an important contributing factor that impedes advancement for American Blacks. As Jason Riley states, "Please stop helping us" (Riley, 2016).

This discussion also brings to light the question whether the leaders of minority groups advocating for governmental interventions are making matters worse rather than better. Their charismatic power to induce an increase in entitlements may not lead to the desired *economic power* for their adherents. As stated by Riley (2017), rarely do those kinds of efforts help people develop "human capital," such as skills to advance and make money within a market system.

Many are concerned that disenfranchised groups will simply funnel into the entitlement system and live dependently within its borders. Without skill development to earn a higher standard of living, they are stalled. The symbolism of racial group membership possessed by a politician does not matter if the policies advocated do not produce more flourishing and self-reliance. Likewise, *not* having a politician of a particular race does not mean that the system will be rigged against the targeted minority, or insensitive to its needs. It is certainly possible that a non-group member could advocate for policies that could be of great benefit.

In pursuit of viable ways to assist, Promoters find it more reasonable to study the problems of those who struggle with a different lens. They would rather look for an array of contributing factors instead of focusing only on matching skin colors for political representation. They want policies that advance financial achievement rather than dependency, and they do not see this approach as victim-blaming. The perspective is simply claiming that everyone involved can contribute to the solution, and they believe that help can take many different forms, even if skin colors between the helpers and recipients do not coincide.

The focus shifts to identifying specific behaviors that need to change, with the goal of finding improvements to the identified hardships. For example, develop behavioral changes where minority students are no longer viewed as "acting White" when they achieve at school. Or find ways to incentivize family stability (Sowell, 2006). Identifying ways to alter these social patterns might be extremely beneficial, although it requires looking at the problem from many different angles. A cynic might say, if your glasses only allow you to see racism, then racism is all you see, but perhaps a different focus will be less myopic.

Unfortunately, according to Promoters, there is a significant barrier when trying to implement alternative explanations for racial disparities. Namely, if a person's political cause strengthens when identifying incidences of racism, then finding those occurrences will yield an increase in desired power and appreciation. Many Promoters claim that the *need* to identify racial bigotry expands well-beyond its actual occurrence, as too many have too much at stake to stop harping on this way to account for societal hierarchies in today's political climate.

It is therefore not surprising that Promoters are pushing back against the current trend of many Protectors to endorse *critical race theory* (Stefancic and Delgado, 2017; Critical Race Theory-Key Elements, 2020). In their view, the theory leads people to see racism everywhere, and it introduces three major problems that could implode society rather than improve it.

First, they contend that advocates of critical race theory assume an incontestable victimhood of disadvantaged groups in society. All of the misfortunes of these individuals are allegedly caused by an underlying racism or other identity oppression (Crenshaw, 2019). For Promoters, this conceptualization recreates the same mentality that occurs with all acts of bigotry. Namely, group commonality trumps personal uniqueness. There is no consideration of individual exceptions. Everyone must align with group characterizations. Oppressors are culpable, even when not cognizant of their disservice to others. And people are victims, even when unaware of how they are being harmed.

Second, proponents of the theory assert that any reticence, questioning, or disagreement with their presumptions are by fiat wrong, depraved, or imbued with a "fragility" that prevents giving up privileged status and pursuing anti-racist policies (DiAngelo, 2018). Similar to most religions, they proclaim a metaphysical truth, there is guilt for not joining, no opportunity to disagree, and they promote an increased vulnerability and disdain toward outsiders who refuse to join in (Triggernometry, 2020).

Third, the theory advocates special compensations and entitlements as remedies, without ascertaining the extent to which those actions might induce dependencies and other forms of ineffectual behaviors that interfere with advancement. Like other Protector interventions, they seem to ignore the possibility that they could be hampering those they are trying to help.

Consequently, while those who endorse critical race theory seem intent on "discovering" presumed racist actions, Promoters wonder what might happen if they stopped inferring that crime with so much certainty and vehemence? What if there is a shift to other significant factors? What if empirical outcomes that are currently indices of racist vectors, have little or nothing to do with that dynamic? What might happen if minority group leaders lead a movement that develops "human capital" instead of expanding the menu of entitlements to offset inferred racism?

Let us take the following example to illustrate these kinds of concerns. There is now increased income disparity between minority groups and others, as single-parent households proliferate in minority communities. Single-parent households have a distinct disadvantage in generating family income, as compared with two-parent households, which makes this a significant problem impacting a family's ability to afford a house, among other important acquisitions.

The American Dream is now more out of reach for struggling minority groups due to the explosion of single-parent families. However, instead of malicious racism causing the problem, it occurs in relation to "two-parent privileges" and the role that *helping policies* contributed to family breakup (Rowe, 2020). According to Thomas Sowell, and consistent with this view, even in the 1980s, two-parent Black households were "out-earning" two-parent White households (BasicEconomics, 2012).

While single parenthood might relate in part to the sexual revolution, it seems that it also relates to governmental programs designed specifically to protect the *well-being* of single mothers and children. However, for years, researchers have claimed that these programs have inadvertently led people away from the institutions of work and having children within marriage (Riley, 2014; Moynihan, 1965; Man-in-the-House Rule).

While the deterioration of the two-parent family norm will affect more people as it metastasizes, it currently helps to explain the widening economic and behavioral fissures between racial groups. Unfortunately, some groups are falling prey to these programs out of necessity, and without any other way to obtain assistance.

In sum, Promoters do not agree with the assertion that when members of historically discriminated groups fail to show adequate representation in admired outcomes, it can only be due to a racially based past and present denial of opportunity, or ongoing insidious bigotry by powerful people. They retain an interest in exploring the extent to which minority group underperformance relates to ostensibly benign political actions, while simultaneously recognizing that historical mistreatments set the process in motion and helped to shape what is happening now. However, they claim that even if it is true that current personal behaviors are logical consequences of bigoted systemic power structures, moving forward entails developing self-reliance rather than the perpetuation of dependencies.

While many Protectors continue to see underperforming behaviors of minority groups as consequences of past and present power intrusions and bigoted actions inflicted by the majority culture, Promoters do not want to invariably revert to that singular causal argument. They want to help those who struggle, develop agency and self-reliance so that they can escape from the social safety net, and they reject the idea that skin color or oppressive historical factors are insuperable.

They point to the absence of school choice, and the omnipresent governmental interventions that stymied previous progress in relation to influencing family breakup, skill advancement, work ethic, and increasing crime. They believe that all of these programs failed to build human capital and self-empowerment, which were happening at a faster pace prior to society's attempts to rescue and abet (Hoover Institution, 2019; Hillsdale College, 2015). As said by Voltaire in 1759, "We must cultivate our garden" (Voltaire, 2014), and Promoters agree with Voltaire.

Affirmative Action: Helpful or Harmful

Given that explicit legal racial injustice has occurred in the past, many acknowledge the need to rectify that harm and provide extra help to those impacted by that injustice. In many ways, the entirety of the Protector position is one of reparation, and *Affirmative Action* is a specific kind of boosting designed to bypass stringent performance criteria and lift people forward.

A Protector claims that it is unreasonable to expect that people can compete with others, when inequity has impeded them throughout their lives. If strict meritocracy prevailed, they would never have a chance to win. The hope is that once they occupy higher positions, they will acclimate and eventually attain the kinds of skills that produce success.

By elevating status without full qualifications and accomplishments, it is anticipated that achievements will eventually fall in place. Protectors note that many individuals lifted in this manner have gone on to have productive and outstanding job performance and careers that would not have otherwise occurred.

However, even if the reparation does not accomplish that positive objective consistently, Protectors believe it is morally imperative to implement the policy when marginalized people have suffered mistreatment and ostracism for extremely long periods. Since obstruction of their "rights" occurred, rectifying that crime should supersede all other interests, and a definitive and bold action is required to boost and compensate these harmed individuals. Changing standards is a reasonable and ethical endeavor to give them a chance to experience a respectful social position.

Protectors also claim that a purity of judging people solely on objective criteria has never existed. They point out that nepotism is rampant; people often gain positions of authority and wealth in relation to the people they know, rather than what they can do. One only has to note the ease with which the children of politicians from all racial groups gain entrance into the most prestigious colleges.

They also point out that we often judge people by their appearance, height, manner of speaking, and dress, and any number of different kinds of ancillary traits. It is untenable to claim that people gain status solely, or even primarily (in some cases), in relation to their feats, projected achievements, or current accomplishments. Since that seems to be the case, why not make *racial (and sexual) characteristics* factors that can push individuals ahead, rather than consciously or unconsciously keep them behind, especially when we know that bigotry has been a significant factor impeding their status.

If it is presumed that some people lag due to the circumstance of their birth, and are segregated from others who might otherwise help them learn behaviors that could assist them, we are condemning these marginalized people to a deficient life. This was the logic to bus students to different schools, as it was thought that "separate could never be equal," according to the preconceptions of experts in education, and the enlightened personal beliefs of influential bureaucrats and judges. It was expected that classroom integration would help excluded individuals manifest abilities to learn and thrive.

Parents are often quite aware of the impact that peer groups and milieus can have on their children. They frequently worry about their child's cohorts, and try to orchestrate variations of the logic of school desegregation to help advance their children. Consistent with these concerns, empirics show that exposing troubled adolescents to other misbehaving adolescents during treatment makes them *worse* rather than better (Dishion, McCord, and Poulin, 1999). These outcomes demonstrate that associates can make a substantial difference, and affirmative action has the benefit of providing increased contact with higher functioning cohorts.

In contrast, Promoters are not convinced about the value of implementing affirmative action policies. While they recognize that criteria for merit is not the panacea that some claim it to be, further diminishing its importance is moving in the wrong direction. Instead, they want to enhance the importance of performance criteria and develop techniques to factor out nepotism. They want to make sure that assessments identify the highest echelons of talent, and not allow secondary or irrelevant criteria to overwhelm the process.

Problems with utilizing performance criteria for promotion do not imply diminishing the utility of the selection method; it implies the necessity to make the system better. Making decisions independent of race is not an incidence of perpetuating bigotry; it is following the *universal principle* that all people should be treated in a consistent fashion, regardless of their immutable characteristics.

This was the message of Dr. Martin Luther King Jr. and the Fourteenth Amendment to the Constitution.

This approach is not a denial that some people need help. It is simply an argument against utilizing racial composition, ethnicity, appearance, or sex to determine whether to offer assistance or promotion. Promoters would rather assess an individual's integrity, emotional stability, and prerequisite achievements, including the overcoming of obstacles, and then decide what to do.

Promoters recognize that estimating a person's merit is not an exact science, but they do not want to make surface characteristics the most important variables. They cling to the belief that race and gender are not flawless indicators of having experienced obstacles; immutable traits do not always correlate with hardships, lower socioeconomic status, or lagging skills. Consequently, if there is an offering of special accommodations, it is preferable to assess the individual's *actual* requirement of an easement, rather than give identity traits bonus points carte blanche.

Additionally, since many different traits may interfere with a person's success within a system, Promoters also wonder why we are only providing affirmative action for performance deficits that correlate with sexual characteristics or marginalized racial group membership. For example, if tall people are likely hired and given higher salaries, do we compensate short individuals? If the physically unappealing suffer social exclusion and implicit systemic bias, do we compensate these individuals with affirming policies? These questions point out that assessing a person's liabilities and assets requires an evaluation that goes far beyond skin color or matters pertaining to gender.

In a related problem, since affirmative action has been operating for a half-century, Promoters fear that we might be denying access to valued social positions by limiting people who have nothing to do with the egregious racial sins of the past, or historical employment patterns between the sexes. Given the plethora of compensations marshaled to help certain categories of groups for decades, these seemingly "innocent" individuals sometimes face a steep uphill battle to gain desirable opportunities, while the incumbents keep their seats. Despite their putative "social privilege" of being in a racial group or gender that has generally flourished, they endure noticeable discrimination based on fixed characteristics they can do nothing about. Essentially, their claim to "equal rights" is taken from them.

Interestingly, the same argument is applicable in relation to many immigrant families that came to this country from the vast expanses of Europe, South America, and Central and South Asia. What responsibility do they bear for the racial injustices of earlier decades in America? Do they pay for sins they have not committed? Do we take their rights away? Are they also guilty due to ancestral connection?

Promoters are also quick to point out that not everyone in the dominant culture committed the transgression of legally endorsed racism. They wonder why it is reasonable to indict individuals living now (and the entire country), and whether there is current exaggeration of racial bias in order to retain affirmative action measures for particular beneficiaries. They wonder whether we are establishing apartheid in the opposite direction, if there is no endpoint or limits to the rectifying policies. For instance, some academics are questioning the utility of admitting Caucasian males into various graduate programs, since diversity and inclusion bureaucracies are not allowing the hiring of these individuals after they graduate (Program on Constitutional Government at Harvard, 2018.)

Despite these concerns, advocates of affirmative action insist that these individuals must essentially pay for the wrongdoing of others who possess the same racial group membership as those who committed past sins of bigotry. Their argument in this regard is twofold. First, since racial group membership (not individuality) is a Protector's primary way to understand social behavior, these individuals are just as guilty as their predecessors are, since they embody the essential traits of their bigoted group. Second, since they keep benefiting from systemic power structures that anoint them with privilege, they should step aside without reservation (Applebaum, 2011).

But Promoters assert that if we expand this logic beyond racism, or other *-isms,* identified by Protectors, anyone who gains advantage from an analysis of personal history must divest of that gain and give it to others. Likewise, anyone demonstrating historical impairment is entitled to compensation. Unfortunately, this situation is likely to result in people exaggerating harms and minimizing privileges.

Moreover, how much of a penalty or advantage do we give to each reported instance? Do we only include racial, ethnic, and sexual injustices, as other historical adversities and advantages also affect an individual's current-day functioning. Additionally, what if people with similar problematic histories end up showing markedly contrasting patterns of current achievement? Do we still compensate these individuals, even though they are doing just fine?

Given these complications, it is unlikely that we can derive a fixed amount of incurred harm or privilege that each individual (or racial group) has endured over time, and even if we could, what is the solution? While a Protector might reject the idea of expanding affirmative action to any kind of hardship, in that they argue for compensations only for people within certain victim classifications that they endorse, Promoters wonder why they have to confine affirmative practices to their limited set of protected categories of people.

There is yet another problem with affirmative action that Promoters find important to address. Namely, people with cultural power cannot receive credit for a personal accomplishment. As noted previously, the distinction between *privilege* and *achievement* becomes blurred in their ideology. Impressive behavior enacted by non-protected identities can only be evidence of an undercurrent of *privilege*; nothing they do can be a viable attainment.

However, Promoters ask what happens when dominant group members start behind minority group members, and then reach respectful levels of achievement? Is their advancement still a sign of privilege? What if minority group members start ahead? Is there no possibility that their present attainments included easements, unearned advantages, help from others, or some other circumstantial gratuity? Moreover, do these successful minority group members now become oppressors adorned with privilege that came from the sky because they are at the top of the hierarchy?

There is an additional complication with the Protector ideology, of amalgamating privileges and social harms. For example, while having a two-parent family is generally a privilege, what if there was domestic violence and frequent mistreatment during child-rearing? Does the fact of having two parents in the home still represent an unearned asset? Do we disregard the personal experiences of these children, merely because the narrative runs counter to the simplistic approach of adding categories of predetermined "privileges," and chastising whoever receives higher scores?

It is not surprising that critics of affirmative action do not want to go down the rabbit hole of summarily penalizing or gifting individuals in certain identity groups without ascertaining *individual need* for external help. They would prefer to assist underperforming individuals (regardless of protected group status) with interventions that match the individual's necessity for assistance, and utilize interventions that have historically worked to create progress and skill development. More specifically, they want to prioritize studying and cooperation with expectations, in-home routines, and enact parenting strategies that stress the value of being knowledgeable. These practices have typically helped individuals, regardless of the penumbra of other challenges.

Critics of affirmative action policies also have growing concerns that members of protected groups, who have not experienced inordinate hardships, are often receiving resources that might be better applied to lower-achieving individuals. Some of these individuals might be achieving appreciably better than many individuals from the so-called privileged groups. In fact, detractors claim that it is the higher achieving individuals from racial minorities (and females) who are benefiting the most from affirmative action policies, while the compensations do very little to help the truly needy. This problem occurs, since *only* the most eligible candidates qualify for the allotted slots (Sowell, 2005).

Cynics also wonder if affirmative action is focusing more on creating a number count for certain races, females, and so forth, so that these individuals can gain entrance into high-status positions and inflate an institution's "diversity of faces" and atypical "lived experience" numbers in order to gain status into the "woke community." The maneuver essentially enhances the institutions social standing when many of these "protected" individuals would do just fine without any special treatment. Similarly, a palatable insincerity occurs when someone emphasizes minority group disadvantages, and then feigns a minority group membership to obtain the *benefit* of a special promotion (PragerU, Candace Owens Show, 2020).

Moreover, some are concerned that affirmative action might be a disservice to the general population. For example, if a person is sick, it is doubtful that the doctor's skin color would matter as much as the doctor's competence. There is also hypocrisy when advocating for affirmative action for admittance into medical school, while seeking medical care for oneself on the basis of a physician's reputation. Likewise, it seems improbable that sports fans would encourage player selection based on anything but merit, and people from all races might feel this way.

This brings up the following questions. At what point do we shift from emphasizing the creation of identity diversities and compensating for past harms (when making promotion decisions), to having advancements based on our best measures of performance adequacy and talent? Are graduate and medical schools, or faculty appointments at universities and hospitals, reasonable places to catapult someone ahead and jettison performance assessments? Is affirmative action the best way to advance a profession or benefit a society that depends on expertise to maximize survival? Whose interests, and what kinds of interests, do we want to prioritize?

Overall, Promoters are concerned about bypassing talented people to foster a political agenda. Advocates of affirmative action might feel morality righteous, but not realize the downside of their policies, such as falling behind other social groups that are not hampering themselves in this manner. This may eventually become a significant problem for the integrity of our country, in that nations often compete with each other.

In that formative battle, lopping from the top echelon can sometimes result in devastating long-term consequences. Adversarial countries are likely to be happy watching their rivals hobble themselves when they overlook proficiencies that might have blossomed. While it seems reasonable to put extra resources into helping individuals needing remediation, there are disadvantages to promoting people when they do not earn their advancement. A more prudent approach is to have a sense of proportion where those who languish receive help, and the successful are not pillaged.

Promoters also wonder why any society with interest in the best that science, technology, and craftsmanship have to offer, would want to diminish the sanctity of the expert class. Granted, with limited slots available, selection decisions must occur, but if we try to prevent failure by downgrading the criteria for success, we are likely doing a disservice to the nation that depends on the advancement of expertise for its health and safety.

Even at this time, some schools are eliminating the "exemplary" rating for teachers so they do not "feel badly" about not getting the highest score. Other schools are inflating or eliminating grades, no longer using standardized testing, or even more extreme, downgrading the complexity of the subject matter in an attempt to adjust expectations to ameliorate the sting of failure (Mac Donald, 2018). While "objective" measures might be a viable way to protect the vulnerable against *subjective indiscretions*, there is drifting from standardized evaluative criteria. Moreover, even if giving everyone a trophy prevents a sense of loss, it is not clear what the trophy represents, or how it advances future achievements for any individual or subgroup.

For these reasons, a Promoter is perplexed by a Protector's efforts to increase decision-making in colleges and universities based on fixed traits such as racial identity. As outlined by Mac Donald (2018), academies throughout the country are frequently giving admission to students of certain races an allowance of approximately one standard deviation in formal test scoring, and hiring faculty with the *primary goal* of promoting department racial diversity. If the original problem is that people have historically used these kinds of irrelevant criteria in decision-making, why are we endorsing and magnifying these practices now?

For the following additional reasons, Promoters eschew affirmative action. First, when people know that certain races gain advancement from affirmative action, they might also doubt the competence of the individuals when functioning in their "granted" position. They might resent the fact that the person received a seat that might have been given to more deserving individuals. Instead of diminishing presumptions about racial inferiority, the system perpetuates invidious stereotyping and rancor. For example, if White males and Asians need higher credentials to advance, some will jump to the conclusion that they must be *eminently* qualified when they see these individuals in their institutional roles. The whole system seems to increase racial prejudging, and perhaps enhance the belief that some identities are superior.

Second, Promoters are also concerned that affirmative action may stultify eagerness to achieve and work hard. Why put in the effort to master a discipline and build know-how, when racial identity trumps competence? If quotas are implemented (legal or not), the possibility of success diminishes even further. When the maximum number is reached in the organization, the game is over, and it is futile to try.

Third, Affirmative Action may also cloud the recipient's sense of accomplishment with suspicions that it was unfairly earned, or that it accrued at the expense of someone more proficient. These individuals might evaluate their stature as artificial, and become self-conscious about their acceptability. While some might try to overcome the perception of inferiority by increasing work intensity, others might accede to their anxiety and become dispirited. The program to advance them could spur the likelihood of an imposter syndrome.

Fourth, our efforts to help could also be placing many affirmative action recipients in settings that increase the likelihood of failure. When that occurs, they can either blame themselves and their inadequacies, or externalize fault and perhaps conjure neglect or persecution by the institution for their struggles (Hoover Institution,

2018). Given the tendency of considerable numbers of people to externalize blame, the latter is a concerning possibility.

Fifth, even now, some are presenting empirics demonstrating that "over-placing" students costs them money in the long term, as students may drop out or change majors when curriculums are too difficult for them. For example, they might shift from STEM to social science in order to mitigate the problem of lower academic preparation. Ironically, instead of enhancing their long-term outcomes, this shifting diminishes their lifetime earnings (Arcidiacono et. al, 2012). If they were appropriately matched, they might have succeeded in STEM (Sander and Taylor Jr., 2012).

Systems that promote diversity over success seem fraught with problems, and these failings have been evident when attempted in other countries (Sowell, 2005). Consequently, many Promoters now believe that the animosities, doubts, and shortcomings created by affirmative action are worse than allowing a neutral system of advancement to play out on its own. They cling to the belief that when rules allow for preferential treatment, everyone suffers in the process (Sowell, 2012).

Alternatively, what might happen if we simply allow people to retain their dignity and rely on their own desires, commitment, and intelligence to compete on equal footing with others? What if the approach of not propelling some people forward helps them work harder, as well as appreciate their success without feeling that others are letting them win? What if *deficiency* results in *education,* and *attainment* leads *to promotion*?

In sum, critics of affirmative action do not believe that the reparation reduces bigotry in society, nor does it bring us any closer to a post-racial society. They would rather allow people of *all identities* to compete on equal footing. They predict that employers, supervisors, and institutions will show less bigotry by reincorporating performance grading in comparison to the consequences that occur when making marginalized identity the *sine qua non* of decision-making.

Promoters would rather endorse the ideology of a liberal society, which advocates the valuing of individual actions and character.

They anticipate that social hierarchies will be less rigid when achievements are unleashed without the social justice tinkering that is presently taking place. For them, the promulgation of equal opportunity performance criteria is the best way to eliminate harms and conflicts that run rampant when there is an attempt to induce equal outcomes by using group identity as a basis to exclude. The aphorism, "It is not where you have been, but where you are going," comes to mind.

The Many Facets of Discrimination

Often, our first reaction to the word *discrimination* is negative. The distasteful association of mistreating particular racial groups and other identities comes to mind. However, in another sense, the word simply alludes to making distinctions and differentiating. In fact, our basic survival depends on making discriminations of various sorts, as we have to know the difference between what is safe and what is dangerous. Starting at birth, the infant has to learn to discriminate mother from stranger, perceive foreground from background, objects from one another, and tell the difference between self and other. Without categorical ideation, life as we know it is impossible. So if discriminating is essential, including having discriminating tastes, what makes for all the negativity?

The basic problem seems related to inferences about intentions—a teleological concern. That is, what is the goal, intent, purpose, or objective of the assessed action? In the case of unacceptable racist discriminations, the following question comes to mind. Is the person imposing needless *hardship* on another person, in conjunction with disdain for the individual's racial group? While some are asserting that "intent" is not important—in that identity oppression, much like ether, colors all of our interactions—what if we want to make distinctions between bigoted and non-bigoted actions? If that is the case, it seems important to study teleological concerns.

When questioning whether to identify an action as an instance of bigotry, we might first investigate the learning history of the individual in relation to members of different racial groups.

This inquiry might help us better understand the "intent" of any questionable behaviors. For instance, if we know that a person suffered an injury from an individual belonging to a certain race, we might understand an initial lack of amicability toward an unknown person in that group as a temporary self-protective response. As long as the person is not creating *unnecessary* harm in the process, we might gloss over the provisional aloofness.

Along these same lines, if we know that a person had a difficult encounter with a proselytizing religious group the day before, seeing a similar group a second time is likely to evoke an unwelcoming reaction. In this case, we might understand the response in a benign light when identifying this recent historical detail.

Likewise, we might have tolerance for avoidant responses if we know a person is anxious in a variety of ways. If the individual is tentative when approaching unfamiliar people of a different race in a foreign neighborhood, we would understand that the person is generally apprehensive rather than racist.

As long as individuals are not creating disproportionate harm to anyone, we would probably understand all of these unfriendly reactions as cautious and self-protecting without the additional inference that the "prejudging" and hesitation is an attempt to induce needless discomfort onto someone else. Yes, the people are making "discriminations" and not being congenial, but the behaviors in question do not seem to coincide with the distaste that the word bigotry evokes.

Each of these concerns might factor into the ways in which we respond to a person's negativity or atypical behavior when responding to others. If we do not want to call every action *racist*, simply because it emanates from a majority group member, many subtleties are worth considering. However, an important issue is who determines whether an action is creating needless *hardship* for others due to antipathy toward a person's identity?

While Protectors are quick to assert that many of our actions are creating unwarranted hardships upon certain identities, and desire censoring to remediate the problem, Promoters prefer to allow individuals the freedom to express themselves, as long as they do not break civil rights laws. Promoters recognize the value of people becoming sensitive to the feelings of others, but they also do not want to lose the gradations and distinctions between innocuous jokes, slurs, insults, social gaffes, derisive comments, ignorance, and inexcusable aggressive acts.

They do not want our interactions to become so muffled and hypersensitive that people avoid interacting to mitigate the possibility of creating a *perceived* injustice that carries a paralyzing consequence. They do not object to helping people learn to be cognizant of the perspective of others, but they do not want to become tyrannical or neo-racist in their quest to diminish perceived oppressions.

In the Promoter view, pausing or questioning a proffered Protector solution to the ills of society does not automatically mean that hesitancy is de facto racism, or a disinterest in improving the status quo. Promoters who question Protector ideology are simply trying to find viable causative factors and improvements within a matrix of concerns that will produce demonstrable upgrading.

Protectors might call them bigots, but they see themselves as benignly considering multiple viewpoints, and this includes all social strata. They assert that social justice activists are jumping to false conclusions when they "problematize" differing points of view as racist, or charge them with blindly permitting inhumanity. They wonder whether the desire for praxis is leading many Protectors into mendacious accusations as a way to enhance their opportunity to gain power. Their so-called moral enlightenment triggers others to jump onboard and foster a revolt.

At this point, an important set of questions arise. What is the basis of an individual's assertion that another person has a particular intent? Is the other person's past behavior the foundation of the inference? Is the assertion of intent simply a projection of what the assessor typically does in similar situations, or what they think is characteristic of most people who are not in their camp?

Additionally, what are the various reasons why people might adopt the belief that other individuals and groups want to cause them harm? Do frequent accusations of bigotry help some people feel morally superior? Do racial accusations distract accusers from their own unacceptable behaviors? Does the accused person remind the individual of someone else, and does that history sway the inference? Do we go along with the accusation of racism, simply because a person reports being suspicious of its occurrence? That is, is the accuser *conjuring* racism, or is the accused *doing* racist behavior?

Another important question comes to mind as well. If the accused is an archenemy, is the assertion of "racist intent" what the observer thinks the adversary might scheme in relation to their ongoing feud? Might the accusation also make it justifiable to act with additional aggression toward the rival? Could this be what the accuser has preferred all along, since the menacing characterization of the other person sanctions the subsequent actions that will annihilate the foe?

Perhaps an alternative to this kind of guessing and condemnation would be to observe the individual interacting with various people from a different racial group, in a variety of circumstances to see if there is a pattern of acting harshly toward individuals in that group, in comparison to those who mirror the person's racial identity. Observers might note the instances where the suspect is inducing hardship when there is ample opportunity to enact more benign responses (Hofstadter, 1941).

This latter method is more "objective," and hedges against inferential parti pris that seems to occur without bounds when inferring the intent bigotry within today's social justice movement. Despite its being cumbersome and impractical, this kind of investigation might help establish a clearer tendency to induce unnecessary harm upon a particular race, and settle some disputes that pertain to racial bigotry in our hypersensitive times.

Despite these concerns, many in the Protector camp are now jumping to the conclusion that individuals are racist, simply because they belong to a racial group that has postulated societal power. Majority-group people (e.g., Caucasians), do not have to do anything at all to be labeled *racists.* Their membership in the dominate culture presupposes that they are perpetually harming other cultures (DiAngelo, 2018).

However, Promoters disagree. While it is always possible to study a culture, and the impact that its structures and authority have on various subgroups and economic strata, they wonder why they have to endorse DiAngelo's understanding. Put differently, why must preferences that coincide with a particular ethnic group necessarily reduce to bigotry, which has the additional connotation of cruelty? For example, is encouraging the use of proper English an attempt to induce suffering? Or is it a way to increase a person's chances of obtaining financial success in America?

While it is always possible to find patterns in society that harm some more than others, it is inevitable that social groups organize in particular ways and introduce a means to determine what is acceptable and what is not. This is not unique to societies populated with Caucasians. It is unavoidable that ways to establish knowledge, such as using the scientific method, or preference for long-term goals, will reflect majority-group values. In the case of America, those traditions have European origins, and people with different cultural backgrounds will have to adjust and work hard to learn the new behaviors.

We might also be concerned that DiAngelo's theoretical construction runs the risk of *increasing* bigotry. It focuses on *skin color* rather than the idea that power structures, regardless of the skin color of the people enacting them, will have consequences on the people in a social group. It is an inescapable consequence of *all* social systems.

DiAngelo might not intend to increase contempt against White people, but using race to describe the ever-present phenomenon of having to contend with entrenched societal structures could well lead to that result. For example, if minority group members have problems obtaining services in their native language, are these events instances of bigotry? Or are they limitations of the society's resources? Do we call the country bigoted every time it fails to accommodate to every variation, social nuance, and need for people who do not share the dominant social practice?

Moreover, even if being Caucasian correlates with success within a society predicated on this group's values and beliefs, it does not mean that the preferences are causing needless harm to others. The fact that it might be difficult to function in a society that has a different culture than one's own, does not mean that the culture is, by definition, injurious. The embedded ethnocentrism could be quite admirable, despite the hardship it imposes on others attempting to learn and adapt to its language, laws, and traditions. Consistent with this perspective, many people of color migrate to countries with European populations, with the preconception that their life will be better functioning within those norms, and as noted, some of these individuals even outperform the indigenous groups soon after arriving.

Given this empiricism, Promoters wonder if, or when (if not already), the majority deploys DiAngelo's conceptualization of racism, will those newly enthroned "majority culture" individuals be labeled racist? After all, when that occurs, they will be impelling others to live within the confines and impositions of their hegemonic power-knowledge and language usages, which include certain presumptions about the acceptability of certain actions, and the importance of equity goals.

Yet many in the Protector camp are adopting DiAngelo's conceptualization with impunity, and this view seems to be increasing animosity against the Caucasian race. Although bigotry has occurred throughout history in every country and for every race, and currently endures in non-White countries, that insinuation persists (Sowell, 2006; 2008). It goes unnoticed that Whites have been enslaved throughout the centuries. And even in America, Blacks owned slaves when that practice was legal (Koger, 2012; Sowell, 2013). Unfortunately, humans have historically mistreated each other in terrible ways; it is not a "White only" phenomenon, and this includes indigenous peoples and other races appropriating each other's land (Sowell, 2006).

Despite these facts, given today's singular focus on Caucasian mistreatment of others, we might be concerned that many individuals will view people with white skin as inherently inferior. They are intrinsically racists, while others are not. Surely, this is not the best or only way to help a country rid itself of bigotry; it is simply changing the color of who has the most inferior skin tone. Moreover, this new perspective reinforces the view that White people are responsible for all the problems currently experienced by "those without power," and denies the importance of any other impeding factors.

Nevertheless, for many within the Protector camp, ambient White racism occurs whenever disenfranchised groups experience strife. The conclusion is that White people must be creating those harms, and Protectors want it to stop. Since people with power are, by default, racists within this enlightened reality, talking or acting in a negative fashion toward racial group members with lesser social power simply makes them *explicitly* and *extremely* racist.

Given this foreboding perspective, Protectors argue that we must find a way to protect and shield individuals from these ever-present harms. They encourage ongoing scrutiny of actions or verbalizations that show the slightest negativity toward groups on their protected list. They want to determine if there are residues of bigotry beneath the surface. Protecting the vulnerable, and those whose ancestors have suffered legalized anguish, is their top priority.

Conversely, Promoters *reject* DiAngelo's conceptualization that racism is everywhere. They argue that Protectors are presuming the occurrence of a racial sin, even though they know little about the specifics of the encounters they are assessing. Often, they do not know about the details surrounding the events they are scrutinizing. They peruse the incident, and if they can *infer* any insensitivity or advantage for the majority-race actors, then racism is the culprit.

Accusations

Promoters find it unfortunate that accusations of racism are occurring without precise investigation. More commonly, many in the Protector camp freely castigate others, based only on a cursory analysis. They impose the scarlet racist moniker, simply because they did not like the other person's behavior when interacting with someone from a protected identity group. For them, inferred negativity can be proof of bigotry, and all other possible explanations for what happened can push aside.

In contrast, Promoters want to introduce nuance when determining instances of bigotry. For example, was the Three-fifths Compromise after the revolution an attempt to diminish the value of Blacks? Or was it an effort to limit the voting power of those who remained aligned with slavery (Understanding the Three-Fifths Compromise)? Those unwilling to adopt a *racism is everywhere* framework, find this kind of inquiry worthwhile before jumping to the conclusion that each enactment has bigoted intent.

In this framework, it becomes preferable to examine mixed racial interactions carefully, and this includes analyzing the behavioral goals of alleged perpetrators. In some instances, Promoters argue that the interactions might have little or nothing to do with racial disdain. However, they recognize that no matter how much scrutiny occurs, it is always necessary to make a *judgment call*, and there might frequently be differences of option regarding the intent of initiators, and the effects that the behaviors had on recipients. Moreover, they point out that people can scrutinize acts of friendship in different ways, and if they persist in analyzing, they could well "discover" some kind of insensitivity or selfishness in relation to their efforts.

An analogous problem occurs within the legal system when it must be decided whether an action represents self-defense, an accident, or a crime. For example, are religious objectors to gay marriage *harming* or *self-protecting* when refusing to bake a wedding cake for customers? Even when carefully delving into the matter, people may differ in their judgments of innocence or guilt, and it is often difficult to determine the party that has the most damage. The accused downplays harms and ablates negative intent, while victims play up the necessity for reparations, and demeans the character of the accused. Rulings often depend on the biases of the evaluators, and a consensus may or may not occur.

Most of the time, it seems that people will identify their intent in socially acceptable cloaks, and insouciantly deny categories of intent that are less acceptable. For example, when the San Francisco legislature advocates lowering the voting age to sixteen, they claim that their primary intent is to get young people to be knowledgeable and involved in the political process. Skeptics, however, might offer a different account. They would claim that the legislature was quite aware that younger voters would be more likely to endorse their progressive agenda.

To complicate matters further, even if we try to carefully tease out the intent of a behavior, there are frequent occasions when even the *people doing the behavior* are not clear about intent. This problem occurs regularly in psychotherapy, especially when people say they want to change, but do not. For example, individuals might insist that they want to lose weight to promote the possibility of finding an intimate relationship. However, weight loss does not occur despite great consternation. Upon further inquiry, it becomes evident that the individuals worry about exploitation and disappointment when involved in relationships. Not losing weight keeps those outcomes at bay. Given this scenario, was the intent of the individual to find a partner, or not find a partner? As you can see, the problem of identifying "intent" is indeed a complex matter.

An additional problem with determining "intent" occurs when assessing international affairs. For instance, people might disagree whether an intervening country is intending to impose its own brand of imperialism on an indigenous group, or whether it is trying to foster the well-being of the populace and protect them from perceived harm. Often, political debate revolves around imputing different characterizations of intent onto the intervening country. Typically, assessments emanating from individuals suspicious of the interventionists will say they did it with little regard for the recipient country. While advocates for the intervening country will say they wanted to help (Steinkuhl, 2002).

On many occasions, the facts are amenable to both interpretations, and each side is able to make a persuasive case. The question then becomes, *What are the criteria to rank order benefits and harms related to the intrusion, and what morality yardstick are we going to impose?* Moreover, how do we judge the intervention's effectiveness when we do not know what might have happened without the intrusion, and what factors are invoked to explain the short- and long-term aftermath? Does the entire debate simply reduce to whether we like or dislike the intervening country?

Despite the difficulties that occur when trying to determine intent, it is now commonplace for many people to make sanctimonious accusations that others are racists. Indictments will take place, for example, when majority group members show negative emotions, distancing, criticism, extraneous derisive comments, insensitivity, disapproval, negative generalizations, impoliteness, sarcasm, and failure to extend preference toward minority-group members. When observing any of these actions (and more), serious consequences can unfold.

The individuals doing the actions might insist that they never meant to harm, yet "the more knowledgeable analysts" may assume, however wrongly, that psychic damage occurred because of racism. The person instantaneously becomes a bigot, and those who indict have a sense of certainty and moral righteousness. Given the extensive social power afforded to the "offended," the identification and exaggeration of harm can be extremely effective in censoring the alleged perpetrator.

However, while activists might deem certain acts as racist and unconscionable, the so-called offenders may often see their actions as defensible, rational, statistically supported, and founded in their personal experiences and observations of behavioral patterns. They feel they are entitled to their point of view, and their right to protect and express themselves exceeds the harm that others are claiming. They would like the accusers to have empathy in both directions. For example, if a minority group is having a lively party with loud music, are complaints from neighbors racist or warranted?

Despite the subtleties to disentangle, if a Protector activist surmises that a person's racial group membership factors into an individual's inimical behavior, many will quickly jump to the characterization that the offensive individual is a racist and should be stifled. While protecting oneself from churlish behavior, or silently disliking certain behavior without others noticing, carries less social risk, any kind of discernible negativity towards disenfranchised identities becomes intolerable in today's age of ferreting out bigotry.

Even when it is difficult to gauge the balance between acceptable self-advocacy and harming someone else, the concerned views of

Protectors are often adopted. The gavel comes down on the crime of racial bigotry, and there is no due process. Not infrequently, these kinds of accusations help individuals indict vast numbers of people in ways that weaken them in society, and the tactic helps the accusers gain significant authority.

After all, they are cleansing society of bigotry, and reshaping the purview of what is acceptable. Rather than look stupid or ill-informed like most others, their ferocity signifies that they are amongst the enlightened few. Their *cause célèbre* is a quest to facilitate for all encumbered groups, at all costs. They maintain the belief that bigotry is alive and well and creating anguish for those experiencing a gamut of day-to-day torments, and they want to turn the system upside down.

They insist that individuals must fight conventional systems, or else they are simply allowing the persistence of bigotry. They must be "antiracists," and renounce the depravity of their privileges that oppress others. For individuals anxious about their social acceptability, this invocation is a powerful message. It is essentially the same social pressure that is currently inducing corporations and many churches to comply with these orders. These institutions risk great social peril if they do not submit to the anti-racist narrative. And not surprisingly, many eagerly advertise their allegiance to the cause.

The Problem of Sorting

Despite the ongoing danger of receiving a racist stamp, we all have a stake in advancing our self-interest. It is essential that we self-advocate so that we can *protect* and *promote* ourselves. This frequently entails making judgments based on incomplete information. Often there is unfamiliarity, and we do not know about the particular actions and deeds of the individuals we encounter. At these times, we must make quick inferences about what is likely to happen from the momentary data that is available.

This will usually include responding to a person's veneer, or other circumstantial information. We must predict what is probable in the context, situation, and circumstance with the particular person or group, and enact a reasonable way to behave, given the assemblage of *discriminations* at our disposal. Only our *conscious or unconscious historical learning associations* can guide us in these matters. Even though we might be making a mistake about safety or danger, this is our typical mode of survival as we encounter the ambiguity embedded in our world.

Unless we get to the point where *everyone behaves in identical ways*, we will likely continue to make rapid and varied inferences about situations and what is likely to happen, and we will base our responses on whatever information we glean from the moment. It becomes unavoidable that this will include what we have learned about people in general, different races, and other identity groups, and this learning history will stimulate our immediate reactions. While new experiences with the same person or groups will help us learn new patterns of adaptation and interaction, this constrained method of adjusting to our social circumstances occurs for all of us as we operate with the available empirics in different contexts and situations.

In short, we are all making *assessments* and *prejudgments* to promote our well-being. None of this is inherently vile or wrong. Our actions are heuristic, self-enhancing, and often preemptive. They are only problematic when someone else decides that our behavior was unnecessary, too extreme, or uncouth. That is, they evaluate our behavior as crossing the line from self-care to *needless* insulting or doing harm.

This is where things get sticky. Some people experience harm when others do not, and people differ in their appraisals of circumstances and likely outcomes. We all have different life exposures, and our responses in certain situations are consequences of our learning histories. What seems like excessive negativity to some, may be reasonable to others, as people see the world from their own perspectives. It is therefore not surprising that one person might claim that an action was self-preserving, while others might assess the same action as needlessly unfavorable and disruptive.

Consequently, there are likely many gray areas and disagreements when assessing the appropriateness of a behavior. Frequently, disputes about a behavior's acceptability will depend upon knowledge of historical events and personal experiences leading up to the situation, as well as knowledge of upcoming events. However, it is unfortunate that observers often do not know about these kinds of details.

Even professionals (such as police officers) must operate according to historical factors that create a bias in responding. In order to do their job correctly, they must enact "discriminatory" actions based on empirical correlations. Police forces call this *data-driven* policing, and it has nothing to do with an interest in denigrating individuals because of racial contempt.

While they might act in ways that are "targeting" individuals within particular racial groups, they may not have any interest in *causing* harm. Decent, respectful, and civil investigations require acts of discretion and logic, which follow a crime scenario and suspect description. Unfortunately, racial correlates might come into play during this process when particular groups have high rates of crime. While it seems harsh, this is similar to what insurance companies do when targeting certain subgroups for higher premiums due to actuarial data. For example, in general, younger male drivers incur more accidents, so *all young men* must pay extra.

A reasonable example of this policing problem seems evident when Gibbons et al. (2020) correlates police "hassling" with subsequent increases in crime rates and incarceration. In this study, when African American youth *perceive* racial discrimination (PRD) from "police hassling" (assessed at four different times from childhood through adolescence), criminal behaviors increase. Moreover, the rates of incarceration rise when the youths experience the "hassling" at younger ages.

While some might conclude that the perceived hassling emanates from bigoted police behavior, which then causes future harm to the Black youths (i.e., outside→ in), a different analysis seems reasonable as well. For instance, one could also infer that youths who *interpret* antipathy from police actions are also more likely to be the subset of individuals who commit more crimes. Moreover, the earlier this disaffection toward the police, the more likely these individuals will develop a criminal record that warrants incarceration (i.e., inside → outside).

While both explanations seem feasible, the question remains, *Were the police "hassling" and antagonistic due to the race of the youths? Or were they doing "proactive" police work and inadvertently disrupting, and unwittingly aggravating, some of the youths?* Of course, responding to this question requires us to invoke criteria to determine the police motives. It also requires us to determine whether the possibility of disrupting the youths was a better option than *not* doing proactive policing, which we know will lead to increased neighborhood crime.

Even if the police showed coercive or unfriendly behaviors that left the youths feeling "hassled," where those actions related to resistive responses on the part of the youths? Was their motive to antagonize due to racial animus, and to what extent were they reacting to the youths' negative behaviors? The latter possibility might be reasonable to investigate, in that empirics show relationships between police negativity and attempts to defy police instructions, which more frequently occurs in minority neighborhoods (Fox Business, 2016; Alpha News, 2020).

However, none of this negates the necessity to help the police learn less callous ways of doing their jobs in order to mitigate adverse interactions between civilians and police. The hope is that the education will help curb the severe outcomes that disrupt the nation and its attitudes toward policing in general. Moreover, none of this denies that some police behavior is going to qualify as bigoted, inordinately hostile, and unjust, and it is important to investigate those incidents and get them to stop.

In our efforts to improve interactions between police and the public, it might also be beneficial to help both sides understand each other in a more positive light. For example, police might learn less threatening ways to approach civilians, and youth might learn to interpret police actions as attempts to *help* the neighborhood ward off crime, rather than maintain the view that police are "pigs" who want to oppress. Both sides could make it clear that they disdain police brutality, and honor public safety (i.e., inside ↔ outside). An added benefit is that these changes are likely to increase neighborhood security and enhance economic development in many communities as well.

When reflecting on the kinds of problems police encounter, what if similar scenarios occur for all of us, as we all have to advance our well-being and achieve certain goals. It stands to reason that we risk creating difficulties for other people, whether or not this was our objective. While we might think our actions are benign or promoting a particular outcome, what if we act in error, and what if the consequences of our actions lead to interpersonal conflict? Even for people desperate to avoid interpersonal strife, there is often a risk that they will offend others. Relatively innocuous attempts to maintain safety might disrupt someone else, which could lead to reprimand or a charge of racism, especially when someone is observing the actions with a "woke microscope."

It seems unavoidable that another person's appearance, language, culture, opinions, likes and dislikes, group identity (Black, Asian, Moslem, WASP, preppie, privileged elite, etc.), name, clothing, hairstyle, mannerisms, male or female, and political garb, and the like, may (in the absence of other information) kindle a variety of feelings and memories, which trigger particular responses. It is a human condition that momentary discriminations will elicit delight, disgust, intrigue, empathy, hatred, fear, escape, and many other emotions. While negativity that seeps into the public sphere could result in provoking social difficulty, it is doubtful that any of us can flawlessly avoid interpersonal strife as we manage our existence from one interaction to the next.

Bigotry Solutions

The solution of never allowing negative responses to occur in public is an option, but it might be difficult to conceal all negative responses and anticipate what someone else might find offensive, including those times when we remain silent. Moreover, how could we learn from each other without expressing our opinions? And if we become intimidated by those who are inferring nefarious intent, we might paralyze each other to such an extent that it is unlikely that we will be able to work out our differences or enjoy each other at all.

In this regard, many are concerned that the "anti-racism" training programs that are *forcing* people to change their behavior are creating these kinds of adverse effects. Many Promoters believe that the coercion embedded in these programs is making the bigotry problem worse. Instead of respectfully helping individuals identify instances of racial overgeneralizations and narcissistic attempts to self-aggrandize, and then encouraging alternative responses that make sense to each participant, people are pressured into a rigid belief system that is capable of finding identity harms in almost any social behavior.

Promoters do not want to go in this direction. They do not want to tell majority group members that they are invariably creating psychological damage to those who struggle, or inform them that they alone are responsible for the failings and feelings of inferiority that marginalized identities internalize. Over the long term, these individuals may not want to endorse the message that they must change solely for the benefit of others, and tolerate their self-abasement whether they like it or not.

Of course, we might increase their compliance by denigrating them if they resist. We might also appeal to their sense of guilt, or threaten termination of employment for noncompliance. However, those measures might only exacerbate anxiety about receiving a negative evaluation, as well as increase alienation and resentment. People do not want to be sullied by others, and many of these programs could increase animosities and self-consciousness during social interactions, instead of enhancing social harmony.

Sadly, and according to some empirics, this is what seems to be happening with many of the profit driven critical race trainings that are burgeoning throughout the country (Data Driven Conclusions, 2020). While it is a noble endeavor to encourage people to eliminate intolerant, inaccurate, and demeaning actions toward racial groups, it is important to find reasonable ways to accomplish that goal. Perhaps the following ideas will help.

First, we want to encourage people to pursue individualized assessments whenever possible, as those kinds of evaluations are likely to be the most accurate ways to predict character and future behavior. Second, since there is much to learn, and early learning is powerful, perhaps we can find ways to help parents and children behave with tolerance within the family, with the hope that those behaviors will generalize to others. Third, we can encourage people learn about multiple perspectives, as this could help them interpret the motives of others with more empathy and understanding.

Fourth, we can encourage people to develop accurate information about identity groups so that their sorting behavior has increased precision. Fifth, we can discourage people from making unsavory remarks about irrelevant identity characteristics that have nothing to do with the current problem or situation. Sixth, instead of presuming deficiency, delay, or defect when people behave differently from what is familiar, we can encourage them to adopt a *difference model*, which does not imply that other people are inferior; they are simply not our replicas. Seventh, we can encourage people to resolve interpersonal problems with the least amount of negativity, coercion, and infringement.

The expectation is that this approach will help to diminish inaccurate derisive stereotyping, help people recognize the positive aspects of different cultural patterns, and help them understand the history of different cultures that shaped those behaviors. We want to socialize people to welcome these learning possibilities, which will then enable them to differentiate their social world with increase precision, empathy, and tolerance. The hope is that this way of socializing people will result in a reduction of needless harm and insult to others.

Stopping the Madness

Although, as noted, even when adhering to the aforementioned advisements, it is unlikely that our efforts will completely eliminate all of our interpersonal problems. Despite our attempts to treat each other humanly and respectfully, many of our actions might still fall short of being perfectly congenial, and often we do not have the opportunity to get to know a person over time, in a variety of situations. Our behaviors at any moment might then increase interpersonal or racial tension, when that was not what we wanted to do.

At times, survival can be difficult, even if we are not setting out to diminish others. Our subtle and sometimes more explicitly unfriendly patterns of behavior may worsen the responses of the offended parties, which in turn creates a cycle of mistrust, avoidance, and negative bias in the ways individuals and groups interact with each other over time. While people might not be acting aggressively, they might still unwittingly add to the divisiveness in society. Moreover, when people self-enhance by denigrating others, interpersonal problems are bound to increase.

This does not imply that the gears of the machine cannot go in the opposite direction. Individuals can perform affable behaviors, or begin to show patterns of behavior that gel better with others, and the divisiveness can shrink without anyone trying to coerce that result. However, getting individuals and groups to be positive and accepting toward each other can be difficult when there is a state of fear and animosity. The problem becomes how to stop the machine's negative direction once it is active. Since *risk avoidance* protects us, and people like feeling superior, the unwinding process may prolong until affinity and safety are unmistakable.

So what does all of this mean? To start, social decorum requires individuals to provide at least some justification when they behave inhospitably toward others. We also require people to settle disputes in the least drastic manner. Otherwise, individuals are likely to be admonished, or perhaps suspected of bigotry, when the offended person belongs to a struggling minority group. Since there is currently a low tolerance for callousness, criticism, or harmful actions, especially when directed towards marginalized identities, accusations of racism are rampant.

Since many Protectors presume that empowered people are, by definition, racist, the label is now simply a matter of the degree to which racism has occurred. For example, *high-degree* bigotry would be inferred when majority-group members make negative comments about another person, knowing only the individual's race. On these occasions, these people would be labeled *very bigoted*, especially if they are not interested in learning more about the person they are deriding. An activist would likely question the reasons for the spirited negativity and lack of interest.

Even if particular negative appraisals about a group have an empirical basis, sarcastic tones of voice might be enough to trigger a label of high-level racism. The tacit belief is that individuals *should* understand the difficulties that certain aggrieved racial groups face. They should not engage in victim-blaming by exuding negative emotions. The person's disinterest in going beyond racial stereotyping, and their negative sentiments become further *evidence* of inherent racism.

We are also likely to characterize people as extremely bigoted when they make blanket contemptuous statements about a given race when observing the mere presence of a person from a particular race, or from their slightest misbehavior, instead of remarking about the disliked *actions* of the *particular* individual. In these instances, the guilty party is not individuating enough, because not all members of the race behave in that fashion, and the pertinent issue is their behavior, not their race. Ironically, this scenario departs from a Protector's usual practice of emphasizing the homogeneity of marginalized-group identity when discussing the essentialism of their suffering. Only at those times is it permissible to make summary comments about these groups.

Another example of what might now be considered overt racist behavior is evident in the following logical fallacy: "If Chinese people drink tea, and the person drinks tea, then the individual must be Chinese." In this instance, the remark implies that *all* Chinese behave in this particular fashion, and that kind of ideation is enough to trigger an accusation of racist intent because it is an overgeneralization. Even though the statement is not disparaging or inciting the persecution of Chinese people, and is unconnected to any bonafide action, consequence, or harm, the mere presentation of this kind of *ideation* is enough to indict whoever utters the words.

Overall, these kinds of response subtleties contribute to the ways in which many people are now assessing others as inordinately racist, and the list is growing rapidly. While people, in general, might have ideation that is derisive toward individuals or groups, and dislike patterns of behavior correlated with particular cultures, social difficulties occur when these kinds of responses become evident to others who want to protect and defend the maligned. This is the case whether or not the "guilty" parties do anything other than make subtle negative vocalizations, sighs, eye rolls, facial movements, gesticulations, or unenthusiastic comments about behaviors that coincide with marginalized ethnicities.

The tacit presumption, whether true or not, is that the *perpetrators* of these "micro-bigotries" are augmenting the harms that befall minorities. This inference justifies an ongoing "anti-racism crusade" to stop the avalanche. The belief is that people require constant censoring and indoctrination to prevent the possibility of real-world harmful consequences. The goal is to stop all behavior that might lead to marginalized people feeling badly about themselves. And by stopping the subtle, and sometimes more explicit, comments about marginalized identities, there will be an end to bigotry—and in time, societal inequities.

While these presuppositions about outcomes might or might not come to fruition or have corroborating empirical evidence, for those attempting to stamp out all identity harms, every *possible* instance of minority-group identity harm must be stifled to the utmost degree. Their primary goal is to eradicate those mistreatments with unlimited intensity. Especially in elite circles, college campuses, and large businesses, this fanatically driven quest gains traction in relation to giving kudos and moral credibility points to the individuals who make the putative discoveries.

In this same group, there is permission to racially slur majority group members, without the fear that they are being bigoted when making blanket indictments against them. Since there are now many Protectors who presume that people *cannot* be racist if they are without dominant social power, individuals falling into that safety net are given *license* to affront majority group members, without fear of any social reprisal. Their membership in defamed groups provides them with this exceptional shielding, and this is becoming an accepted norm. Since they are oppressed, they must have this extra authority to emote, protect, and deter.

However, disgruntled Promoters opposing this practice wonder, *If we reversed the races, would we still sanction the person who behaves in that manner? If not, have we stopped looking for universal principles in our ethics and social policies?* While some might think they are helping to rebalance power asymmetries, others want to maintain ethical principles that apply to humanity as a whole.

They want to increase and protect the liberties, opportunities, and achievements for everyone. They remain concerned that the lack of evenhandedness will exacerbate problems between people, rather than create more harmony, and they doubt whether the over-compensations will have any leveling effects (Pluckrose and Lindsay, 2020). They also object to the premise that people without power cannot be racist, since that "proviso" has never been part of any previous definition of racism (Sowell, 2006). Moreover, they fear that we are now encouraging people to do the kinds of behaviors that most want to eradicate.

For Promoters, it is more important to develop consistency for *all people,* and show concern for long-term consequences. Promoters insist that we must always weigh pros and cons of our social policies. They believe that there are always trade-offs when we act. And this is the case, even when addressing the problem of bigotry. Sometimes a particular way to rescue can have grave consequences for everyone involved, and backfire. As the saying goes, one more person in a life raft might sink the boat.

Due to these kinds of concerns, Promoters want protective energies to expand to subsequent consequences. A common example of this problem occurs when flight attendants instruct parents to put the oxygen mask on themselves first so that they can remain physically able to save their children. In this respect, social justice can be a difficult calculation that varies across situations, and in relation to the benefits and harms that can play out in subtle ways. In the process of being "socially just" and allowing bigoted behaviors from some groups and not others, harm can occur to many people, problems can worsen rather than improve, and devolve into who will be the sacrificial lambs.

From this perspective, we must carefully evaluate solutions that advocate favoritism for some people at the expense of others, within a larger context and timeframe. That is, how much harm are we doing to which individuals, and what are the likely short- and long-term consequences of one remedy or another? They ask, *In what ways are anti-racist strategies beneficial or problematic, and what will happen after those without power ascend to authority?* If we reinforce the belief that they have permission to harm others because of the harm that was done to them, what will stop the carnage and impel them to lay down their swords?

In sum, we all make inferences and guesses about the motives of others. However, it is now common to see people berating others about their racial bigotry and their virulent intent to harm, despite the fact that accusers may know little about the circumstance, the person's usual way to deal with disputes, and their frequent emotional responses with a wide range of people. With the certainty of a judge or jury, they assign blame, and this occurs despite the problem that interpersonal behavior can be nuanced, situational, and difficult to unpack.

While not every instance of maltreatment between individuals of varying races foments in racism, an assertion of racism has gained veracity, especially within the new Protector's canon, which is determined to protect the vulnerable, and see every social problem as evidence of racial power dynamics creating a storm. All it takes is for an onlooker to infer that an aggrieved-group member is experiencing negativity, and that there is disinterest in popular renditions of critical race theory.

While this kind of appraisal is gaining ground and taken as gospel, Promoters believe that the "dogma" is not sacrosanct. They question current trends, and rather than presume bigotry, they find it important to *investigate* whether bigotry is a significant factor when observing mixed race interactions. For them, it is essential to obtain a more thorough understanding of the variables involved, and show openness toward alternative interpretations of what is transpiring. While there could be numerous scenarios where people have attitudes that certain racial groups are globally inferior, and exhibit revilement for that reason, it is important to investigate that hypothesis with some rigor, and not automatically rule out other possibilities. Promoters do not want to make racial identity (or any other identity) the only way to account for problematic interactions.

Promoters have a growing concern that when activists presume *racism,* simply because an individual is a majority-group member, they are only perpetuating a new *acceptable* racism. They see this approach as another barebones instance of undesirable bigotry where the names have changed, but not the morality of the actions.

As an alternative, they prefer to give all people the benefit of the doubt when there is no apparent risk to do so. They remind us that attributions ascribed to groups (whether majority or minority) might tell us very little about individual people. However, they also recognize a sobering thought. Even when we think we know a person, we still might proceed incorrectly, as we are always operating on limited information when we interact with each other.

Racial Hatred

Racial animosity can occur with intense emotion, as dislike sometimes transforms into hatred. Occurrences of differences of opinion are understandable, but why the boundless acrimony and lack of concern for the health and safety of the loathed adversary? What is bringing about this apex of emotion, which seems to be fomenting in America?

First, it is not unusual for people to tolerate mild difficulty when it occurs only once. We might attribute the misfortune to bad luck, or to a problem that will pass and never haunt us again. The characterization that the displeasing event will not recur is soothing, and we are not likely to expend much time or energy protecting ourselves going forward.

In contrast, when unwanted events or behavioral themes repeat, we must consider whether we need to take a shielding action to prevent future harm. Effort is expended to keep the repetitions at bay, and our anxiety may become intense in the process. Self-preservation may prompt responses that are fervent.

The following illustrates this problem. When a person bumps into another person, it might be disruptive. If the individual passes by, the recipient may likely infer accidental carelessness, and escalation is unlikely. In contrast, if the other person does the same behavior two times in succession, a different assessment comes to the fore. Emotions are likely to intensify quickly, and questions arise whether the perpetrator is *intending* malice. In this scenario, aggression ramps up and we observe an emotional response analogous to hatred.

With this in mind, when noticing that some people are reacting with intense negative emotions, the question is, why this might be the case. Does the event signify an instance of an old bruise being rankled? Does it cue an association to something vexing and significant? If the answer is yes to either, we can provide an account for the extreme riposte.

In this current framework, *hatred* signifies that the unwanted event is triggering extremely bothersome ideation, and the individual is gearing up in self-defense. For example, if an individual comes across a person who ignites the memory of another person who was disruptive, the resemblance can produce an extreme reaction that seems incredibly unreasonable to current onlookers.

Second, when an emotion becomes hatred toward another person, often the distinction between person and behavior coalesce. It is not that we hate particular behaviors; we disdain identity traits. The loss of this distinction is self-protective, as the mere presence of the individual immediately signals a blanket reaction that has strong shielding power. The hatred attaches to the physical presence, which is discernible at all times, and there is maximum alerting.

In much the same way, when we have repetitious negative incidents with individuals belonging to particular groups, it is more likely that the intense emotion of hatred will attach to group membership rather than to the actions of some or many people who belong to the group. Examples of this problem are occurring presently with the categories "Trump supporters" and "leftists."

In these instances, the group label signifies that everyone in the group behaves in a particularly negative fashion. Like spilled ammonia, the presence of an individual in the category spews an unwanted aroma that repels. Those individuals, as evidenced from their group affiliation, become avatars of possible harm and deservers of drunken hate. Individuals feeling vulnerable become impelled to take no chances, and any accusation leveled against the hated other is instantly believed.

In this way, category identity becomes one of the practical ways that signify the need for bolstered preparedness and animosity. It becomes shorthand for the potential of despised behavior, as we associate an entangled set of repugnant actions with the people in the group. As soon as we recognize that a person is a member of a hated group, our emotions ignite. However, as is always the case with the occurrence of false negatives and false positives, *hating or liking everyone* within a category of people is fraught with mistakes.

With *racial* hatred, the inherent problem is that people cannot change their racial group membership, while they can change their actions and moral behaviors. The identified "pariahs" cannot do anything about the negative attributions foisted upon them. If the "hater" allows for further interactions with the despised other person and something positive transpires, the situation may relax. However, and as noted previously, it may take many future encounters with numerous individuals belonging to the hated group to change the hated attributions ascribed to the group. Hatred relates to self-preservation, and people are unlikely to let down their guard and preconceptions about the jeopardy associated with the *person type,* without exerting caution.

Undoing learning that pertains to what is harmful and deserving of hate, and what is safe and worthy of peaceful interaction, may take significant time and consistency of outcomes. Only under desperate or unique circumstances do people recklessly expose themselves to possible danger. When there is long-term acrimony, it may become increasingly difficult to extinguish built-up negative emotions, off-putting prejudging, and suspiciousness. Rather than operate to enhance togetherness by showing compassion, trust, and understanding, many conclude that it is wise to remain alienated.

Third, people responding with hatred no longer see themselves as having anything to do with the problem. When this orientation predominates, demolishing the perceived evil becomes the primary focus and panacea for an individual's long-standing misery, failure, and hardship. Individuals essentially become obsessed with destroying the wickedness associated with the professed external enemy, who is now dehumanized and worthy of severe retribution. There is a fantasy of an idyllic life after the destruction of the hated other (i.e., outside → inside).

Moreover, if the animosity continues to the point where all parties involved feel threatened by each other, hatred becomes a bidirectional event. As with other feedback loops, the failure to find solutions results in repetitious harms going back and forth. Heightened loathing, and a loss of the distinction between person and behavior prevails and escalates. When there is ongoing bitterness, the negativity perks at the slightest mention of the detested other.

Fourth, and extremely important, reinforcement of this heightening of emotions can frequently occur when beneficial results take place in relation to the spiraling escalation. For example, people might show great intensity in their emotional responses, and if those excesses lead to conciliation and amelioration of the problem, then there is likely to be repetition of the intense behaviors. We all know that giving in to a tantrum will increase its recurrence. In this way, hatred is reinforced rather than extinguished. It can effectively get the hated persons to recognize the harm that they caused by their present or past behavior, much like what happens with "White guilt." The constant hammering and exposure to the litany of their crimes keeps them anxious about being labeled purveyors of injustice.

When understanding hatred in this fashion, Protectors are not surprised that victimized groups show emotional intensity, and sometimes aggressiveness and rioting, when confronting signs and symbols of past mistreatment. They recognize that certain stimuli trigger irritation of old bruises, intense fears, and exasperation. Rather than deriding the extreme emotional reactions, they have empathy and are willing to make reconciliations. They are aware that any behavior remotely connected to past abuse will ignite an emotional discharge, and they have no compunction to rectify the fury when it occurs. The possible downside of reinforcing the extreme behavior pushes aside. They recognize the behavioral intensity as a justified sign of desperation to produce change, and those who want "change" are more than happy to indulge the hate.

CHAPTER FOUR

THE SEXES AND THE UNHINGING
OF THE PATRIARCHY

Similar to economic and racial group conflict, understanding relationships between males and females plays out in comparable ways within our two camps of thought. As you might guess, Protectors see females as victims within a system that favors males, while Promoters see mutual benefit and downside for both in the arrangements between the sexes.

Much like the debate about capitalism, the dispute revolves around whether *reciprocity* or *oppression* prevails. For Protectors, females are victims of *The Patriarchy*, a system that normalizes and endorses bias against females, while Promoters claim that both males and females have discretionary authority to influence behavioral patterns that change reciprocally over time (Scorzo, 2015; Straughan, 2020). One view sees females as acted upon, while the other view sees ubiquitous cooperative actions and complimentary achievements in an ongoing attempt to maintain comfort between the sexes.

While both sides agree to outlaw aggression between the sexes, Protectors see the core of the system as licensing perpetration of the strong against the weak, much like what occurs in a Marxist analysis. In juxtaposition, the Promoters see an ever-changing distribution of responsibilities, obligations, and repayments in response to the ebb and flow of environmental changes and situational demands. This view recognizes that social arrangements between the sexes might be relatively static for some societies, in some environments, while they might be changing rapidly in other societies operating within different circumstances.

The Battle of the Sexes

The first concern is to whether male and female interactions are characteristically adversarial or mutually advantageous. Protectors generally equate male-female relationships with the same sense of rivalry as what occurs between racial groups and economic strata. That is, one faction asphyxiates the other and gains, while the other deteriorates and loses. Protectors allude to the civil rights movement as a clear attempt to get the suffocation to stop, and to get different races on equal legal footing. They cite historical asymmetries in laws as blatant examples of one race oppressing another, and they identify similar patterns of subjugation when observing how males and females coexist.

They believe that women must fight back against male-inflicted tyranny and unbalanced privileges. Whatever is found wrong with society, it surely has a male profile. In their view, the postulated nemesis, known as *The Patriarchy,* causes most of the lagging and hardship experienced by females. If an individual fails to realize this scenario, that person is a victim of the ominous indoctrination that males have always perpetrated.

In contrast, Promoters insist that male-female interactions are not synonymous with race relations. Promoters believe that the sexes develop differentiated patterns of behavior and achievement in relation to childcare and other functional arrangements within the family, whereas racial disparities evolve from other factors (Sowell, 2011). In this belief system, there isn't a battle of the sexes; there is a reciprocal and joint effort for males and females to mutually facilitate, increase survival, and procreate. The behavioral roles for men and women might be different, but this does not mean that the disparity is a predicate for mistreatment.

In Promoter ideology, males are typically interested in fostering well-being for females. Males are more likely to compete in achievement and physical prowess with other males for status in the male power hierarchy, which includes enhancing their sexual desirability, but they are not typically orienting to oppress females. Rather than presume that masculinity is toxic, many behaviors associated with "maleness" are valiant and advantageous to society when harnessed within social norms. Their increased strength and willingness to take physical risks helps to save lives in many different situations, and their readiness to do jobs that are inherently dangerous fulfills a variety of social necessities.

But Protectors are not swayed by this argument. They point to numerous examples that illustrate exploitation. These include acts of physical and sexual aggression, historical voting restrictions, property control, higher wages and earnings, and the overwhelming presence of males in positions of power in both the public and private sectors. In their view, societal laws are *made* by men, for the *benefit* of men, and they want the shackles on females removed. Women are victims of restrictions that have never been imposed on men, and Protectors are convinced that this pattern is adjacent to the systems of power that help us to understand systemic racism and other identity degradations.

Promoters, however, offer a different perception. Rather than understand male-female interactions as adversarial, they presume that each gender adopts a behavioral pattern that permits the best chance of survival within particular milieus. For example, in the past, males hunted for food, while females cooked and cared for the young within the confines of shelter and safety. Clearly, the correlated pattern today is that more males sustain full-time employment, while females donate more time to care for the children.

Given the circumstances occurring throughout history, and the perils in the world, this division of labor characterized family life within community groups. Both males and females, *in tandem,* generally favored this arrangement, which included protective restrictions on females, and the imposition of increased risk on males. Punishments for transgressions might have been severe for both sexes, and there was more danger when male aggressiveness at the extreme went awry, but in general, this is what helped the group persist.

As a corollary, when females depended on males to support them during childbearing years, males had to concurrently maintain fiscal responsibilities. Within this social arrangement, females generally preferred males who could function as benefactors with upward social mobility, and economic arrangements between males and females developed accordingly. However, this did not imply that there was an ongoing male plot to deprive females and keep them poor.

While some might interpret these historical asymmetries as evidence of male ascendency, these arrangements may not have been an attempt to denigrate females. Males might have been given privileges to encourage work productivity, and for many, self-sacrifice for the group's prospering and defense. However, that did not mean that their lives had more happiness or value.

Forfeiting males for the benefit of society has always been less detrimental than foregoing the well-being of females. Instead of portraying males as wanting to harm females, in this perspective, males' greater concern has been to *defend* and *provide* for females. Since females have the unique capacity to bear children, their safety is crucial for every group's survival. Promoters note that when the ship goes down, females (and children) have priority to get a seat on a lifeboat.

However, in modern society, it is less necessary for males to provide, insure safety, or do heavy lifting. Not surprisingly, the idea of the "disposable male" is gaining traction in relation to this fact, and it is doubtful that this moniker would attach to females who still retain their child-bearing importance. With the advent of sperm banks, assembly robots, security alarms, and other sophisticated weaponry and machinery, there is increasingly less need for traditional male involvements. In that females now have employment opportunities and government subsidies, male economic participation is significantly reduced. Females can simply secure an outside repair professional with their own money, have a family without a male, and machines can do the rest. More bluntly, it is not surprising that males are losing credibility in First World countries.

Therefore, when social scientists evaluate patterns of male-female behaviors within given eras for particular cultures, it is essential to recognize that restrictions imposed on females to protect them and enhance monogamy are also likely to also coincide with the requirement for males to assume greater duty, obligation, and peril. Extrapolating further, if societies must safeguard females, then boundaries on females are likely to tighten in direct proportion to the magnitude of extant threat.

For example, prior to the advent of reliable contraception, and the acceptability of abortions, females had significant hazard associated with sexual activity. The social and religious mores of those times imposed comparatively strict limitations on females to guard against unwanted child birth that could have devastating consequences. The intent of the policy might have been noble in order to protect females and society, but the restraints were vast.

Not surprisingly, when looking back, it is possible to conclude the existence of a *patriarchal oppression*. However, with changing sexual mores, changes in the law, and the contraceptive pill, patterns altered rapidly and sexual prohibitions diminished for everyone. Given the swiftness and ease of this conversion, it is difficult to believe that The Patriarchy had any significant power to keep the former social order. Many inner desires were set free, and a new age of self-gratification unfolded (Trueman, 2020).

The apparent malevolency of clamping down on female sexuality, and their ventures into the environment, quickly altered in conjunction with cultural and legal transformations enacted conjointly by both sexes. If they so desired, women could now be more like men. While some males and females maintained traditional patterns of monogamy and family structure, a more cavalier attitude toward sex became acceptable. Both sexes now had significantly more living in the world of options and sexual choice (Eberstadt, 2021).

As is often the case, when the necessity to maintain any given male-female arrangement subsides, the sexes generally reorganize into different relational patterns. This is why Promoters argue that studying the hardships associated with one gender, and listing the privileges of the other, is not a wise approach. It is alternatively advisable to consider the balancing of obligations, constraints, and advantages associated with each gender within particular frames of time.

For instance, in years past, females typically yielded to males' legal and economic authority. They also fulfilled domestic and child-care responsibilities, and were obliged to be proceptive on a regular basis. This arrangement reinforced males to be chivalrous, committed, and willing to risk life and limb in support of the integrity, safety, and stability of family. Both sexes endured these discrete expectations in conjunction with the accommodations they received. So who was in control?

The essential point is that females will generally require more protections, and therefore, more confinements when there is danger, while males must be more willing to promote the security of others and risk their health. However, in order to get males to accommodate for the benefit of family, community, and country, it was necessary to give them extensive power to govern the institutions and laws that they were required to defend. After all, who would sacrifice for something that they did not find worthwhile to protect? While the roles might blur in some situations, this was a frequent arrangement.

The moral to the story is that there are no free rides for either males or females when understanding their intermingling in society. Their arrangements can be tacit or explicitly written in formal laws. While the balancing of duties and privileges can be discrete and more differentiated when males are needed for physical labor and defense against danger, they are less distinct when societies are tranquil and replete with a social and sexual safety net. Not surprisingly, this blurring of roles is exactly what is occurring in all societies that are replete with the freeing advances of modern technologies, birth control, and government caretaking.

In short, patterns of male and female behaviors develop in relation to the proclivities and talents that each gender demonstrates within particular sets of conditions. The social roles evolve in response to the average tendencies of each gender, even though not all individuals will find satisfaction in the social norms that support and facilitate the general patterning. Although, when there is a sufficient social backlash due to outdated arrangements, in America, the behavior of both sexes typically transforms at a noticeable pace.

For Promoters, it is not that societal patterns between males and females are birthed from oppression; they are ever-changing *consensual arrangements.* The *power* of the arrangements comes from their *temporary usefulness* to both sexes. For example, females did not learn to drive in the past, not because males wanted to imprison them, but because families had one car, males needed it to work, and females staying at home had less need to drive.

Even if *submissiveness* of various kinds seems evident within a particular social system, it does not automatically mean that the system is abusive, unreasonable, or designed to exploit. An example of this is evident in *Sleeping Beauty*, which, according to Protectors, indoctrinates females into a coercive male-dominated belief system that promotes female dependency. However, in response, Promoters claim that in previous times, both males and females pleasantly immersed in this idealized fantasy. The storyline reflects females' desire for admiration and ultimate protection, and males' aspiration to receive respect for their bravery, and their wish to obtain social value for their achievements.

Once again, for Promoters, it becomes essential to more thoroughly investigate the *intent* of male-female patterning at the time in which the patterning occurred, rather than hastily conclude that males are guilty of hegemony. For example, were past voting laws an attempt to quash females? Or were these laws perpetuating views held by many women at the time as well? Namely, were many females disinterested in politics? Were many concerned about taking on new responsibilities, including military service? Or were others identifying societal problems that might result from changing the voting laws to include women (Opposition to Women's Suffrage, 2020)?

Regardless, when enough women got on board, the voting laws changed. Moreover, even prior to the advent of females occupying political positions, having voting rights, or holding down full-time employment, female empowerment was evident. For instance, while males earned more money, women had considerable influence over family spending, and they had significant input in the decision to enact prohibition laws, despite the detail that males signed the documents (Chalberg, 2019).

Given these facts, were most females against the previous economic and social arrangements, or reinforcing their occurrence? While the enhancement of male earning power was clearly not in the best interest of *all* females, especially when males behaved selfishly, it might have been perpetuating an arrangement that many females favored at the time. Since most jobs were dangerous or dependent on physical prowess in times past, they were not well-matched for female consumption, even though that has since changed.

However, on the downside, it is now cost prohibitive for many women to stay home and raise children even when they might prefer that option. For these females, the new social arrangements have created some heartfelt restrictions. They are enduring the unfortunate side effects of an evolving social pattern that is not working for everyone, and doubtfully related to a patriarchal intent to deny women a positive life.

In yet a further attempt to challenge the belief that men want to harm women, Promoters sometimes ask Protectors to identify the empiricism that supports that view. They take this stance because they do not believe that males form in-group alliances to benefit themselves at the expense of harming females, their intimate female partners, or their female children. They do not believe that social policies creating disliked results for numbers of females are designed by a male conspiracy to accomplish that purpose. Instead, they claim that the social arrangements are simply mismatched for some women, or are outdated patterns that require revision. While claims of oppression usually make for a fast-paced upheaval and reorganization, the accusations do not prove that there was a *desire to harm*.

Interestingly enough, present-day *economic data* seems to cast doubt upon the view that males are orchestrating a society to oppress women (Bolotny et. al, 2018). For example, current wage discrepancies seem to relate to unforced occupational decisions, years of uninterrupted employment, and the prioritization of monetary acquisition and career, at the cost of other preferences, including child-rearing (Sowell, 2011). Moreover, in that males have historically shown greater extremes in performance in relation to certain traits (e.g., mathematics), and an interest in the inanimate rather than people, it is not surprising to find them occupying certain well-paid positions in technology fields and skilled (sometimes dangerous) manual labor jobs (Murray, C., 2020).

Those arguing against *patriarchal oppression* also point out that criminal sentencing, suicide rates, workplace injuries, amenities for hiring, medical care, shelters for homelessness, gender-based family law, reproductive rights, and entitlements for education, all favor women. While Protectors assert that these "privileges" are counter maneuvers and necessary to fight the ever-present patriarchy, objectors point to that data as evidence that disparities go in both directions, and do not axiomatically imply that one gender is oppressing the other.

Finally, those pushing back against the "toxic male" metaphor are also concerned that we are making young men pay for our disapproval of the past. While Protectors are adamant that current societal gratuities and overcorrections for females are not instances of misandry, Promoters remain cynical. They wonder how so many special privileges are possible in a system that is designed to repress females. They wonder how a system that is derisive toward females is willing to accept the dictum to "believe all women," which has the power to remove a male from social standing, and essentially implies that females have moral superiority. They question why a society that is bias against women, is often reluctant to prosecute women who falsely accuse men of rape or other crimes, even though this canard represents severe harm to an innocent person.

Protection or Oppression

As discussed throughout, whenever there are differences in the way in which people are treated, either legally or informally, questions arise about the reasons or intent of the disparate treatment. Parents run into this problem with their children quite frequently.

For example, when one child has the option of a later bedtime, or more opportunity to venture from the home, the other children might wonder whether the parents favor this child in comparison to them. They might think that the rule is a cipher for incompetence, or restricting them because of parental malevolence.

Parents, on the other hand, know that they are gauging their child's independence and sleep requirements based on the best interest of the child. Even though there comes a time when limits change because children mature and danger subsides, parents know that their parameters are not attempts to be unfair, hurtful, or unreasonable. While oppressive behaviors do occur within families, for most parents, limits and relationships are not predicated on inducing harm.

However, when individuals view a situation as if they are being cheated or degraded, it can be difficult to distinguish whether differential treatment emanates from concerns that relate to protection, or from a desire to create subservience or oppression. Those ascribing to the evils of The Patriarchy assert the latter. In their view, when they observe differential treatments for females that have associated hardships, they are likely to claim an instance of male-orchestrated malfeasance to create those privations. They read intent in a negative light, much like what happens when a law has disparate impact on one identity group compared with another.

For instance, if marriage is hamstringing some females due to limited financial resources to escape, the explanation magnetically draws to the belief that males have created a system designed to hold females captive. The idea that females might be participating consensually in the social institution of marriage eludes them. Even when females are proceptive, many see females as vulnerable receptacles for male sexual dominance that borders on something akin to rape. Likewise, if unmarried females have sexual restrictions, it is not that both sexes want to promote safety and a family structure; it is that only males desire the asymmetry in sexual behavior.

Those who oppose these male-blaming inferences provide a different account. They see reciprocal benefits to social patterns. For example, while chastity for females might benefit males because they would have reassurance of a genetic link with the child, as well as help them feel valued, appreciated, and special, it also benefits females who could reap the benefits of having and raising children, with the security that a male will offer increased dedication and conscientious support. This benefit might occur because males are more likely to share acquisitions and services toward the goal of family protection if they know they have sexual exclusivity and a genetic link to the individuals they protect.

When considering additional mutual benefits from committed relationships, Promoters find yet another advantage for both sexes. They make the case that both sexes might accrue greater satisfaction and safety from a loyal, respectful relationship, which includes a variety of caring behaviors during day-to-day life. On paper, these kinds of arrangements allow both men and women to be the kings and queens of their own small domain. For many, this magic is lost, but the institutions of sexual exclusivity, marriage, and family life derives from this predicate.

Overall, Promoters believe that when society maintains the sanctity of an exclusive male-female bond within marriage and family, both males and females retain power over their lives. They are more likely to be economically viable and have more autonomy within this arrangement. Promoters note that it can be facile to indict the entire institution of marriage when outcomes create small pockets of harm or discomfort. In their view, particular social patterns come into existence because they yield more positives than negatives for most of the participants. As long as the good outweighs the bad, the patterns continue. When it stops, change takes place.

Changing Patterns

In Promoter ideology, the basis for restrictions on females, and impositions of risk on males, will change as environments become safer. The historic vulnerability of females, and the emotions tied to doubts about security, have led females to opt for safety over freedom in many instances. Since the workplace has gotten substantially less dangerous over the years in relation to technology and female advocacy, venturing into the world of work is now a viable option as feminine-friendly environments evolve.

Now, more than ever, many women actively seek jobs and careers that are conducive to their preferences and skills. With modernity and automation, managing the home is no longer an intricate and all-encompassing activity. As time goes on, more jobs and careers are available for eager females to fill. Whether the shift from family to workplace creates more life satisfaction for either gender is unclear. However, employment is now an incentive for both sexes, and behavioral patterns correlated with each gender are morphing and intertwining in new ways, with an ever-present blurring of distinctions. As noted, females can now live in the world more like males and still be safe.

While Protectors persist in claiming that "glass ceilings" and obstacles for females remain, Promoters insist that society as a whole is readily acknowledging women's interest in changing the old arrangements that are now outdated. It simply takes time to replace incumbents. However, as a way to speed up the process, it is now commonplace to see "gender diversity" initiatives in all kinds of industries. There are numerous affirmative action programs for hiring and promoting females, even though males are falling behind in many areas, including educational attainment and in many desirable careers (Greenstone and Looney, 2011).

Many Promoters point out that it has been relatively easy to change patterns between men and women, despite assertions about The Patriarchy. They note that for men who want the approval, sexual interest, and the partnership of females, there are limited options, other than going along with what females currently advocate. For example, many men doing Internet dating frequently encounter the message that they "need not apply" unless they are in alliance with feminism, and do not "vote for Trump."

It is, however, worthwhile to consider some problems that are occurring from the rapidly changing social order. As government takes over the care and protection of people with limited family support, women and children rank high on the list to receive assistance. The unforeseen consequence of providing this aid (and the ease of divorce) has unfortunately incentivized subgroups of fathers and mothers not to remain together. For increasing numbers, two-parent co-habitation is becoming less frequent (Buckley, Jr., 2017).

It is now feasible for women to have the freedom of childbirth without the necessity to find a kind and responsible person to share daily family responsibilities. They no longer have to risk harm or disappointment from a potentially unsatisfactory partner, as the government can aid and abet.

While this new arrangement could have a concerning impact on children having to adjust to parents living apart, the extra financial burdens of maintaining two households, teenage motherhood, amplified domestic violence, and multiple-partner fertility, the new social arrangement is beginning to substitute for the traditional family. According to Amy Wax, except for pockets of educated individuals (i.e., primarily middle-class Caucasians and Asians) who still maintain the traditional family norms of remaining together, this new child-rearing structure is gaining in frequency (Buckley, Jr., 2017).

Since a Protector's primary concern is offsetting immediate hardship for those who suffer, giving females increased opportunity to remain viable (especially with children involved) is a worthy goal. Welfare rules and other subsides might regrettably eliminate males and threaten traditional family structure for those living in poverty, but Protectors are willing to advocate for social change, which permits increased security for those in need. Struggling females can obtain flexibility and leeway with governmental backing, and if male "toxicity" occurs at any time, females gain the option of ridding themselves of this harm, with the government swooping in to take over the job if they lack financial means.

Females in all economic groups now have less need for a long-term commitment from a male to flourish or to have children. Since men can now have children and sex (due to the sexual revolution) without having to limit themselves to a marital relationship (with all of its requirements and pitfalls), fewer males are buying into a monogamous lifestyle as well. While the two-parent intact family is still an optimal way to provide for a child's well-being, this form of social organization is sinking into the shadows for greater numbers of people.

For Protectors, however, these societal changes are equivalent to overturning the barriers that stifle marginalized identities. They are comparable to helping the impoverished by redistributing money to promote their economic security. While we do not know about the long-term consequences of the new social order, it is likely that this reformulation of society will have considerable impact on the behavior of both sexes, as well as the children growing up within these changed conditions.

Perhaps, instead of complimentary, which can make relationships easier and more predictable, the sexes will become functionally similar in many or most ways. There could also be a realization of the Radical Protector's goal of sameness in the future. Perhaps individuals will delay marriage, shy away from raising children, and endorse misogamy. Moreover, if society continues to see males as persona non grata, males might become more alienated towards traditional family roles, and withdraw into activities that expose them to less shame, financial risk, and negativity (Grace, 2020; Straughan, 2012).

Not surprisingly, with all of the affirmative action programs and emphasis to promote females throughout society, it seems that young males are beginning to flounder in notable ways. As this occurs, it might become increasingly difficult for females to find acceptable partners. Since females have historically been reluctant to integrate their lives with males who have comparably lower earning power or social status, the steady decline of males' financial prowess and value in society is likely to have at least some impact on the success of heterosexual patterning and the gratification of female hypergamy.

Moreover, in that large numbers of females (and males) are now growing up with father estrangement, many women are frequently reaching adulthood without the benefit or familiarity of being close with a male who is caring and concerned about their well-being. They learn long-term survival without male interdependence or the knowledge of what it is like to be involved in a gratifying heterosexual relationship. This is likely to significantly influence mating patterns as time unfolds.

In sum, as the government becomes the primary source of protection and need-fulfillment, and replaces functions that had formally been the responsibility of males and females within a family context, changes in society will certainly be marked. Protectors are much less likely to fear these kinds of transformations, because they believe that the current social order has always been oppressive. Promoters, on the other hand, fear that both males and females are likely to lose discretionary authority over their lives, and suffer a depletion of happiness as these patterns entrench. They worry that many will lose the joy of what male-female intimacy can provide, and perhaps regret early life decisions. They lament the fact that many modern societies are following this path.

Consent

The topic of *consent* is critical when studying interactions between people. The term signifies the demarcation between coercion and volunteerism, and pertains to other important dichotomies such as the difference between compliance vs. agreement, oppression vs. freedom, rape vs. sex, and the difference between slave and employee.

For both Protectors and Promoters, the idea of consent is noteworthy in any discussion of male-female relationships. There is significant debate about its occurrence, or lack thereof, during sexual encounters, and during day-to-day interactions. While it is always possible to define the word in a particular way, subtle problems arise in different situations and circumstances when trying to discern whether or not it meets an imposed criterion.

First, mutual permission, or affinity with others to take particular actions, is much easier when writing legal documents. These kinds of circumstances permit individuals the time to specify contingencies, create a degree of exactitude, as well as specify when opting out can take place. In many instances, people hire professionals to stave off the pitfalls and difficulties that might otherwise occur during future interactions. All of this takes place *prior* to signing documents, which then provides legal and binding limits and the necessity to behave in particular ways.

However, day-to-day life often plays out differently. While there are times when individuals can ask about the acceptability of a particular action prior to enacting the behavior, often people interact within a flow of action and response. Individuals generally do not find out that other people do not like their actions until they have *already* taken place. All they can do at that point is clarify, apologize, or not repeat the behavior, with the hope of preserving a semblance of the relationship. The dilemma is the same as what occurs with "freedom of speech."

The important point is that individuals may commit an objectionable behavior without knowing beforehand that it is a violation, and nothing can change that fact. If others want to claim harassment, bigotry, sexual inappropriateness, or other crimes and misdemeanors, they can do so. The receptive individuals can subject initiators to scrutiny and evaluation. Their appraisals are contingent upon such factors as their biases, moods, and tolerances for behavioral variations. If the responders have significant social or legal clout, their opinions rule.

Often, the only difference between whether an action is problematic, acceptable, or passed over without a second thought, is the particular way that the receptive group or individual *interprets* the action. If enough people agree, the enactors have trouble on their hands. Behaviors that might be bearable in a different crowd (or even applauded), might be deemed horrendous in a scrupulous milieu with different preferences and beliefs. When that happens, individuals might be ousted by the majority rule or prattling loud voices. Since it is not always possible to gauge the reactions of others and their proclivities, there is significant risk with many initiated behaviors.

As a way to deal with this problem during interactions between the sexes, males can learn the ins and outs of what females are likely to prefer, and in the extreme, become so cautious about their actions that they are catatonically transfixed to mitigate the possibility of being exiled. In today's guarding of the vulnerable, "consent" is in the fragile eye of the beholder, and this is paramount when recipients are females. In these instances, all the power resides in the females' gauging of meaning, and their right to impose restrictions.

Promoters voice concern in response to this scenario, which is without an easy remedy. For example, if we require permission prior to taking each action, activities could be spoiled to the point of being ludicrous. Just think of enacting this solution during a sexual exchange. Even when participants are trying to be cognizant of the receptiveness of the other partner, this is a cumbersome remediation.

A second problem arises when males gain "consent" with a head nod or other affirmation, but then recipients change their minds *after* behavior proceeds. If the initiator recognizes the revoking and stops, then the problem is less severe than if the unacceptable behavior continues. However, whether or not initiators discern the change may depend upon the explicitness of the rescinding. That is, was there lack of compliance, or was the halting message unclear? Was the tone of voice unequivocal or ambiguous, or was it voiced at all? For example, some individuals might become privately uncomfortable and blame others for not recognizing their inner emotions. They operate with the premise, *If you really cared, you would have known how I felt.*

Given these kinds of complications, it seems unreasonable to deem initiators guilty because they could not read minds. Yet recipients feel coerced, and they do not interpret the interaction as a consensual endeavor. They might blame their inhibitions on others, and say they were "intimidated," even though "perpetrators" had no idea that this was happening. When unraveling this dilemma, we might ask, *Were the individuals timid, or were the other people daunting?* Who to blame seems like a messy puzzle, and judgment often reduces to the biases of evaluators.

To complicate matters further, there are occasions when it seems that the *outcome* of the action determines its acceptability, instead of the agreement *prior* to the exchange. For instance, sometimes people are reluctant to engage in a particular activity, but then find out that they liked what happened after the activity begins or is completed.

They might even thank the individuals who nudged and poked them to join in.

However, events play out quite differently when individuals feel mildly pressured and then have a bad experience. The coercion prior to the event might have been the same in both instances, but the outcome creates resentments and desire to chastise. Depending on the extent of the negative reaction, the reprimand and consequence could vary in considerable ways.

Moreover, even without any prior coercion, feelings of shame or disappointment *after* the encounter might trigger an externalization of blame. People may assert that individuals "made" them participate, as it is often easier to blame others, as opposed to taking at least some personal responsibility for what transpired. Not surprisingly, this response pattern occurs frequently in the aftermath of frivolous sex when shame and guilt are more likely for many people. It also occurs when individuals are insecure and anxious to please, and then feel *exploited* when there is no reciprocity.

Additional problems arise when individuals involved in various kinds of transactions have discrepant wherewithal or authority. While the weaker person might give consent to proceed, it is difficult to see the transaction as mutual due to power dynamics, naivety, or incapacity of one of the participants to understand the consequences of what might happen. This problem is evident when adults interact with children, when employers interact with subordinates, and when one individual is intoxicated and the other is not.

In these instances, the person in power, or the cognitively competent person, is held responsible for any adversity encountered. However, while most people agree that it is important to protect vulnerable people, many problems arise when it is difficult to ascertain how "impaired" the other person might be, or when competence might not be consistent with age. In these situations, the usual deciding factors are vague or at odds.

There is yet another complexity to the problem of consent. People might give consent, but have very different ideas about what they believe will happen. For example, what if an individual behaves in a manner that indicates care and concern, and the other party reciprocates, divulges personal information, and permits a sexual encounter? If the philanderer gets up in the morning, leaves, and is never heard from again, the aggrieved party might feel victimized. The "exploited" individual might insist that there was a tacit agreement about future interactions, and see the other person as conniving, disingenuous, and outright fraudulent.

While there was putative "consent," the aggrieved individual was not agreeing to experience what eventually happened. The distressed person feels harmed, and may want to get retribution. While there was no explicit coercion or physical restraint, the individual has a profound sense of having been mistreated and defiled. As stressed by many Protectors, the construct of "volunteerism" is often used much too flippantly by many within the Promoter camp.

A similar problem with "consent" occurs when couples are on the verge of a sexual encounter, and one person indicates the presence of birth control. Whether or not there was prevarication, a pregnancy ensues. Clearly, one or both did not agree to conceive a baby or to support a child for over two decades, but a child is conceived. When people become entangled in these kinds of scenarios, little do they know what they are "consenting" to when they say the word *yes*.

As is evident from each of these different social exchanges, there are many nuances when deciphering whether interactions are mutual or consensual. It is not always clear what is in store for us when we supposedly "agree." Small fluctuations in authority dynamics, and what transpires during or after the event, can lead to different conclusions regarding comfort or regret. All of these concerns are relevant when determining whether interactions contain even a modicum of kindness or permissibility.

Given these concerns, Protectors often insist that consent is difficult (or impossible) to achieve when males and females encounter each other. Since there is *buy-in* to the construct of The Patriarchy, males have a power advantage by default, and this intimidation factor must be taken into account at all times. At its core, male-female "consent" is a fallacy in this system of belief. For example, if the male and female are intoxicated, it is still reasonable to hold the male liable due to the presumed unequal power dynamics, and the more severe consequences that females must endure from the possibility of pregnancy.

For Protectors, females might accommodate males in a variety of ways, but we are not observing instances of consent or mutuality; we are seeing the consequences of male oppressions unfolding. They implore everyone to be suspicious of what transpires between men and women.

They want to eradicate "mansplaining," which is an ongoing pattern of males trying to dominate females during verbal exchanges. They want to stop the undercurrent of repression that has continued for ages, and they put forth a myriad or examples of females conforming to male preferences because of *implicit* bullying. They believe that males relentlessly subjugate women, even if it is not overtly seen by others. The parallels between sexism and racism are astounding, and it is not surprising that the two have coalesced.

In contrast, Promoters are less apt to outright assign blame to males. For example, if both parties have been drinking and the female regrets the sexual encounter, they might analyze the situation from a neutral starting point, and look to see if there are contributions to the dilemma coming from both sides of the aisle. Rather than begin with the premise that patriarchal enactments beat down females, they see females in a more powerful light, with the possibility of agency, rather than characterize them as easily manipulated automatons.

While keeping in mind the possibility that physical strength does tip the scales in many instances, Promoters presume a modicum of equality in females' ability to behave assertively, ferret out ruse, stop unacceptable arrangements, and anticipate problems. For them, exploring the possible contributions from all participants is not equivalent to victim-blaming; it is presuming that both sexes have comparable responsibilities and analogous competencies. Alternative explanations, in this view, can be entertained before venturing into the undercurrent of male intimidation. Again, while Protectors flush out harm incurred by females (i.e., outside→ in), Promoters consider the interweaving of actions, and are willing to entertain the notion that females can be violators as well.

Domestic Violence

Even if we presume that males and females want cooperation and mutual caring, there are numerous occasions when there are conflicts of interest that escalate to an intolerable degree. In the commonly accepted view of domestic conflict, females are more likely to be viewed as victims, and males as perpetrators. The popular conception of domestic violence, called the *Duluth Model*, leans in this direction. However, contrasting with that perspective, Williams and Frieze (Sex Roles, 2005) present data showing that domestic conflict is perpetrated at equal rates by both sexes.

In the latter view, rather than indict males as a nocuous poison in domestic matters, statistics about domestic violence might not be as lopsided as they first appear. Often, conclusions depend on the definitions of mistreatment and interpretation of the data. Prior to locating blame solely on males, some claim that it is important to have a comprehensive understanding of what is happening during the reported altercations (Scorzo, 2015). While the mere questioning of data might trigger accusations of misogyny, victim-blaming, or rape apologies, in many circles, some are pushing for a more detailed and balanced analysis.

Given this backdrop, what are the consequences of adopting the perspective that assigns blame to one gender, especially when there are numerous times when both parties might be contributing to the problem? Do we still advocate for the weaker person, even if the presumed recipient of harm initiated the violence? Is the physically stronger person always at fault if a conflict ensues? Does the identified vulnerable person always retain the power to punish the other person and dictate what happens legally? Do we persist in holding males accountable in all circumstances?

In response to these questions, and in an effort to be even-handed, Promoters are concerned that interventions routinely taking sides and assigning blame are overly simplistic. They are likely to create many other problems as well. For instance, the cosseted individual has less fear of accountability and is essentially given license to act with less civility. That individual can control the relationship by using the cudgel of victimhood against the other person.

Moreover, while authorities might think that they can easily identify the perpetrator when couples have conflict, that determination can be a subtle problem. The bias induced by belief in The Patriarchy directs authorities to indict the male, but what are the criteria used to decide that the male is responsible for the uproar? Is it who complains first to the authorities? Is it who is physically injured, or who complains the loudest when the authorities arrive on the scene? What actions are perpetrations, and what actions are defenses? Are there any conditions that justify physical force? If the accuser recants, which rendition has veracity, and is the retracting simply evidence of "The Patriarchy?"

Like the claim of racist harm, the claim of domestic abuse can result in many severe consequences. The accused is often expelled from the home, special services are granted to the victim, and the crime of domestic violence can negate the possibility of gaining child custody in court decisions. If recipients of domestic violence have this kind of power, then accusations of mistreatment may be reinforced by outcomes beyond the opportunity to escape from subjugation and danger.

There is yet an additional consequence associated with domestic violence that might influence participants. The aggrieved individual's suffering induces guilt upon the other person. This often leads to the "aggressor" having increased interest in maintaining the relationship. The person who was seething, and the source of physical harm, then becomes the identified blameworthy party who is regretful and apprehensive about rejection. The accused might then attempt to gain forgiveness by going to great lengths to please the victimized partner, and this pattern of obsequiousness is seen throughout the society.

During the aftermath, more affection and concern is often evident than what occurs without the prior fighting. It is common for couples with domestic violence history to have repetitious patterns of fighting and making up, which include contriteness, consoling, declarations of commitment, and passionate sexual encounters that rarely take place at any other time.

However, and importantly, rather than jump to the conclusion that this is implying that couples *like* to have domestic violence, discerning this sequence of events is only saying that the pattern can be insidiously, and often unwittingly, reinforced within relationships. This is the case not only for couples, but for friend relationships, and for parents and children as well. Frequent examples of this pattern occur when a partner brings home flowers or cooks a gourmet meal in reaction to a previous mistake.

It is not that Promoters want to minimize instances of blatant one-sided domestic violence, which should be stopped and prosecuted. They understand that there are horrendous stories of violent crimes perpetrated by individuals who have ongoing contact. Additionally, they know that quite often it can be easy to determine a pattern of unilateral abuse. However, they recognize that these easy-to-adjudicate scenarios do not represent the largest sample of domestic violence cases.

In the interest of fairness, they argue that it is important to investigate what happens in a neutral, case-by-case fashion when there are claims of domestic violence. They recommend investigations that proceed without the presumption that males are invariably guilty, or that females cannot be perpetrators because of inherent vulnerability to the strength of male oppression. Much like their rejection of the assertion that *people without power* cannot be racist, they do not want to accept the view that females cannot have accountability.

In contrast, Protectors are reticent to endorse any claim that brings female oppression into question. They do not want to entertain the possibility that some instances of domestic violence might be perpetrated by females. They hesitate to consider that some conflicts might be mutually initiated or mutually reinforced, or that there is any power associated with victimhood. They are instead concerned that these kinds of ideas will undermine, and perhaps undo, efforts to protect vulnerable females. They abhor any perspective that could be construed as "victim-blaming."

Despite these kinds of concerns, and the strong social pressure that backs the Protector position, Promoters want to consider the actions and deeds of all involved. They want to be cognizant of possible remunerations that can occur in relation to claims of ill-treatment, and look at the downstream consequences that sequence with such claims. They want to investigate whether gainful results might be reinforcing exaggerations of suffering and entitlement for compensation. They make the case that these alternative concerns are especially pertinent in the context of divorce and child custody decisions.

While they have no problem remediating the trauma associated with the victim, Promoters delving into this matter entertain the possibility that there could be possible *reinforcements* for couples to engage in highly charged repetitious physical altercations. They might also examine previous exposures to anger and violence, including what happened in their parents' relationship, and then explore how that history and role modeling might relate to the current situation.

The expectation is that this kind of approach is likely to yield better and more lasting effects for all the individuals involved. Promoters are concerned that domestic violence behaviors are more likely to repeat at other times and in other relationships, if these matters are not addressed. This does not discount handling cases in the traditional fashion when unilateral perpetration or psychopathic behaviors are evident, but Promoters advise against seeing every case in that light.

As a general policy, Promoters do not want to downplay the need to penalize those responsible for violent domestic crime. However, they want the occurrence of *nonbiased interventions* without the presumption of one-sided fault. They desire an accurate depiction of the altercation, even though many take offense in response to this approach. Moreover, they are open to the possibility that some relationships with domestic violence might be worth saving, as there can be pros and cons related to this matter, for both the couple and their children.

Promoters do not want to perpetuate unjust treatment of males by presuming their guilt, since that will edge metaphorically close to a lynching. This includes backing away from recent attempts to reduce due process for males accused of sexual misconduct on college campuses, which is currently accepted practice by recent changes in law (Rubenfeld, 2016). In their view, preserving a presumption of innocence remains important human right.

In sum, while Promoters acknowledge that there are males who harm and oppress females without remorse, they argue that these males are a small minority of men who, in most cases, are violent and harmful in a variety of other ways. Many of them are also more likely to have suffered abuse themselves, including abuse from females (Groth, 1979). They emphasize that this small faction of repeat offenders is not characteristic of males, in general, and there are psychopathic domestic behaviors initiated by females as well.

One only has to acknowledge that the label of "wife beater" is certainly not a status symbol that most males like to wear on their chest or have as an epitaph. While society, in general, shuns maltreatment, this is especially the case when directed toward women. This taboo has been in existence for centuries, across the world. Interestingly, and consistent with this assertion, the highest rates of domestic violence rates occur between bisexual females and lesbians, while homosexual and heterosexual males have the lowest rates (Evans, 2017).

Abortion

When the mother desires her baby, the fetus is treasured, and anyone doing harm to the unborn child is a criminal and prosecuted severely. Assuming that the woman is competent, problems arise only when she outwardly objects to the pregnancy. This scenario gives rise to the abortion controversy, which was exacerbated after the *Roe vs. Wade* Supreme Court decision claimed that state laws that banned abortions (except to save the life of the mother) were unconstitutional. Given the virulent debate concerning this matter, understanding the positions of our two camps is an important endeavor.

The crux of the debate is whether the baby or the mother requires protection, and under what conditions is killing permissible. Since Protectors typically safeguard visible harm, they argue to rescue pregnant females who suffer from the pregnancy, while Promoters focus on the unborn fetuses that have the right to live. Importantly, what accounts for this difference in priorities, and how does the inside ↔ outside psychodynamic exhibit itself?

For Protectors, pregnant females are likely to *suffer* if they are unable to obtain a proper medical abortion. Women might seek illegal abortions that could be harmful, and they do not want to put females in this compromised position. They argue that it is not the right of others to force females to increase overpopulation, endure pregnancy, childbirth, or the responsibility of childcare, when the other people do not have to bear those consequences. It is their *right* to protect their bodies and life preferences, and they should be able to defend themselves (i.e., outside → in).

These "right to choose" advocates claim that fetuses should not be given the same status as fully developed human beings. The stage at which the fetus attains full status might vary (e.g., heartbeat, brain activity, viability, etc.), but fetuses have lesser standing in this view. If it is necessary to pick the one to protect, it should be the individual who is fully formed and autonomous, and the one whose suffering is urgent and clearly discernible.

Promoters often take the opposite stance. They insist that both fetuses and mothers are alive and should have equal rights to exist. In their view, no one has permission to kill the innocent, and the suffering of mothers pales in comparison to the crime of murder. Provisions can be made to ease a mother's suffering, and perhaps have the baby adopted, but promoting the integrity of each fetus's life is paramount. In the small number of cases where a mother's life is at risk due to the pregnancy, many in this camp will concede to safeguard the mother.

In response, Protectors are repelled by the stance of "pro-life" groups. They wonder why individuals from that camp might permit going to war, and tolerate the collateral damage of innocent people during military invasions, yet eschew abortion because it represents "killing of the innocent." They see the argument as hypocritical.

On the other hand, pro-lifers fire back in relation to that contention. They claim that killing in those instances is actually saving more innocent lives than doing any other tactic. The actions are the better of two evils, and not unlike saving the mother when pregnancy might kill her. They are still operating under the guiding principle that the right to innocent life is supreme.

As you can see, the abortion debate is often *not* about whether a fetus is alive; the controversy usually focuses on when it is permissible to kill. For example, anti-abortionists might advocate the death penalty for certain crimes, some might permit euthanasia under some circumstances, and they might make abortion exceptions when females are impregnated from rape or incest. Under these conditions, it is acknowledged that females are the innocent victims and should not have to endure the consequences of the pregnancy, even though killing the innocent is still taking place when performing the abortion. In these cases, *liability for the problem* seems to be a guiding factor that determines whether it is permissible to kill.

Let us explore another scenario. Often, the argument to permit abortion occurs in relation to the assertion that it is permissible to kill a fetus because it cannot sustain itself without the female's body. For this reason, the fetus should not be given full human status and value. However, many of these individuals would not advocate withholding medical care from a person on a ventilator who would otherwise die without external support. Moreover, the issue of viability relates directly to the medical care available, and this could change markedly, depending on the time and place of the dilemma.

In a similar vein, a "free to choose" advocate might claim that fetuses do not have fully developed brains. In this view, their suffering cannot compare to the suffering of mothers who are lucid and have to endure the ordeal of pregnancy and its aftermath. However, they would likely object to killing people with dementia or brain injury, even though they also have diminished brainpower and reduced facility to remain alive without support from others.

Overall, it seems that both sides have reasonable responses to the arguments of the opposing camp. Both sides make assertions about when it is permissible to kill, and when it is a crime. While the debate can sometimes take the form of whether or not a human's life starts at conception, the debate often devolves into a dispute about the conditions under which it is allowable to terminate a human existence. This includes instances where it is permissible to kill the innocent, such as when it is necessary to bomb areas where weapons are located in highly populated areas.

However, what rationale accounts for the proclivity of the Protector camp to defend and support pregnant females at the cost of fetuses, and why does the Promoter camp frequently advocate for fetuses? More precisely, why does the faction that is intent on rescuing the weakest in society align with the mother over the helpless fetus, while people most often accused of being devoid of compassion, work so hard to defend the least powerful entity in the equation?

The answer to this question seems to be threefold. First, it is usually the case that Protectors are concerned with the suffering that is most evident at the moment. Their interventions are often directed at relieving immediate hardships, including subsidizing an abortion with governmental funding, and pulling people out of vulnerability as quickly as possible. Those urgencies have priority, and pregnant females fit the bill. Much like allowing needy immigrants to enter the country without exception because of their dire straits, the downstream consequences push to the side. The first and primary concern is to rescue, and pregnant females require immediate attention.

Second, why wouldn't the Protector camp align with the pregnant female? Women are typically fervent allies with this bloc. They are one of its major constituents and purveyors. As acolytes to the motto, *Protection reigns supreme,* they are in sync with identity groups clamoring for a shielding status. Taking a position that might induce increased suffering for women, who are vocal about the right to choose, would be inconsistent with the value to fight back against the oppression of traditionalism. Limits on abortion, like systemic racism, are simply another unwanted hardship society imposes on the vulnerable. The invisible fetus cannot undercut the quest for their identity freedoms.

Third, since pregnancies occur in relation to an act of a male, the hatred of The Patriarchy might also factor into the rush to protect females. Since many females want to promote liberation from the barriers of male oppression, releasing females from the harness of childbirth, childcare, and male entrapment is certainly a valiant endeavor. For some within the Protector faction, pregnancy itself is evidence of the imbalance of power between males and females. In the name of equity, since males do not have to endure pregnancy, why should females have that obligation thrust upon them?

In contrast, since Promoters advocate for personal responsibility, they argue to hold people accountable for their actions and deeds. They want people to deal with the consequences of their "voluntary" sexual behaviors (i.e., inside → out). Why should we unremittingly kill the innocent because some people behave recklessly or change their minds as an afterthought? For them, the requirement to endure consequences is what shapes mature, considerate, and reasonable behavior that ultimately benefits us all. They believe that people should be accountable for their behavior, and when people are protected from the consequences of their actions, the frequency of those behaviors inevitably increases (Allen, 1993). This phenomenon is known as a *moral hazard*.

Given the opposing views on abortion, it does not seem that the debate is easily resolved. What principle can we invoke to tell us when it is permissible to kill, even if we assume that the fetus is alive? We can adopt the truism that it is unacceptable to harm the innocent, but that can transform into a discussion about whether one action saves more innocent lives than another. However, if we follow that logic, it seems clear that those innocents that are going to be killed would not want the "tyranny of the majority" to determine their fate. When seen in that light, it is ironic that the Promoters, who are most vocal about the unacceptability of "mob rule," adopt this stance.

One final thought. Even for Promoters who are neutral about abortion, their solution to the problem is markedly different from those within the Protector camp. For example, while Protectors want to increase abortion *services* to rescue struggling females, many Promoters recommend adoption, vigilant birth control, and sexual restraint. In their view, if society begins to largely embrace those three norms, the frequency of terminated pregnancies will significantly decrease.

Gender Dysphoria

Currently, there is increased acceptance of many sexual behaviors that were prohibited in the past. In some circles, it is easier for individuals to announce their sexual preferences and gender identities, as compared to disclosing political viewpoints that vary from the majority in the room. In contrast, individuals wanting to transition from one gender to the other continue to create a significant social and political stir. Often, there is controversy about the safety of undergoing the medical treatments, and significant problems arise when children and their parents claim a child or adolescent's desire to transition (Goodman and Nash, 2019).

The acceptance of sexual transitioning requires many different kinds of social adjustments in beliefs, language and institutional behaviors that can affect medicine, sporting events, restroom usage, insurances, and living arrangements. Due to these factors and the medical consequences of the transitioning, this phenomenon is an important problem to address carefully, even though proponents see this matter as an advancement of each person's identity expression.

Complicating matters further, while gender dysphoria and an interest in transitioning has previously been associated with early onset in young boys, it is now common for growing numbers of middle-class adolescent females to report that their assigned sex is not their correct sex (Shrier, 2020). Since many of these "rapid onset" cases are occurring more often when their cohorts make similar claims, many are concerned that social contagion, augmented by social media and progressive sex education, is influencing the burgeoning rates of its occurrence (Littman, 2018). Rather than accepting the assertion that *nature* has committed a mistake, these individuals are encouraging an investigation into the interplay of psychosocial factors, with the claim of having the dysphoric condition.

However, given the active voices in our current politics, of not wanting to create additional hardship for marginalized identities, there is ongoing affirmation of transgender assertions. Practitioners are rapidly moving forward with medical treatments and neglecting the possibility that there might be transient psychosocial influences. This trend continues despite the concerning fact that in less than a decade, transsexual treatment has increased in the UK by over 4,000 percent (Van, 2018).

While Protectors acknowledge these tendencies, they do not want to inhibit an individual's opportunity to get relief from sexual and emotional discomfort. They point out that in the past, there was significant rejection of sexual variations, and this forced people into treatments to "convert" them to traditional patterns of sexual patterning. They know that those coercive approaches failed miserably, and they do not want to repeat those oppressive mistakes. Even though it is primarily teenage girls, a group that historically shows susceptibility to cohort contagion that exhibits the rapid increase in gender dysphoria, Protectors maintain that it is simply a freedom to "come out of the closet" that accounts for the amplified numbers (Jordan Peterson, 2021).

In their view, a truly ethical society must accept transgender claims at face value. Otherwise, the society is inherently cruel and oppressive (Giordano, 2008). They believe that it is unconscionable to make pre-adolescent youths endure the unwanted bodily changes and social responses that occur during puberty, without providing help. Those post-pubescent changes will only exacerbate the oppression of living in a sexually mismatched body, and make it more difficult to obtain the bodily characteristics of the opposite sex (Prestigiacomo, 2021).

Given the mushrooming of this medical viewpoint, sexual transitioning is increasing, and the general culture is also becoming increasingly receptive to this trend. For example, according to the US 2015 transgender survey, one-third of individuals in the younger generations see gender identification as protean. The culture is definitively moving toward the approval of all kinds of sexual variations, including transgenderism (James et. al, 2016).

In accordance, Protectors discount the cautionary alarms pertaining to the proliferation of adolescent females desiring a sexual transition. In their view, since females suffer the extra hardship of patriarchal oppression, it is no wonder that numerous adolescent females are captured by this movement. If these females are actually males, the transition will emancipate them from all of the problems associated with being female in a misogynistic society. When coupled with the significant and uncomfortable body changes that adolescent females endure in comparison to males, of course they are receptive when given the opportunity to be set free.

Advocates also believe that regrets after transitioning will subside now that society is more receptive to the transgender identity. While the empirics are not yet firmly established, proponents remain hopeful that de-transitioning and suicide rates will eventually decrease in conjunction with the newfound societal welcoming (Williams, 2015). They anticipate that outcomes will eventually be similar to other civil rights movements.

As a result, medical providers aligned with the Protector camp are now more willing to administer the hormones, perform the surgeries, and make the necessary accommodations in order to alleviate hardships and suffering currently experienced by transgender individuals. Their hope is to curtail the "arbitrary" roles that society imposes on all of us, including differences between males and females. Not surprisingly, while the results have since been retracted (Van Mol et al., 2020), there was initially much excitement when it was reported that the surgeries had psychological benefits, as those findings were consistent with Promoter ideals (Bränström and Pachankis, 2019).

Protectors believe that the transgender issue brings their political concerns into a laser-like focus. They see societal forces imposing suffering on yet another minority contingent, and they want to add this subgroup to their growing battalion of maligned groups that can stand up to traditional family norms and ways of life. Any attempt to shift transgenderism to conventional standards becomes equivalent to endorsing the harms of racism, misogyny, and xenophobia. The failure to provide instantaneous relief is slurring and demeaning to a person's true identity potential, and this is exactly what oppressive societies often do to minority voices.

In their idealized world, transgender people must be free to venture into possibilities that have always been taboo within past systems of oppression. They welcome people holding grievances toward previous restrictions, and if they are able to sanction the extreme of sexual transitioning, then all other identity limitations will be even easier to emancipate.

In Protector ideology, denying the premise of "sexual misassignment" is harmful. Naysayers are implicitly blaming individuals for possessing an immutable characteristic, much like skin color. Similar to the claim, "believe all victims," everyone should condone the assertion that the person is paired with the wrong body, even if the declaration comes from a very young child.

These first-person reports are considered factual, and they have nothing to do with experiences or patterns of coping. Promoters note that many social changes occur for people with other kinds of physical misfortunes, so why question or hesitate to make changes for individuals who struggle with this particular unwanted bodily variation. In that many are agreeing with the "biological mismatch" assertion, there is an ever-present legal push to prohibit interventions that are hesitant to promote the transgender activist perspective.

Interestingly, while some might see this new social movement as deviating from the Protector's usual constructionist metaphor, which claims that sexual preferences are created by societal coercions and not biological essentialism, this is not the case. Transgender individuals, like other minority groups, are facing imposed adversity. Like these other minorities, they are powerless victims of a "force" that resides outside of their true self. In the case of racial minorities, the force is eternal racism. For females, it is the baleful Patriarchy. For the poor, it is the greed of the wealthy capitalists. And for the transgender individual, it is a mistaken body. As with all explications within Protector ideology, personal agency for the sufferer does not come into play. It is society, or other impinging sources of oppression (in this case, biology), that impede the liberation of one's core distinctiveness, which is unmodifiable (i.e., outside → inside).

In stark contrast, Promoters question whether it is reasonable to encourage and accept the kinds of claims currently espoused by the transgender community. They are also skeptical of medical procedures that seem experimental, especially when a child's physiology permanently alters with surgeries and puberty blockers (Hruz, Mayer, and McHugh, 2017). They point out that "watchful waiting" has worked reasonably well in the past, because many young children become comfortable with their bodies over time, and simply identify as homosexual (Sho, 2020).

Consistent with this analysis, conservative estimates are that about two-thirds of children typically grow out of their "gender dysphoria" (Steensma et. al, 2013). Promoters remind us that in cases of desistance, early transition and surgery would have led to significant misfortune. They remain unconvinced that *all individuals* in the transgender group suffer from a biological mishap, and prefer to investigate the extent to which transgenderism has psychosocial components that might be resolved without major surgery. They want to see whether feelings of mismatch could morph over time, into body acceptance or other sexual propensities.

In this view, it permissible to ask questions prior to taking actions that have serious psychological and medical consequences. While this approach certainly extends personal hardship, they remain cautious and do not recognize questioning as equivalent to pressuring, blaming, criticizing, or attacking. They believe that it is *prudent* to explore psychosocial variables that relate to transgender assertions.

They do not believe that this kind of inquiry is repeating the implosive sins of past conversion therapies that tried to *compel* homosexuals to become heterosexual. For them, competent therapy does not proceed in that fashion. Just ask most therapists whether they can effectively *force* individuals to change their eating, drinking, or smoking habits.

Generally, it is more acceptable for therapists to help their clients understand the development of their feelings, beliefs, desires, and reinforced behaviors so that they can identify changes that will help them live more satisfying lives. Many non-activists are currently lamenting the fact that numerous practitioners and agencies either shun or do not perform these *neutral* psychotherapeutic interventions due to political, legal, or personal bias governing the transitioning process (Kerschner, 2020).

Today, many practitioners are summarily avoiding transgender treatment as a way to side-step accusations of "transphobia," while the therapists that stay involved continue to align with unadulterated confirmation of transitioning. These hesitant practitioners believe that it is too easy for the gender activists to interpret neutral inquiries as clandestine attempts to convert, and they will not tinker with that time bomb. Since parents also fear reprisal for standing in the way of the transitioning process, many are reluctant to express their objections, questions, and concerns as well (Shrier, 2020). Similar to many current trends, activists with particular political views are taking control of the way we socialize our children.

However, adversaries worry that if no one speaks publicly about the current partialities in the field, there could be higher rates of *de-transitioning* in the future. This might occur as recipients gain distance from current media partiality, subtle cohort pressures, and the positive mood changes that initially take place with the ingestion of the prescribed hormones. When that dust settles, they predict that more transsexuals will experience patterns of regret.

With that in mind, some professionals are finding it reasonable to help people voicing a desire to transition glean a clearer picture of what kinds of living-in-the-world problems they anticipate resolving by making the advocated medical changes. They want to inquire about the kinds of behavioral and emotional changes that individuals anticipate occurring for themselves and others in relation to the transition.

These mavericks, for example, might explore the significance of some individuals wanting to stand while urinating as an objective to having bottom surgery, as well as look into the reasons for some transsexuals to detest their breasts or penis. They might probe how sex might be more comfortable after the transition, and inquire about partner preferences. They might investigate statements such as "starting over" in one's life, feelings of social isolation, and tendencies to be preoccupied with singular concerns. They might delve into early sexual exposures, including pornography, and feelings about homosexuality and autogynephilia. They might explore possible resentments toward family members, and parental wishes to have a child of a particular gender. They might inquire about problems identifying with the same-sex parent, or domination and lack of closeness with the opposite sex parent. They might ask about trauma, vulnerability, self-disdain, and discontentment with the power dynamics typically occurring between males and females. They might explore body self-consciousness, anxieties related to aggression, or the enhancement of one's sense of value, desirability, and command in the world as people show concern, change language, and make accommodations to their new identity.

Rather than accept the view that surgeries are removing *mistaken* physical structures, they proceed as if the individual is considering a plastic surgery that may have serious consequences. They want to know if an anticipated outcome might be obtained without the extreme of an operation or the ingestion of health-threatening hormones. The intervention has nothing to do with disrespect or phobia. A more detailed psychosocial understanding can be empowering and clarifying. If the result is that the *adult* remains intent on transitioning, then so be it.

While trans activists might vehemently object to this approach, Promoters think that it is preferable not to base best-treatment practice on who is most adamant. Moreover, they do not want social science "experts" seeking a predetermined outcome to advance a particular viewpoint where they determine what questions can be asked and what conclusions can be reached. More succinctly, they do not want the power of sophistry to shape professional intervention. They wonder if societies endorse transgender claims without inquiry or questioning, then what assertions about "identity" will society not accept, and on what grounds?

One final point seems important. Yes, prenatal exposure to testosterone levels (Hines, 2011) and brain scans (Ponseti, et al., 2020) are consistent with the view that biology co-occurs with sexual behaviors and preferences. However, those data do not establish a "born this way" causality. As with "intelligence," that kind of data only shows the consequence of the intermingling of biology and living in the world, or that certain kinds of biology increase the *likelihood* that certain sexual proclivities will become apparent. However, since different patterns of sexuality occur in relation to the same biological starting place, further inquiry seems reasonable.

Within this view, and irrespective of whether sexual behavior occurs early or late, whether it is acceptable or shunned, or whether it is likely or unlikely to change, Promoters believe that it is not criminal or disrespectful to examine psychosocial developmental influences. The approach permits an investigation into the individual's history of living in the world, and patterns of learning within that history. The belief is that this kind of inquiry will help to put pieces of the puzzle together in the interest of each individual's self-understanding and well-being.

While a Promoters reticence to adopt trans activism will offend many Protectors, they claim that an alternative approach can be helpful. This is particularly true when children are involved, since many children change their minds about their body's sexual identity during the course of development. For that reason, they find it crucial not to act too quickly. Moreover, since the hormonal and surgical interventions have risk, and have not yielded unequivocal positive outcomes (Anderson, 2018; Shrier, 2020), they assert that there is ample reason to temper those procedures. Promoters find it important *not* to allow politics or galvanizing social influences to decide the issue. They want oversight, not advocacy, and they deny that their reserve is vitriolic.

CHAPTER FIVE

FAMILIES AND THE
DRIFT TO PROTECTIONISM

Thus far, there has been illustration of the inside ↔ outside dynamic when addressing poverty, racial group hierarchies, and patterns of discontentment between the sexes. The same framework is also useful for family interactions. This chapter examines what family members frequently do to settle disputes, and exploration of the social and political consequences of the different patterns of socialization.

A child-rearing option that blends the favorable aspects of our two camps is embedded in this chapter, which may help to promote civility, self-reliance, and cooperation—behavioral patterns that are pertinent and necessary in a well-functioning liberal society. The hope is that the included recommendations will not only assist family members, but also help the outlying society as children venture into the world of school, work, and new family relationships.

The presumption is that children will keep doing what benefits them, and stop doing what is not advantageous. This includes those times when they grow up and do the opposite of what happened in their childhood, as a way to compensate for what they believe went wrong. They essentially make a concerted effort *not* to be like the individuals who negated or disrupted them.

What follows is a smattering of family behavior that commonly occurs in daily life. It identifies current trends in child-rearing that emphasize rescuing, dependency, and accommodation to satiate the child. It illustrates patterns of interaction that unwittingly reinforce complaining, blaming, and allegations of denial and victimhood that seem so prevalent.

Nowhere in psychology does a particular starting point invariably lead to a given outcome, but the kinds of family patterns described in this chapter portend the likely ways children will behave when they leave the family. The early occurring patterns are also likely to influence their sociopolitical tendencies, and the kinds of helping interventions they advocate as adults.

Of note, and much like our legal system, family prohibitions and punishments attempt to wipe out unwanted behaviors. Although, within the family and in politics, there is no system that can monitor people enough to stop them from wrongdoing. Since oversight and threats of punishment may not adequately socialize people to function with civility when no one is watching, it is essential for children to self-monitor and *want* to enact decent and kind behaviors. This chapter promotes that outcome, and the favorable aspects of Protector and Promoter ideologies may be very helpful in this regard.

Safety and Outside Threats

In our post-scarcity society, the trend has been to advocate for protection over risk. With the vanishing of the frontier, and the withering of subsistence farming, it seems that most of us are moving away from a peril-laden existence. When people were destitute, they had to take more chances just to survive. In those conditions, "safety-ism" was less likely to predominate. However, in times of plenty, it became easier to focus on maintaining comfort. People could work at relatively safe jobs, and with their own resources live comfortably, while those with fewer resources could look to the government to provide a standard of living that exceeds the deprivations of past generations.

When parents do not need children to labor for the family's survival, they can focus their energy on *giving* the readily available wealth. It is no longer necessary to insist upon contributions from the child, which was the case when people worked on farms, and throughout human history. *Happiness* rather than *work* takes precedence. There can be chauffeuring, pampering, and provisions without any requirement that children endure hardship or inconvenience. The family can persist without a child's effort.

Moreover, when families have fewer children, each child can receive even more enhancement. In a country already focused on promoting self-actualization, this emphasis is growing astronomically. While parents have always been concerned about the care and protection of their children, over recent times, efforts to fend and facilitate for children have blossomed into a preoccupation. The smaller family size makes it easier to enhance each child's contentment and welfare. It is now commonplace to see adults catering to the child, adolescent, and college student; emancipation often extends well into the second decade of life.

The trend to protect children's well-being and safety is also exacerbating in relation to the growing numbers of "mother-only" households. Mothers, in general, are more willing to comfort and protect, and they more typically fear akrasia, in comparison to allowing for more opportunities for risk-taking, which could help to build anti-fragility. Many studies show that females are more likely to worry about the possibility of uncertain dangers (Wikipedia Contributors, 2019), and this emphasis in child-rearing seems enhanced in families with lesser involvement from adult males.

However, there can be notable consequences when children are the family's centerpiece and treated as fragile works of art. When there is extreme emphasis on promoting the child's health and safety, there is often reluctance to permit unsupervised time. The encapsulation is relieving for anxious caretakers, but the constant overseeing, or "helicopter" parenting, impedes autonomy, hedges against trying and failing, and negates the freedom to explore. The mantra of "Be safe" takes hold, and the more the parent finds out about what could damage the child, the more the hovering. One only has to remember the freight imposed on parents when "missing" children's faces appeared on milk cartons in the 1980's.

While some parents might be reticent to have their children live within a protected bubble, they welcome the opportunity to stave off trouble. It is no wonder they do not want to allow their children out of their sight. Currently, many parents are inclined not to allow children to leave the house unsupervised, well into middle childhood, which is much later than in previous generations (Lukianoff and Haidt, 2019).

The current trend to monitor is quite different from the past, when frequent autonomous playtime was the norm. During the era when one parent was typically at home at all times, children often played outside. Even when mothers began to enter the workplace, children still had more unsupervised time, as the more self-assured latchkey children grew in prevalence as a transitional step.

However, and very soon later, institutional childcare became more frequent. Children began to spend more time in larger organizations operating within a top-down authority structure. They had supervision from the moment they woke up to the time they went to sleep. "Big Brother was watching," and they became accustomed to surveillance and institutionalized care. Handholding was the norm right up to the school's front door, and the more parents heard about danger, the more they defended. The trend was to create absolute shielding, and putting a yoke on the child became a preferred parenting strategy.

Given this scenario, instead of allowing children to incrementally create their own safety and resolve their disputes amongst each other, in the name of unqualified protection, adults rush in to mediate. However, the consequence of this parenting is that children become less adept at conflict resolution, and learn to rely on others to rescue and relieve. There is reinforcement for an outside→ inside orientation, as harm prevention orchestrated by others becomes the modus operandi.

In addition to these concerns, numerous other factors seem to be creating fear, dissatisfaction, and fragility for the younger generation. Excessive time spent on electronic media can distance children from in vivo relationships. Responding in isolation within the protective barrier of electronic interaction can also lead to hearing about frequent exaggerations of personal successes, which may increase anxieties related to failure or missing out. Ironically, with so many available options, satisfaction is often more difficult to achieve both with friends and material items, as alternatives are constantly available.

When communicating through digital space, it also becomes easier to taunt, bully, discard others, and perpetuate lies that could destroy the reputations of many children (Downey Jr., 2020). Social harshness may increase, as communicators can hide behind the ubiquitous electronic barrier that the medium provides, much like what occurs when people become enraged while driving within the confines of their shielded cars.

All of these factors can imprint more apprehensiveness in young people just starting to learn about status, desires, and social appeal, and increase everyone's concerns about vulnerability. The medium allows the instant transmission of danger, ignorance, and hate, and accusations can fly without supporting evidence. Rather than politeness and decorum, behavior can become extreme and contentious, in comparison to face-to-face exchanges. Moreover, what used to be circumscribed can expand quickly, and like many trends in society, localism becomes globalism, discussion becomes polarization, and no one knows who is lurching in the shadows.

While some children might gain connection from social media, and show increased empathy for others when finding out about their difficulties when staying in touch electronically, it is worthwhile to consider unwanted effects that can occur with this form of networking. For example, claims of suffering, angst, and victimization might increase in relation to the extra attention, social bonding, and drama that resound when teens emote to their friend groups. Social contagion and a viral interest in joining in can reinforce more youths to copy these behaviors.

This does not mean that individuals in past generations did not have nasty phone calls, drama, or conflicts between cliques and gangs, but it does mean that a preponderance of time spent in electronic modalities may yield adverse effects on children and families that have not previously occurred to this degree. For example, some empirics show that problems with anxiety and depression are rising (particularly for females), and there is speculation that excessive time spent on social media is exacerbating those emotions (Hunt et. al, 2018).

Overall, since we now have a sophisticated electronic network that connects us with whatever happens in the world, it is now possible to hear about every pitfall and harmful consequence that can occur. If people were dissatisfied and anxious beforehand, their emotions and interest in protection seems to worsen with an exponential trajectory. With so many "experts" supplying families with information about what could go wrong, everyone ramps up with an arsenal of protective measures.

People are now working diligently to build a world without anguish. They become interested in protection, and focus on eradicating what could harm. Seat belts, safety helmets, filters, and the identification and elimination of toxins become the focus of our energies and the preoccupation of "green" organizations. When there are complaints of distress, instead of strengthening brittleness, there is a growing readiness to eliminate all objects of complaint. The notion of resilience, desensitizing, and overcoming are falling to the wayside (Lukianoff and Haidt, 2019).

The quest for ultimate security and control extends everywhere. Increasing numbers attempt to harness the global climate, which then justifies the necessity to undo the entire society. Like firefighters to a fire, they rush to squelch the harms caused by the evil supremacist wrongdoers that created the difficulties they experience in their day-to-day lives. They lash back at those people, and vie to palliate the environment, not only to protect it, but also to prevent it from hurting them.

In these ways and more, recent generations perceive greater vulnerability. There are now increasing numbers of events that people identify as traumatizing and leading to disruptions in mood and feelings. The numbers of people labeling themselves as wounded are proliferating, and mental health workers are now focusing their energy and professional time developing ways to relieve the consternation. Relaxation and meditation therapies are propagating the mental health scene, as these treatments purportedly help to comfort individuals from distasteful outside experiences.

While this trend is certainly an attempt to assist people when they encounter deeply disturbing events, there is an increasing tendency to expand the *trauma* category so that it captures almost any experience that is disconcerting. Instead of having a consensual listing of events that we deem traumatic, or likely to evoke post-traumatic stress disorder, as long as a person indicates deep distress, the experiences obtain the trauma label.

Consistent with other trends, the person's *reaction* determines the vileness of the event. The cause of their suffering *is the event*, and not the way in which the individual might frame or *interpret* the incident. Rather than encourage the individual to desensitize, energies focus on getting environmental sources to change. Treatment orients to ease the person's life requirements, and the recipient of the intervention feels valued in relation to the care and concern *received* (i.e., outside → inside).

The unfortunate consequence of this frequent pattern of intervention is that many of these individuals grow up and repeat these behaviors with their peers, cohorts at work, care providers, and others. They anticipate that removing all imperfections in the outside world will eliminate all of the sadness and anxiety they denote. When getting the message that society includes the evils of racism, sexism, and malfeasance from capitalists, they crusade for fortification, and look for something powerful enough to stop the bombardment.

For many, it can only be the revered intelligentsia and civil service agencies that can produce a rescue mission that is sagacious and powerful enough to get the job done. Rather than have suspicion that nodes of power can oppress, they foresee governing bodies as doting parents. These individuals eagerly mix into the Protector's recipe affirming a trouble-free life, as long as there is succumbing to the guidance of the higher-ups.

However, while many financially secure children live within the confines of safety, a subset of lower-class children endure social patterning in communities that are diametric. Instead of tethering to a safety-oriented regime, they spend extended time unsupervised, in rowdy neighborhoods that are highly unpredictable and perilous. Many of these individuals connect to peers who promote risk-taking and rule breaking as well.

For this group, there is little social control or environmental safety. Many of these children grow up without adequate protective boundaries or routines, and their world provides little refuge. When others tell them that the sins of the establishment create their discomfort, their well-being can only occur by destroying the societal structures that others have callously foisted upon them. When penalties for recalcitrance diminish, then even more opposing behaviors occur, proliferate, and intensify.

Rather than adjust to meet traditional expectations that seem out of reach, many of these children find other ways to gratify. These efforts are likely to include greater frequencies of avoiding standard achievements, sexual promiscuity, rule-breaking, and forceful tactics to resolve problems. In this fashion, they demonstrate prowess.

Fatherless young men may be particularly susceptible to these influences. They may look to other males in their surroundings for camaraderie and role modeling. As stated by Denzel Washington, "If the father is not in the home, the boy will find the father in the streets" (Larry Elder, 2021). When that happens, young males (and females as well) are deprived of whatever advantages *competent* and *caring* fathers might bring to their social training. These benefits may include increased aspiration for achievement, obedience to authority, empathy for others, more security, and a sense of family responsibility.

Echoing this view, Farrell and Gray (2018) note many different ways in which father-enriched boys have increased probability of lifetime success, in comparison to those who are father-deprived. Similarly, Peterson points out the negative consequences of diminishing "rough and tumble play" that fathers often promote and initiate (Bailey, 2018).

Nevertheless, and despite the differences between deprived and cosseted children, both groups retain the general belief that the world is a dangerous, unfriendly place that engulfs people in perpetual harm. Children brought up without adequate security, family resources, or supervision may develop a focus on what is happening to them, just like overprotected children. Both groups learn to pay more attention to the ways in which they are being deprived or mistreated. While family dynamics are quite different, it seems that the extremes of overprotection and under-supervision will lead to a similar increase in environmental blame.

It appears that both social strata are learning to complain and reject their outside world. They expect change to come from destroying societal structures that purportedly created the harm. When most of the younger generations focus on the evils that bear down upon them, it is not surprising that an outside → in orientation spreads throughout society.

While protected children bandwagon to stamp out all sources of environmental imperfection, those in poverty despise their world because those who purportedly detest them manufactured that world. Rebellion takes precedence over adaptation for both groups, and cries of victimhood create a loud voice to change the "climate" of everyone's existence.

As you can see, the key issue is that the responsibility for well-being shifts from the individual's coping resources to changing the outside world in order to make it benign like a protective angel. This magical incarnation of an idealized parent, or an entitlement program, creates a remedy for every grievance. Both overprotected and under-protected children argue for a world that organizes for their benefit. While adolescents have always gone through a period of idealism, and an interest in changing the world, this orientation is expanding and not remitting.

In sum, it seems that protected children are imitating their parents' hyper-concerns about possible harms, developing a low tolerance for risk, and becoming wary of whatever might disrupt their equilibrium. Their claims of victimization and suffering produce a firestorm of remediation from their adoring parents, and from others who might attend to their complaints. Analogously, children growing up in truly unsafe proximal conditions are also seeing their safety problems as caused from without. The "system" is the foundation of what keeps damaging and impairing them.

In both instances, the world is not something to adapt to, but something to rebel against. The first group rebels because worldly bombardments interfere with the revered safe haven, while the others skirmish because the world offers little nurturance and blocks them from having assets and social value. Both of these polarities eventually become the formidable subgroups of the protectionist camp, and neither promote an inside → outside orientation.

However, those concerned with these trends claim that the quick responsiveness to cries of discontentment weakens individuals, as they become increasingly reliant on others to provide shielding remedies. In their view, the eagerness of others to relieve the snowballing of complaints simply reinforces the recurrence of those behaviors.

The Diminishment of Conformity and Mutual Accommodation

Our current willingness to adopt an outside→ inside orientation reinforces the belief that we are victims with little agency to reframe events, maintain composure and poise, and not become beleaguered. When we define problems as residing outside of us, and highlight how devastating they are, we create more interest in changing what happens to us. We orient to alter what we do not like, rather than adapt, compromise, and adjust.

Today, people often justify requests for accommodation by claiming they are tired, depressed, bored, overwhelmed, stressed, anxious, or distressed. These cries for relief provide the reason for others to alleviate burdens and provide a remedy. For example, children might insist that a school assignment is "too hard." Parents might then do much of the work for them instead of helping them learn routines and ways to resolve complexities.

To the extent that individuals with the most gripping troubles and complaints get the most remarkable accommodations, the behaviors proliferate. These cries of negative emotions and neediness seep into the political sphere as well. They justify the requirement for legal assistance, and impel others to make the desired analgesic remedies (i.e., outside → in).

This pattern alone accounts for the preference of many young people to endorse *socialism*. For them, this form of social organization is empowering. They want to own the *means of production,* just like they want to rule the family protocol. Since they should not have to struggle or endure a reduction in say-so, they assume they have a right to take the property of others, and they envision a government that gives them license to do so.

The idea of tolerating another person's orders goes hand-in-hand with their view that they should not have to subject themselves to any kind of authority. In many of today's families, children are emboldened with extensive power to dictate and govern, much like tyrannical bureaucrats. Not surprisingly, they object to anything that sounds constraining or repressive, such as having to submit to someone else's expectations. While this discontentment was notable during the uprisings against being drafted during the Vietnam War, pushback against authority has grown and continued over the past decades.

With the advent of social media, and the youth's mastery of this industry, compared with adults, children and adolescents now have unprecedented influential power to communicate and direct other people's actions. We now have a society that is overtaken by this demographic. With knowledge turning over so rapidly, the conventional wisdom of adults is diminishing rapidly, and so are traditional norms.

Since many of these individuals function for long periods with a *controller* or *cell phone* in hand, it is not surprising that they find domination to be quite easy. In their world, if they encounter something they dislike, they can immediately switch it off by a simple push of the button, and they anticipate the same response from others when they announce boredom or discontentment. Like a jack-in-the-box, many adults eagerly chauffeur their children from one activity to the next as their first priority, and children get accustomed to having a waitron.

When households become *child-centric* and indulgent, there is notable deference to the child's preferences and initiatives, which essentially override all else. In these scenarios, parents might instantly drop what they are doing to satisfy the child's desires, and the child learns to provoke attention as soon as the parent shifts attention to other concerns. Often, this pattern occurs between mothers and sons when the father is absent, in that the male child does not have to share his mother with a competing male figure. However, it also occurs whenever parents have little opportunity for an outside social life, or other diversions.

When parents are disengaged from relational closeness with other adults (whether married or not), child-centric patterns are more likely, as it is often easier for children to monopolize when they do not have to yield to the adults' involvement with other relationships. Moreover, when parents face loneliness, they might frequently over accommodate as a way to keep their offspring close.

The children get accustomed to ongoing extravagances and entitlements, and these social conditions make it easier for children to be excessively demanding. Unfortunately, this early social conditioning portends the likelihood of these patterns repeating in adulthood, where no amount of conciliation will be enough to quell the expectation for increased accommodation and gratification from others.

With their extraordinary spending power due to family affluence, the youth now have a prominent voice in the economy that demands serious consideration. It is no wonder that academy administrators kowtow to all the demands of their "student customers." It seems that no accommodation is too difficult to enact to keep them coming with their large checks and government loans. The students closed down the schools in the late 1960s, and the trend continues at an increasing pace.

The young now have the unparalleled *chutzpah* to ordain that their parents and the society they built are wrong and morally corrupt. Many of these children go off to college and assert their views about reorganizing the world into a tableau of their desires. They presume it is their prerogative to orchestrate a magnificent symphony with other people's lives. They demand to be catered to, and they envision a society that conforms to their hedonistic panorama. They have been ruling their families, and now they advocate ruling the world.

Not surprisingly, the expectation for accommodation to the child extends to the school system as well. Often, when children complain about their teachers or school policies, it is common for parents to insist that the teacher and school make changes, rather than vice versa. When school culture is complicit with the quest to tear down traditional ways of operating, or are required to do so by new laws and executive orders to "leave no child behind," there is a lesser emphasis on conformity from the school system.

Many parents are now rushing to the school to obtain accommodations, and less often are they exploring ways to help their children acclimate to traditional curriculum norms. They pressure the school make individualized alterations, and the emphasis is solely on getting the school's methods and expectations to shift. The child does not learn to modulate behavior and cope with the institution, which can never be totally what the child prefers. But this does not keep the family from trying.

While it makes sense not to neglect any child, what does it mean to help children thrive? Assuming that parents are not objecting to a lack of scientific neutrality, or improper discipline within the school, must all solutions require changing school procedures and standards? Might some interventions also look into ways to help the child adjust to time-tested curriculum expectations? Are many enacted changes underestimating students' competence to adapt and overcome? Are they inadvertently lowering achievement outcomes by going full-fledged into accommodation?

Given the declining test scores of many children, it seems important to gauge the value of such extensive accommodating. Perhaps students were served better when there was more emphasis on helping them adjust to the school, rather than the other way around. Since giving schools more money does not automatically translate into better educational outcomes (Burnette II, 2019), something else has to happen to enhance the child's skills and adaptive prowess. Often, it seems that interventions address complaints without regard to outcomes, as if attainment robotically occurs through the gifting and satiating, even though it is not financially prohibitive to teach basic skills and critical thinking.

There are now growing numbers of children requiring special curriculums and deadline exemptions that tax the educational system. Given limited resources, these excessive adjustments for some individuals may well lead to a diminishment of resources for others. However, when accommodating complaints takes precedence, the boat tips over to that side, even if it is at the expense of everyone else.

This problem becomes even more concerning when schools require a *psychiatric diagnosis* or *learning disability* to justify making curriculum alterations. Under this pressure, many succumb, and an added bonus is that the struggling child's test scores do not count in the school averages submitted to governing officials (Wipond, 2014). While some might insist that this trend is improving recognition of who needs assistance, others claim that families and schools are finding ways to meet legal requirements in order to qualify for extra services and subsidies. Yes, the costs will rise and resources go to the "impaired," but what about the rates of learning across the spectrum?

There are now innumerable reasons why children *cannot* meet expectations. In an attempt not to appear coldhearted or morally corrupt, there is constant giving in. While the remedies may produce immediate relief to the aggrieved, what happens, for example, when compassion leads to passing children to the next grade without mastering the content of the previous grade?

Approaching the problem differently, what might happen if we put greater emphasis on requiring children to meet heralded standards? Instead of contorting the system, what if we focused on giving approval when children attune? In this solution, before focusing on altering externals, parents might explore changes that the child could make to improve the situation. After the child makes some initial changes, parents can reassess what is happening; it may or not be necessary to put the onus solely on school personnel or other environmental sources to transform.

This change of approach does not mean that all current patterns of addressing problems at schools are unworthy. It is simply pointing out that an extensive shift in the direction of *giving up* standards and accommodating to blaming accusations may have problems that require careful examination. An alternative is to let changes evolve when they move children *closer* to accepted objectives, rather than move the goals closer to the child.

Families that advocate this approach are likely to question the kinds of remedial programs currently monopolizing our schools. For example, they wonder whether having the child stand while doing work helps the child learn to relax and ultimately sit, or whether having the child do only part of the assignment eventually helps the child do all of the tasks. They ponder whether having a teacher's aide sitting next to the child eventually helps the child work more independently.

These parents question whether some or many interventions are presuming ineffectuality for numerous children when it is not the case. They are concerned that schools are making permanent accommodations with the belief that the child is incapable, and they are apprehensive that current ways to remediate will *insure* that result. They fear that children will believe that their lack of achievement is due "the system," or due to permanent impairment, instead of focusing on self-improvements. For example, it is conceivable that the child could develop consistent rule-following, as well as overcome aversions related to scholarly activity.

Of course, the proviso is that parents and teachers must first learn how to accomplish these behavioral changes. This might entail asking children what they are saying no to when refusing to do schoolwork. Parents might look to decipher the child's history with academics, and the family's way of managing school achievement. They might explore the child's reactions to mistakes, the value that the family places on education, or examine historical factors that might make schoolwork uncomfortable, or feel like drudgery, for the child and the parent.

Instead of withdrawing, becoming sullen, or enraged, resolving these kinds of problems may help many children learn to retain their composure and fine-tune their actions so that requirements are met. Personal integrity and anti-fragility could take over, and increased *accommodation* to schoolwork and other expectations might ensue.

As a way to exemplify this kind of socializing within the family, let's look at a scenario that requires a child to adapt and cope with the family's necessity to move to a new apartment. While the child might initially believe that the transition will be overwhelming, parents wanting to nurture adaptation might patiently wait for that initial negative reaction to subside. They might then begin a discussion that addresses the child's grievances and fears that the move will create irreparable and inescapable hardship.

The parents' goal is to help the child acclimate to the idea of moving, and eventually react with less perturbation. Parents might then help the child recognize that there are options to respond in a variety of ways; the world does not "make" the child react in a singular hyperbolic fashion. The child might have negative feelings about the new living arrangement, but the discussion helps the child construe the situation in a more benign light, and identify behaviors that make the situation tolerable.

The child might continue to cajole the parents to stifle the move, but the child eventually acknowledges that adjustment is necessary. As a way to accomplish this outcome, each person recognizes that concerns are "heard better" when there is equanimity during discussions about pros and cons. If the child withdraws, whines, or becomes disrespectful with claims of suffering or threats, parents remain calm and matter-of-factly ask what is bothering the child, but the objective remains the same.

The emphasis is less on what the move is *doing to* the child, and more on finding ways to make the transition palatable. Over time, this pattern of discipline helps children gain the skill of acclimating to transitions and working out mutually acceptable arrangements when there is room to compromise. This newfound skillset helps them develop the savoir-faire to cope with their ever-changing social and physical world.

While some might insist that children must unequivocally accept parental directives and adjust without any protest, allowing children to voice concerns and objections reinforces their value. It encourages them to do the same for others. If it is feasible to make outside changes and everyone agrees, what is the danger? When parents respect children in this manner, they might get more respect in return.

Overall, this more collaborative pattern is not recommending that parents relinquish leadership to please the child; it remains necessary for the child to adapt to family necessities. However, if it is possible to accommodate to modifications that the child prefers, then this can also help the child learn about the benefits of give-and-take and pleasing each other.

Considering the child's point of view, and helping the child understand the reasons for particular parental actions, is not equivalent to spoiling or permissiveness. If the child's requests are not feasible, and if the situation calls for obedience, the requirement to conform remains. Nothing terrible will happen if the child must sometimes take no for an answer. This will not harm or traumatize the child, as some parents fear.

Although when looking closely at what happens in many families, it seems that not enough parents are helping their children learn to compromise or conform when necessary. Instead, many specify solutions for the child, neglect to give the child's concerns adequate consideration, or placate the child to avoid conflict. Unfortunately, those patterns of socialization are far less likely to develop adaptation or reciprocity.

Finding ways to help children learn to accommodate and identify a middle ground is difficult, but it can mitigate a wide range of problems. It can help with perspective-taking, and help people learn about the effects that their behavior has on others. Truly competent parenting requires more than the production of an immediate effect that occurs when giving in, or when asserting dominance by saying, "I said so!"

In total, the recommended patterning avoids reinforcing the belief that parents must fabricate a child's *happiness.* It also avoids encouraging children to expect others to change without making changes themselves. The goal is for children to confront adversity and inure through problem-solving, which beckons an inside ↔ out dynamic.

With guile, these parents want their children to adjust to hardship and overcome anxiety rather than distance, complain, or revert to histrionics as their only options to cope. However, in order to accomplish these goals, it is crucial for parents to role model these desirable behaviors, with the hope that the child will learn and imitate.

One final topic seems relevant. In addition to the isolating effects of encapsulating electronics, it seems that the proliferation of family instability also factors into the trend of children having difficulties establishing mutually satisfying interactions. For many, there is less pleasurable *family time* due to work schedules, and this can make it difficult to stay coordinated and enjoy time together. The lack of consistent routines, the frequent time spent with non-family childcare workers, the absence of family meals, and ongoing parental stress can make relational commitment disappointing. The ramification is increased negative attention provoking, reduced interest in conforming, and diminished closeness to other family members. Under these conditions, emotional assistance within the family may be a short supply.

In general, when families frequently move, when adults come and go, when siblings are partially related or not related at all, or when there are relational problems between the adults that the child depends on, family discomfort is likely to increase. When children are unmoored from traditional family patterning and experience frequent disillusionment, unhappiness, and loss, it might be difficult for them to align themselves with a family identity. Instead, alienation rises to the surface, and as claimed by Eberstadt (2021), it is not surprising that more of our youth are finding their affiliations in their "identity politics" rather than in their family connections.

However, this is not saying that family breakdown will preclude the development of cooperation and the acquisition of social skills that enable effective functioning in society. It is saying that it might be more difficult when parents struggle to steer the boat, when family members have less gratifying time with each other, or when the adults in the child's life are experiencing incompatibility.

Accountability and the Externalization of Blame

The problem of accountability and blame is important whenever disputes between people occur. We have an intricate legal system to help produce a sense of fairness. The same kinds of concerns occur in families, although with less formality. Many different patterns of establishing family justice seem to take place, and each pattern socializes children to have certain kinds of beliefs about what is *fair* and who is *responsible*. Some of these patterns seem consistent with an outside → inside emphasis, while others reflect an inside → outside psychodynamic.

In general, when parents function as the family judge and jury, they resolve the problem of deciding on who is to blame and what is fair (much like the court system). However, what are the criteria to determine who started the fight, who overreacted, and who had alternatives available to mitigate the conflict? Given all the complexities in determining accountability, parents have the difficult job of determining justice, much like what happens in our legal system.

When exploring the problem of accountability in families, it seems reasonable to start with disputes between siblings, since they are frequent and require decisions about blame and victimhood. The question becomes, what are parents teaching children about these matters, and what effect does this have on the children's behavior? Let's examine typical conflict-resolution patterns in many families.

Often, children learn quickly that their disputes lead to parental involvement, much like other negative behaviors. They might be arguing about something, but their fighting takes form in relation to the way in which the parent intervenes. Usually, parents try to determine the identity of the infractor by doing an inquiry, and often they adopt a consistent pattern. For example, they might show a tendency to blame one child based on age or past behavior. They might attempt to make the solution exactly *even* to be fair, or they might stay neutral and want the children to negotiate a resolution.

Each pattern has its own consequences, and the likelihood of sibling conflict seems to increase when the adults in the house are frequently arguing with the children, or are at odds with each other.

If age determines accountability, then the older child has accountability, regardless of what happens. An *immutable characteristic* determines fault and liability. Since they are older, they should have known better and resolved the problem without escalating conflict. Much like what happens with members of racial groups that have historically discriminated against minorities—they are forever guilty. Category affiliation (i.e., being older), rather than actions and deeds, are the grounds for culpability. The same problem occurs if one child is responsible because of being stronger, smarter, the birth child or stepchild, boy or girl.

Interestingly, in families where not all members are related biologically, often birth parents side with their birth children and accuse non-biological parents of not treating their stepchildren with enough compassion. In contrast, non-biological parents more frequently accuse birth parents of permissiveness and favoring their birth child above all else. Not surprisingly, these typical alignments and accusations mimic what happens when racial groups clash. One group accuses the other of oppression, while the putative oppressor group impels the other side to show better discipline and self-control. As is the case throughout society, each side stays aligned with "their tribe."

However, when there is assignment of blame in relation to unchangeable characteristics, defended children may learn that they can transgress, hit first, and not be liable for what happens. If they have grievance with their sibling for any reason, they can provoke until they get a reaction, and gain ascendency when the parent intercedes. In this fashion, defended children accrue benefits when their sibling suffers, and a zero-sum game is born. However, these patterns of conflict are likely to increase the blamed individual's resentment toward the sibling that the parent coddles, much like the disapproval of many who watch marginalized-identity groups aggressively rioting with meager culpability.

While frequently blamed children might learn to ignore their sibling's provocations, many of these children continue to retaliate for a number of reasons. First, some find it preferable to strike back and admonish the provocateurs, given the minor chastisements that they will endure. Since they are dominated by their parents, they certainly do not want their younger siblings to rule them as well. Second, some prefer punishing the parents by hurting the "favored" child, even though they will receive negative consequences. Third, when the parent takes sides against them, they might accuse the parent of bias, and this might lead the parent to do compensatory behaviors to prove this is not the case.

Generally, a partiality to one side rarely reduces conflict, as blamed children become resentful that their siblings obtain preferential treatment. From their point of view, there is justifiable reason to enter into a squabble, given the negative behavior of the siblings and the lack of support from the family. Likewise, protected children will continue to aggravate their siblings because their siblings continue to reject them, and they like the fact that their parents align with them. Getting their sibling "in trouble" becomes a way to gain retribution and acquire dependency gratification within the family, much like what happens in politics when governments swoop in with protective laws to quell the complaints of marginalized groups.

So how might parents resolve sibling conflict more effectively? This is quite complex, in that the acrimony might be occurring for a very long time, and the intensity of the emotions might relate to other problems not yet resolved. Determining who is instigating, who is retaliating, and what the fight is about can be a multifaceted problem, much like trying to establish "social justice" or "domestic justice."

Parents might have confidence that they have acted fairly, but they might be far from the mark. The decision to hold one child responsible may disaffect that child in a variety of ways, especially if falsely accused. For instance, the disparaged child might stop pleasing the parent and hold a grudge. This might take the form of not completing schoolwork, chores, self-care, or whatever will create parental distress and concern. In its extreme form, the child might detach from the family when feeling excessively admonished, much like dropping out of society.

While parents might try to locate fault, there are significant side effects with this method of settling disputes. There is the risk that children will learn to externalize blame, as pointing the finger at the other person redirects blame away from them. Not surprisingly, this pattern reinforces an outside→ in perspective. Someone else always causes troubles, and no one looks at their own contribution to the crisis. The individuals most effective in smearing and identifying the misbehavior of the other person is the victor and the sole possessor of parental support.

Moreover, when parents take over the job of resolving conflicts to expedite an ending, the children involved do not learn those skills. They become reliant on having emissaries intervene, similar to depending on government programs. They become more inept in their social interactions, and unless their parents help them learn to compromise and understand multiple perspectives, they are likely to flounder with peers as well.

They will always be dependent on others to brandish some form of "social justice," and become adept at finding reasons why others are causing them harm. They are likely to continue to hold others accountable, highlight victimization, and alienate others when finding fault in their behaviors. As is evident in our politics, these behavioral patterns seem to generalize when these individuals grow up and function away from their families.

In contrast, when the goal of parenting leans toward developing negotiating skills and willingness to cooperate (i.e., outside ↔ inside), coordinating with others is likely to improve. While it is always necessary for parents to take over and stop physical altercations to obviate physical injury, in this approach, parents function more as ambassadors rather than directors of solutions or assessors of blame.

Parents might ask the children to define the argument from each other's perspectives. They might ask them what they think is upsetting the other sibling. They might help the children understand the history of their relationship in order to have a better understanding of what might be contributing to the intensity of the dispute. For example, if one child often feels rejected or diminished by the other, the slightest indication of that "old bruise" might ignite ferocity and rapaciousness.

In an attempt to establish some progress, parents might ask the children if they *want* to figure out a way to make their relationship better. They might ask if the children would like to promote goodwill and demonstrate that they understand each other's point of view. Clearly, some of the children's responses will be nonproductive, but it is often possible to help children specify the ways in which they contribute to problems, as well as identify ways to help each other make improvements (i.e., inside ↔ outside).

While it is difficult to train competent conflict-resolution skills, it is certainly a commendable parenting endeavor. At first, parents are likely to hear the children saying "I don't know", and/ or not hear a positive contribution from either child. Often it is necessary for parents to learn ways to make it comfortable for the children to describe what happened, and make it safe for children to offer suggestions to alleviate the dispute. They might ask, "What if you take a guess?" to promote that objective. Since being frank and sincere risks condescension, it may take appreciable time and repetition to develop an environment that is conducive to mutual problem-solving so that family members can be diplomatic and forthright with each other.

Overall, shifting the discussion from faultfinding to mutual understanding and compromise is the objective. Giving attention to the children when conflict is not occurring also helps to build relationships that are not predicated on animosities and their aftermath. Similar to couples who often *fight and make up*, it is important to establish relationships that do not inadvertently reinforce frequent conflict. In short, there has to be a way for individuals to hear each other and feel valued without the precursor of escalating a fight. One can only imagine how this enlightened social patterning might transfer to the political sphere, and to the frequency rates of domestic violence throughout society.

In a related topic, what might be a way to resolve the problem of children smugly vexing their parents, in the same way they are incendiary with their siblings? Annoying the parent effectively irritates, punishes, and creates an escalating drama that can evoke an intense reaction from most caretakers.

However, in today's family patterning, often the parent becomes the guilty party when overreactions occur. In these instances, parents frequently bemoan that they did not behave maturely, and they subsequently inform the child of their regrets. The response is similar to what occurs when celebrities apologize to their retinues when they know their approval ratings are dropping.

Ironically, the child is doing the instigating, but the parent is self-abasing and apologizing. The onus externalizes to the parent, who accepts blame for not being exemplary. Parents accept the edict that they are responsible for their child's unhappiness, and they become failures whenever they act imperfectly. As this interactive template proliferates, the budding adolescent and soon-to-be adult persists in finding fault with numerous authority figures, their culture, and society, just like the way they treated their parents.

Children essentially learn that guilt is a powerful cudgel, and parents shriving for excellence reinforce this outside $\rightarrow$ in trend. Strengthening of this pattern occurs each time parents are quick to notice their own insufficiencies, while at the same time not saying a peep about the child's unacceptable behaviors. The more the parent functions as the patron of the child's contentment and incorporates all accountability, the more a child believes the narrative of being a faultless victim entitled to "reparations."

Over time, many children socialized in this fashion learn to abdicate all personal contribution to the problems. When the parents are anxious about conflict and rejection, and give into the child's accusations and demands, the child learns to highlight being offended and emotionally hurt. The parent backs down to avoid the negative attribution of being insensitive and unfit, much like the ad hominem attack of being called a racist, sexist, or homophobe. Only the child's martyrdom counts, and diversity of perspectives does not occur.

When parents are soaked in guilt, they are easy to control. Many of these parents are copying their parents, who were also anxious about disapproval, although others are doing the opposite of what was imposed upon them. These individuals experienced chiding and subjugation during their childhoods, and they do not want to burden their children with the same difficulties. When they hear disapproval from their children, the complaints become the image of their difficult-to-please parental figures. They give in to avoid rejection, and they do not want to be stern or cold-hearted like one or both of their parents.

But unfortunately, their children become more domineering and more like their dictatorial parents as time marches on. Due to submissiveness, the parent becomes easy prey. Rather than identify ways for the child to change or foster a sense of shared contribution, incommoded parents continue to offer services and gratuities to gain approval and make up for their so-called misdeeds and mistakes. It is easy to see how these same patterns of interaction are occurring throughout society, as accusation of causing harm to others becomes a powerful way to incite "guilty parties" to "jump through hoops."

Not surprisingly, when children feel victimized within the family, there are likely to be similar reports when children socialize outside of the family. A good example of this occurs when children complain about being bullied or gaslighted. While these hyperbolic descriptors were once used for only the most egregious instances of harm, there is now a growing tendency to accept the "wounded" person's renditions of the maltreatment. As long as they claim victimization in the form of bullying or gaslighting, it is true, and others proceed without questioning this rendition of the story.

Frequently, parents and others dash forward to offer relief; the focus is on stopping the perpetrator without examining different interpretations of what transpired. There is ignoring of other ways to describe the event, including the possibility that the harmed individual could have responded differently or contributed (even minimally) to the problem. While there are times when children are unquestionably powerless and victimized, that is not always the case, and seeing any questioning or inquiry as "victim-blaming" only permits an outside→ inside understanding, and nothing else.

When socialization permits the ongoing externalization of blame, the internalization of remorse and personal liability do not enter into the equation. Individuals are convinced that they are entitled to rectification. They learn that they can establish a claim of innocence from others by grousing, accusing, and criticizing. They may even learn to despise the perspective of others, as that only obstructs their desires and makes their life difficult. The world is at fault, and this parallels an outside→ inside preference in politics as well.

As a way to counteract this behavior and make it less extreme, some parents explore the possibility that children could learn to be less sensitive and accusatory. They help these children handle the perception of persecution, browbeating, and intimidation in ways that build anti-fragility. Rather than direct the intervention solely toward the alleged perpetrator, parents focus on helping these children recognize that some of their reactions might inadvertently reinforce the provoking rather than squelch it. Moreover, and importantly, they help the children understand that the "bullies" have their own problems which are unrelated to them, as depersonalizing the problem can often relax the offended child.

However, this strategy is not recommending that parents show insensitivity toward the child who is reporting bullying. Parents leaning in that direction will likely create other problems that could be equally detrimental. For example, if they react callously, the child might distance from them and others as a way to self-protect. Only focusing on requiring the child to change may also leave the child feeling unsupported, misunderstood, and diminished. The hope is to help the child learn assertiveness and ways to adapt to what the browbeater is doing. The parent does not want to give the impression that the child must assume all the blame. Effective parenting strikes an outside ↔ inside balance.

Likewise, parents are missing that mark when they insist that they are "always right." When behaving in that fashion, the child has full accountability for all problems that transpire. These dominating adults are often showing an unwillingness to recognize their part in the disputes. In these instances, the parent locates blame solely within the child. It is the child's responsibility to conform, even if the parent's behavior is unconscionable.

When parents ignore the child's perspective, and only impose their own demands, the child has no voice. They might be trying to get the child to adapt, but they might also be increasing the child's resentment. As these children age, they might identify with the weak and vulnerable, and learn to fight for various causes against those in power, when they are free from their parent's dictatorship. In the child's view, authority is unreasonable and does not afford respect, and they may identify with the oppressor vs. oppressed way of understanding society.

Frequently, parents behaving in this dominating fashion are preoccupied with their children *not disappointing them*. Their children's acceptability depends on gratifying their desires. These parents might withhold love and affection until the child conforms and ingratiates, and there are admonishments when the children do not kowtow to their wishes and demands. The children have the sense that they have "hurt" the parent in relation to their failures to meet expectations, and may fear abandonment in response to the parent's displeasure.

Often, these children are easy prey when they venture into the world. Others may effortlessly dominate and control them with disapproval similar to what happened during their childhoods. The slightest indication that they have behaved inappropriately will result in apologies and efforts to please. The necessity for acceptance and inclusion becomes imperative.

In this pattern, other people have all the power, and these children essentially surrender as a way to cope. There is ongoing dependency on the assessments and reactions of others, and they garner security when their actions help them avoid the anxiety of being unlovable. They maintain a preoccupation with possible wrongdoing that includes a great deal of fretting and self-censoring. Instead of outright rebellion, there is distancing, distractibility, and escaping to prevent being controlled, and to bypass the judgment of not being "good enough." The pattern shows a distinct outside → inside dynamic.

Under conditions of domination (including corporal punishment), there is the potential to wreak all kinds of havoc on younger individuals. Children subjected to various forms of domineering discipline might report consternation throughout the day. They may conform to avoid mythical social catastrophes, please others indiscriminately, or evade as a way to mitigate failure and exploitation. They become preoccupied with "what others think."

However, after the buildup of resentments, they might eventually explode, just like the parents they resent. Regrettably, without diplomatic role-modeling, many will not learn sensible boundaries or ways to compromise. They might anticipate oppression and respond within that framework throughout their lives. Their powerlessness will leave them focusing on what the others do to them, and they might incessantly complain without any sense of how to contend with the perceived onslaughts.

When considering these kinds of problems, it is reasonable to hypothesize that this kind of rigidity in child-rearing helped spawn the crusade to make child-rearing a more user-friendly endeavor. It aided in the creation of a rebellious backlash against inflexible norms. Many felt overly controlled by the requirement to meet expectations (e.g., keep hair short, women do dishes, stringent endogamy, etc.). Not surprisingly, large numbers of these individuals grew to sympathize with liberation movements to free society from the social mores that created a sundry of identity repressions.

Overall, there were simply too many side effects associated with social practices founded on unyielding constraint and conformity. Growing numbers of people began to identify with the cause of protecting those with lesser social power. The extant social norms seemed to be too much like servitude or slavery, which was part of the shamed heritage of previous generations.

However, there is a middle ground between the extremes of domination and permissiveness in child-rearing. A preferred alternative is to discipline in ways that are neither neglectful nor callous, while and at the same time not overly indulgent. The aim is to find the sweet spot where socialization occurs without inducing powerlessness, disinterest, resentment, stagnation, or entitlement. In other words, find a way to alter the "outside" to assist individuals to develop self-reliance and cooperation on the "inside."

While some might question whether advocating for mutual liability or *collaborative interacting* is a recommendation for adults to be obsequious with children, this is not the case. This pattern of socialization is simply an effort to help parents show both firmness and kindness, and a way for children to develop a sense of contribution and willingness to accommodate. It is a recommendation for parents and children to recognize that their actions can help, as well as adversely affect others, which includes appreciating the importance of respecting each other's privacy and right to express an opinion.

The hope is that children learn to *enjoy* contributing, instead of waiting for others to make their lives better for them. Their *buy-in* to help the family operate establishes the *central point* where multiple perspectives conjoin. For example, if the child has a good idea, it is reasonable for parents to give it some respect.

However, and just as important, we want the child to recognize that the household will not magically run itself. There is nothing terrible about doing non-preferred activities that might be "boring." We want them to learn that mutual caring and responsibility are crucial in the quest for happiness. Enduring discomfort, inconvenience, not interrupting, taking turns, and showing punctuality can facilitate everyone's well-being.

The goal is for children to understand family functioning as a cooperative, rather than a police state or "Pleasure Island." Parents socializing in this manner develop positive ways to talk with their children so that the child initiates and develops a fondness to assist the family. The child learns to anticipate what is necessary and essential, without the requirement of constant oversight and reminder, and learns about the positive reasons for limits and routines (Wiener, 2012). The hope is that when these children grow up, they will more likely cooperate with their supervisors, experience the success that accrues from conscientiousness and work ethic, and show increased reciprocity in their future families and peer relationships as well.

Parents operating in this framework want their children to recognize that interacting with others is not simply a matter of what others do *for them,* or how they are victims of what others do *to them*, but a melding of preferences. These parents prepare their children for social situations that require a give-and-take. They want them to recognize that teamwork, which sometimes entails conformity, is necessary for many desirable outcomes. For example, if a parent wants a child to make a phone call to check in when visiting with their friends, the child might accommodate that request as a way to *care* for the parent, even if the call is inconvenient. The hope is that the relational benefit supersedes the downside of having to make the call.

In this approach, parents orient the child to work hard and save, as those behaviors will reduce the necessity to impose on others. Children socialized in this fashion are likely to have a better understanding of what it means to lose, since they are more likely to experience the hardship of what it takes to achieve, earn, and win. These individuals might also acquire a better understanding of the Golden Rule when responsibility is both absorbed and given to others. They might be less apt to see the achievements of others as examples of "unearned privileges," as if success simply falls from the sky.

A practical example of this issue occurs when parents extend children advancements on their allowances, or give them extra money after the children spend frivolously and cry poverty. Parents who recognize that these patterns of socialization reinforce irresponsibility are careful to set firmer limits. They prefer that the child prepares and salts away money in order to make a purchase. They want the child to develop financial accountability and planning, and adopt the belief that if you want to have something, you have to be thrifty and do the work *prior* to getting it. This method induces consequences for frolicsome spending, gambling, or employment refusals, as there is no stork flying in with a money delivery to enable those behaviors (i.e., inside → outside).

Unless children have some skin in the game, they can advocate for all kinds of thrills and fatuous behaviors that only have consequences for others, while they get off scot-free. This problem is vividly evident when teachers keep extending deadlines for assignments, with minimal consequences, and when children have so many toys that none of them matter. Children do not learn to be conscientious under these conditions, since rescuing and replacement are frequent. There is essentially no liability. The child believes there will be inevitable rescuing to minimize any hardships that might occur (i.e., outside → inside).

When children are frequently released from obligations, they are not learning about the long-term risks of being negligent. Why are we then surprised that increasing numbers of our youth prefer instant gratifications? When impetuousness has no consequences, there is little downside, as individuals (and corporations) are invariably saved by loved ones, or the government, down the road.

Today, many children are not learning personal restraint, and this is happening within the family, and the society in general. Our current renouncing and laxity toward many traditional limits and mores, and lack of consistency in applying rules, seems to be affecting a large proportion of our social group. In a society predicated on loans, credit cards, bailouts, trust funds, frequent gifting, entitlements, and the allowance of bankruptcy, people can take actions without having to do the responsible behavior of accumulating resources prior to taking the labors of others. This does not discount the fact that providing loans is a viable business, or that a social safety net has no merit. But it does suggest that there is more tolerance of self-gratification, and an increased prerogative to do so.

Overall, there seems to be a diminishment of austerity and preparedness in our social patterns. It is now possible to avoid consequences or defer them well into the future. As long as a person has a source of "coverage," there can be gratification without contribution. If the individual reneges, or others rescue and compensate, accountability and respect for the property of others does not develop. In that sense, the behavior is not very different from stealing. People are essentially taking from others without earning, and they do not appreciate the difficulties that people face when attempting to work hard and save.

Interestingly, this same pattern of entitlement lays the groundwork for people to traipse to the ballot box and vote for the government to siphon money their way. Internalizing a sense of restraint, concern for others, and accountability goes by the wayside. Children learn that they can do what they want without adverse repercussions. Moreover, when the child's neighborhood peer group reinforces rule-breaking, civility diminishes without the recognition that the behaviors are problematic.

In contrast, parents that recognize the importance of developing the child's sense of responsibility, focus on role modeling politeness, austerity, and a work ethic. They do this with the hope that the child will imitate those behaviors and distinguish them from profligacy and the right to have what others possess. They are careful not to reinforce the child's exaggeration of deprivation, as this can intensify a sense of entitlement and justification to *take* from others without remorse. They do *not* want to socialize children to believe that they *deserve* whatever is desired at the moment. These parents prefer to condition the child to focus on *earning* rather than being *owed* (inside → outside).

However, this outcome is unlikely when fairness means that people should have exactly what others have (i.e., no one should feel deprived). Under these conditions, participants become focused on comparing and counting. Claims of neediness increase, as everyone gets preoccupied with minuscule differences that invariably occur. When people believe that assets must be equally distributed, measuring to the finest detail becomes the primary concern, and demands for compensation increase. Instead of finding ways to *earn* more, they keep highlighting reasons why they should *have* more, and there is no end to the scenario. We are now seeing the consequences of this in the distressed states of our youth.

Dependency and the Increasing Reliance upon Others

Many believe that parenting is a quest to help infants transition from a helpless state to a state of independence. Much like a bird that can eventually leave the nest, parents help their children obtain self-sufficiency. However, since families want relationships that are sustaining, there is sometimes a push and pull between attachment and autonomy, and depending on vulnerabilities in the family, one or the other tendency may predominate. For example, parents anxious about abandonment might inadvertently reinforce dependencies, as fostering the child's autonomy is not as important as maintaining the child's availability. When people believe that "doing for others" is a sign of love, passive reliance might be conditioned as well. Overall, whenever there are circumstances that make independent prospering difficult, there is likely to be a greater reliance on others, as everyone benefits from the power of the herd.

Another roadblock to the advancement of independence is that developing self-reliance in children can be arduous. When children are very young, it takes extra time to help them do autonomous achievements, in comparison with doing activities for them. When parents are in a hurry, they will often rush to put the child's coat on or tie the child's shoes. This solution is faster and easier than waiting for the child's self-completion.

Parents having to abide by rigid schedules recognize this problem on a daily basis. Children wanting additional attention might also ask questions they could easily answer on their own as a way to promote parental involvement. Children unhappy about where they are going may slow the pace in a variety of ways, and this includes not completing tasks that are routine. The evolving pattern finds the parent rectifying problems in a desperate attempt to meet time requirements instead of promoting the child's self-management to meet scheduling demands. Not surprisingly, an outside→ in pattern develops as the parent takes over.

A similar tendency occurs when parents have guilt associated with not spending enough time with their children due to their outside responsibilities. Rather than require children to adjust to the limits of their availability, they make up for this by overextending when they are available, even if this entails significant personal inconvenience. These patterns are now increasingly prevalent due to the higher percentages of family breakup, and the requirement for custodial parents to work. The apparent consequence of this pattern is that parents reinforce greater reliance on them to complete day-to-day tasks, as the parents try to gain back their child's favor while operating within shortened frames of time.

If the parent feels sorry for the child for other reasons, such as misbehavior from the other parent, or for other struggles that the child might be enduring, there is even more justification to placate the downtrodden youngster. Parental remorse may also be intense when parents are contrite about divorcing the child's parent, or when the other parent has abandoned the family. In these situations, available parents do not want to induce additional hardship, and indulging dependencies accomplishes that objective.

Parents identifying with the underdog, for any number of reasons, are also likely to advocate for the "hurt" child. They do not want the child to suffer as they have suffered, and have the same negative memories. Often, this pattern occurs when parents did not have enough help or supervision when they were young. They become eager to rescue so the child will not endure similar privations. There is frequent pampering and spoiling, and all the child has to do is keeping claiming hardship for the gratuities to keep flowing. Doing for the child supersedes the long-term advantages of building grit and skill to self-manage.

However, children subjected to this kind of parenting become less tolerant of inconvenience. They are often less willing to work hard to self-satisfy. The children expect others to satiate their moaning by making life easier. They quickly become uncomfortable, demand immediate rectification, and they will lack introspection as to how their behests adversely affect those around them. They learn to wait for others to relent and oblige like empty vesicles, while the secondary consequences of reduced autonomy go unnoticed.

Moreover, when there is a broad array of impairments and disabilities that create a necessity to adjust traditional standards downward, there is an ever-growing requirement throughout society for others to assume responsibilities that these individuals claim they cannot do. With the presumption of diminished capability, the expectation for independence subsides. There is now an ever-expanding pool of adults and children swirling within this unfortunate circumstance. Others must provide them with increasing amounts of care and protection. The fostering of "self-management" becomes a lesser concern for the growing numbers that are labeled as incompetent in one way or another.

Unfortunately, an example of extensive leaning on others is evident with health promotion. Even though it seems preferable for individuals to contribute to their physical well-being, it often seems that people are becoming increasingly reliant on others to manufacture their body integrity. For instance, type 2 diabetes is treatable by altering lifestyle in relation to diet and exercise (i.e., inside → outside). However, individuals can also rely on medication to control their insulin levels (i.e., outside → inside). Often, professionals find it increasingly difficult to get individuals to change their behavior. The overwhelming majority opts for dependency on medication to produce health on their behalf instead of relying on personal resources, and the proliferation of this solution becomes economically disastrous for the health care system (Makary, 2021).

Analogously, with computer search engines and social media, children can now obtain what they want without having to do a great deal of work. While some might take advantage of automation and delve deeper in order to obtain more intense and varied learning experiences, many others simply do less and complain of boredom when the pace slows or obstacles occur (outside→ in). This pattern of reliance on external sources such as "artificial intelligence" seems to be the new standard. While it is pushing some people ahead, it is also creating passive dependency for many others.

There is yet another problem creating dependencies in American society. Despite the opulence available to vast numbers of people, others find it increasingly difficult to function independently due to financial hardship and the cost of living. There is now a growing population of younger adults and other subgroups relying on either their parents or the government to support them in one way or another. Certainly, expensive college degrees not leading to financial advancement, as well as the difficulties associated with mastering the necessary skills to make money in modern societies, contribute to this problem. There is now a toggling to an outside → inside dynamic, which finds others picking up the slack and providing assistance.

It seems that all of these patterns, and more, trend toward creating additional dependencies. Many children learn to rely on others to meet expectations and needs, and there is less emphasis on utilizing personal resources to promote autonomy. Child-rearing patterns seem to be reinforcing increased reliance, and designated impairments entitle more children to receive assistance that would not otherwise occur. In other instances, parents may smother the child for their own psychological reasons, or frighten the child so much that they squelch the child's initiative and autonomy. While some children might push back against limits, react to protections as innuendos of incompetence, and become oppositional, "jumping through the hoops backward" will not result in self-reliant functioning any better than mindlessly following orders.

In a variety of ways, many more children are learning to rely on the resources of others, much like the small few that could rely on trust funds rather than their own judgments and work productivity in previous generations. The percentage of the US population operating under conditions of dependency is ballooning. The requirement for extra assistance is expanding beyond the resources of the deteriorating primary families. Reliance on community and governmental agencies is growing exponentially to aid and abet the burgeoning crowd of struggling individuals (i.e., outside → inside).

In contrast, parents who want to condition their child's autonomy will discipline in ways that promote self-management. Operating within the belief that their child is competent to succeed, they might delay offering of help until they observe unmistakable futility, and at these times, give only enough assistance for the child to resume independently. The child might complain, but they remain focused on the goal of self-reliance.

For example, rather than hand the child an object, these parents might wait for their children to reach for the object. Whimpering may ensue, the child's hands might seem like mittens and the parents might feel heartless, but they desire skill development when possible. Likewise, they remain patient when the child struggles to remember or articulate ideas, instead of abruptly giving the answer or enunciating for the child. They believe that minor achievements will build self-efficacy over time. They realize that moderate struggling, disappointment, and failure can often provide motivation to persevere and gain competency (i.e., inside → out).

There are numerous ways to promote skill advancement. For example, instead of listing available options, much like a multiple-choice exam, parents can ask the child to derive those possibilities. Instead of telling the child what is essential for preparation, they can give the child the opportunity to figure out what to pack. In other words, in lieu of solving problems *for* the child, parents can solve problems *with* the child. For example, they might ask: *What might work for us? What thoughts do you have? How do you want to handle the problem? What might happen if you behave in that way? What changes do you want to make?* Or, *What are the risks if we do it that way?* Parents are essentially helping children develop their frontal lobes rather than exercising their own.

When fostering this pattern of socialization, children learn to value independent accomplishments, and they have more opportunities to resolve dilemmas prior to receiving assistance. However, parents fostering self-reliance also recognize the importance of respecting the child's requests for help when task requirements seem inordinate and beyond the child's current skills. They do not want to dissuade the child from reaching out and utilizing them as a positive resource when growth would not otherwise occur. For example, a child might become disheartened trying to untie a shoelace knot, but with a little help and role modeling how to proceed, the child becomes capable the next time it happens.

There is always a balance between *promoting* independence and *providing* needed assistance and direction, which helps to maintain progress and mutuality. For example, it can be beneficial for the parent to provide help when noticing that the child is unlikely to pour a drink without significant spilling. However, at other times, it can be advantageous to refrain from locating an object for a child when the child could figure out a way to retrieve the object with a modicum of effort and concentration to retrace steps.

Within this parenting style, instead of relying solely on what the parent thinks is best, the child develops problem-solving skills and clearer thinking, as parents more often employ the Socratic method. This approach mitigates the development of an external locus of control where children frequently depend on others to make decisions, plans, or judgments. When enacting this strategy, parents more often ask children what they think or feel about what happened, and then orient the discussion around the child's reactions. For example, they might ask an older child, *Are you satisfied with your grades?* and then utilize the child's response as a starting point to explore problems and possible solutions.

There are many opportunities throughout day-to-day living for those wanting to develop a child's self-reliance and "executive functioning." For example, instead of waking up the child, the parent might help the child learn to wake up independently with an alarm clock. This might entail helping the child develop a routine of setting the clock in the evening. Similarly, parents might foster the habit of independent dressing in the morning, help the child learn how to coordinate colors, and help the child develop the routine of selecting clothing the night before to avoid the morning rush.

Parents interested in garnering autonomy can also help the child implement strategies that assist the recall of expectations without reliance on them to cue, remind, or nag. For example, they might ask their children where they *want* to place their homework assignments in order to remember them in the morning when leaving the house. Even young children can often learn to identify environmental cues that will notify them that it is time for bed. For example, the ending of a television show can signal the young child that it is time to begin the bedtime process. The child becomes cognizant of time because this will result in having extra minutes to share bedtime stories with the parent.

At first, the promotion of self-management will be more difficult than functioning as the child's personal attendant, but the long-term effects can be worthwhile. For children claiming that they "can't" remember on their own, parents might ask, *If someone were to give you one hundred dollars to remember, what would you do to remind yourself?* The parent might then ask if the same strategy might work for a variety of different tasks and activities.

Parents can also promote autonomous family contribution by taking notice of the child's efforts to *take charge* of various aspects of family functioning, including helping with cleaning, managing belongings, cooking, repairing, and the completion of many other everyday jobs. They eagerly observe the fact that the child completes these tasks without any reminding or assistance.

As a way to reinforce the continuation of these admirable behaviors, the family develops a norm that provides participants with a weekly sum of "family money" to use at their discretion when they operate with that kind of maturity and autonomy. Parents let the child know that they are grateful that the child is promoting family unity.

In general, children raised in this manner will likely gain the confidence that they can take the lead and function adequately with less aiding and abetting from others. To promote these outcomes, parents might emphasize the positive consequences that are likely to occur for both the child and the family when the child functions with such command. The child learns that increased cognitive maturity and reliable self-management enables a variety of new opportunities and adventures.

When parents operate within these guidelines, they learn to gauge the child's current abilities by assessing the child's flair and competence when doing activities the child initiates and enjoys. They perform this assessment prior to deciding that the child is too incompetent to succeed. This procedure is advisable, in that enjoyed and self-initiated activities are likely to yield the best-case scenarios of what the child is *capable* of doing.

For example, if children can organize miniature figures into a hierarchically arranged military force ready to do battle, they can find ways to keep bedrooms and backpacks in an acceptable order. If they can remember the names of professional wrestlers, their talents, matches, and personalities, they can remember subject matter at school that requires similar categorical skills. If they can follow rules for their picture card games, they can learn and comply with numerous family and classroom rules as well.

Parents might then help their children generalize the skills that they develop in favorite activities, and talk with them about applying those commendable skills to a wider range of achievements, including schoolwork and other kinds of activities that require proficiency. Parents might admire children's model building, drawings, and game skills, and help them recognize that competence in these endeavors can help to create success in a wide variety of activities, including those that are expected, assessed, and graded.

The hope is that this parenting approach will encourage perseverance toward long-term goals instead of employing a feel-good approach that applauds vacuous accomplishments and indiscriminate prize-giving (e.g., a trophy for everyone). Instead of giving into complaints of disinterest, or claims that expectations are too difficult and boring, these children learn that it is important to meet expectations through effort and perseverance, even if they initially feel jaded or hopeless. Extolling effort is preferable to condoning grievances, and parents commend instances of stepwise progress.

Incidentally, often children avoid and resist achieving when they compare themselves unfavorably to others, such as when a child reacts to a competent sibling. At these times, they might balk at participating because they do not want others to perceive them as inferior. They might think that they have to be flawless in order to be acceptable. Although, some children might enjoy the dependency gratification that takes place when parents show impassioned concern and the provision of special help when they are refusing or reluctant.

If we consider these possibilities, when the child is disinterested, power struggling, crying, waiting for others to supply an answer, or showing laziness, rather than become frustrated, ease requirements, or threaten, parents might delve into the subtle emotional reasons for those responses. Parents might ask, *What will happen if you make a mistake?* or, *What is bothering you?*, and remain patient throughout the process. If there is going to be meaningful advancement, it is important to figure out the specifics of what needs addressing. There are numerous reasons for children to react negatively when adults dictate and evaluate their actions.

In contrast to settling on the explanation that the child is simply indolent or disobedient and requiring coercive intervention, the adult maintains achievement goals, while simultaneously considering the child's concerns about failure and vulnerability. The parent helps the child identify possible reasons for giving up, and works with the child to understand the situations that trigger avoidance behaviors, including fidgeting, squirming, and distractibility. This way of assisting helps the child overcome the problem, as something is disrupting the child, interfering with immersion, and creating a barricade.

It is also prudent for parents to steer children away from invoking alibis for failures. They might also avoid telling their children that an external force such as bias against them, or a diagnosis, prevents them from attaining. Parents might instead admire their perseverance and highlight the value of incremental progress. This is what leads to success for most people (Manhattan Institute, 2019). This message will empower the child and reduce procrastination, external blaming, and waiting for others to solve problems. The "learned helplessness" that occurs when people lack personal agency is less likely when there is optimism that problems are solvable by accessing internal resources (Condra, 2021).

The aim is to help children develop a vision of the future, which includes recognition of functioning competently apart from family members—the belief that they can succeed on their own, even if tasks seem insurmountable at first. Moreover, when there is a focus on both short- and long-term *positive incentives*, achievements are more likely to continue without the necessity for others to coax, coerce, or monitor (Skinner, 1976). The developed mindset of hard work and independent achievement combats the depression and nihilism that is evident in so many of today's youth.

Put differently, struggling to achieve is not a nemesis to discard. Striving for excellence and learning from mistakes is not an automatic cause of stress or intimidation. Slow and steady progress, or "iterative prototyping" towards a lauded goal is how noteworthy achievements come to fruition. When upholding the child's skill building, parents notice the kinds of ambition, curiosity, and proficiency that is characteristic of many artisans, musicians, and writers of the past. They reinforce the belief that lofty goals are commendable, and children enjoy the fact that their parents value their accomplishments and fund of knowledge.

Rather than standards being too high, the greater problems are diminishing the child's anxieties, patterns of reacting to criticism, or to resentments related to being berated and controlled. As a way to mitigate those tribulations, parents might carefully gauge the child's initiative and immersion when doing the activity. If they notice reluctance, avoidance, or other extreme behaviors, it is necessary to resolve those reactions.

The hope is to reinforce achievements by making them a cherished family value that the child enjoys, as striving for an ideal can be positive rather than imbued with travail. A question to ask is whether the child *dreads* the consequences of failure (outside → inside), or whether the child is *thrilled* by the possibility of success (inside → outside).

Emotionality and the Contingency Management Solution

We go through life emitting sequences of responses in relation to context, situation, and circumstance. We call some of these responses "emotions," and the list usually includes fear, disgust, anger, surprise, pleasure, and sadness. While we sometimes settle disputes without easy discernment of these kinds of displays, often people obtain accommodations, control, or receive reprimands in relation to exhibiting emotional behaviors.

Emotional displays can establish who has preference, power, and entitlement to establish what they want. People might argue right vs. wrong in a formal debate predicated on logic, with little emotional ting. However, in daily life, emotions can be a powerful way to intimidate others with rejection, and sometimes aggression, when others do not respond in the desired fashion. We often modulate our actions based on emotional dynamics, as the facts can dim in comparison to an emotionally driven charge.

While the origins of emotional responding have their beginnings in infant temperament, very quickly, children learn about the repercussions of emotional behaviors. They often imitate the tirades, hyperbole, lashing out, banging, displacements of anger, and aggressiveness exhibited by those around them. They learn that temper tantrums can be effective, and they may learn to threaten, destroy, or yell when they have objections, if those behaviors are reinforced. They might develop patterns of whining or sulking until others give in, cry or whimper until accommodations occur, or show anxiety and fearfulness until easements take place.

There is now reluctance to do any kind of socializing that might negate a child's *emotional* insistence or putative anguish. This general pattern now plays out in politics of our time, as identity groups claiming a lack of power and privilege show the same emotional enactments currently tolerated and reinforced within many families. However, if the goal is to ameliorate this trend, what can we do instead, as there some advantages to tempering histrionics and introducing more instances of logic and reason both in the family and in the outside world.

Keeping in mind that many people do not always outgrow frequent emotional displays, we ought to consider if we prefer that children learn to cope with and meet expectations in more sedate and reasonable ways. Clearly, there are situations where emotionality is advantageous and ill-advised to discard, but there are many opportunities to help children learn equanimity in a wider range of situations. Moreover, it is often easier to find a common ground when people remain calm and patient with each other. Of course, to accomplish this social patterning, it is important for significant others to model emotional composure and not reinforce histrionic behaviors.

Not surprisingly, many adults are looking for ways to extinguish hyperbole, and the usual method adopted is *contingency management*. That is, reward acceptable behavior and punish the unacceptable— and presto, conformity comes to fruition. Children's access to their resources will occur in conjunction with their adherence to rules and limits. Emotions become irrelevant; only the facts matter, and parents gain control with this method.

Contingency management discipline is present throughout our society, including within the penal system and most institutions. Professional psychologists have helped to fine-tune the method for use within families, and frequently advocate the technique. While corporal punishment is largely in disfavor, many parents find it acceptable to settle disputes with children by *controlling* their resources to induce instantaneous compliance. For example, parents might say: *Study, or I will take away your cell phone. I will buy you a video game if you get ready on time.* Or, *Stop yelling, or I won't take you to your friend's house.*

The approach often produces immediate obedience. However, it also has side effects that are not always examined or recognized. First, the inherent value of an activity usually diminishes in relation to the value of the external contingency. For example, if we use the cell phone to promote studying, then the phone becomes increasingly precious, while schoolwork retains only the instrumental value to keep the phone. Unfortunately, the consequence of losing the phone is often the only topic of concern. Problems associated with not studying, and the intrinsic benefits of learning, sink into the background, and children will likely study less when bribes are removed (Lepper et al., 1973).

It often seems that parents overlook important problems with this form of disciplining, such as failing to do the detective work that might help them understand the possible reasons for the young person's lack of cooperation prior to making their ultimatums. For example, is the teen not studying due to phone time? Or does the teen not understand the work? Is the teen angry with the teacher or parent and refusing to do assigned work as a protest?

Given a wide range of possibilities, resolving these kinds of concerns is vital for both the current dilemma, and for the teen's long-term adjustment. Since there will be many occasions where the teen will have to deal with failures to meet expectations and people behaving poorly, this kind of analysis is valuable. Resolving the teen's *emotional* reactions (including spiteful behaviors) may help the teen comply in reasonable ways without cutting into phone time one iota.

Another drawback is that both parents and children may learn to use the coercive practices of contingency management against each other by finding ways to counteract each other's attempts to control. There can be escalating demands for more rewards, and punishments might have to intensify to be effective. For example, children might continue to resist schoolwork until their parents continue to raise the payments for higher grades.

Moreover, many children may learn to circumvent, lie, sneak, and oppose in order to outmaneuver the system. For example, while parents might take away prized items in an attempt to induce compliance, children might reduce their interest in the object to counteract being controlled. If parents punish by inducing isolation, the child may eventually prefer to be alone. When there are struggles for power, children might forget responsibilities, become careless, detach, delay, or imitate the parents' actions and take prized objects from them. Children, like everyone else, will protect their self-interest, and they are likely to copy the patterns of coercion used against them.

There are numerous reasons to question the use of contingency management as a *primary* way to socialize. First, it is often deficient in helping participants learn the gentle art of compromising; it predicates on one-upmanship. Second, the contrived system of bribes and punishments may induce compliance, but not help people repeat and generalize the desired behaviors when the system is not in use. Third, it can add to our preoccupation with materialism, since consequences center on resource distribution. Fourth, while the method works well to resolve urgency and helps to induce the completion of simple tasks, the approach has limitations when the objective is to master complex tasks requiring long-term commitment. (Pink, 2009).

Parents aware of this latter problem will shy away from contingency management. For example, if they desire their child to play the piano, they might gauge the child's interest and work out a practice routine that the child advocates. Rather than punish non-compliance, they solve problems that might be influencing the child's lack of engagement. Most importantly, they promote achievement by enjoying and admiring the child's playing instead of coaxing with a variety of bribes that they control.

In short, the many deficiencies of contingency management become blatant when observing the clandestine activities that frequently occur in prison where rape, stealing, and aggressive behaviors run rampant despite the strict overseeing by prison attendants. In fact, this is what we mean when we say a person has been "institutionalized." Individuals become accustomed to having someone else manage and control, and many find ways to outmaneuver as much as possible. Mutuality and empathy do not enter into the equation. Decisions occur dispassionately, and those in charge herd the enslaved like cattle, while "the inmates" think of ways to escape and overcome. When managers are not available to force compliance, there is no reason to conform.

So what might be an alternative way to discipline children without the hysteria of emotions overwhelming reason and logic, and without the side effects of contingency management? Perhaps an answer to this question is to help children to learn about the relational benefits that occur when cooperating. For example, instead of bribing or threatening to produce punctuality, we can help children recognize the positive consequences associated with respecting the time parameters of others and fulfilling responsibilities. As children learn to value those relational benefits, trust and consistency develop, and this opens up a wide range of possibilities that everyone involved may enjoy. As the saying goes, "A handshake is better than a fist."

Moreover, when rewards for participants revolve around reciprocal caring, the exchange of material items becomes merely an aspect of the ongoing relationship, but not the primary focus. The driving force is not quid pro quo, which is a mercantile exchange. The distinction between prostitution and mutual sexual pleasure illustrates this point quite well.

While the formality that is characteristic with quid pro quo interaction is typically necessary in society at large, where relational connection is vague or nonexistent, if we do not emphasize relational reinforcements within the family, in what setting will people learn those behaviors? If beneficence does not occur with loved ones, what is the probability that the maturing child will show remnants of those behaviors outside of the family? Again, if we focus on taking objects away to stop transgressions, the focus is on the object rather than the unconscionable action and its effects on others. Is that the learning objective we want to nurture?

For those interested in advancing camaraderie, human decency, and empathy, a different pattern of parenting comes to the fore. As long as the child is capable of enjoying relational pleasures, even very young children can benefit from an admiring comment, a smile, or a hug as possible ways to facilitate valued behaviors. As children mature, parents can bring additional relational consequences into focus during the socialization process.

Importantly, building a society that can tolerate the risks associated with allowing personal freedoms requires child-rearing that reinforces adequate concern for others, so this social training is invaluable. Parents might let children know about the harms they create for the family (and others), in relation to certain inconsiderate actions, as well as help them identify the benefits that occur when cooperating. For example, they might point out, *If you help clean up, we can have more time to play before it is time to sleep.* The child learns that teamwork leads to an ongoing exchange of favors, as well as more pleasant time together.

Some might worry that this pattern of disciplining is a form of permissiveness, but this is not the case. As a last resort, and in lieu futility, frustration, or anger, parents can always stop accommodating in a variety of ways to thwart unwanted behaviors. If there is no other option, they can revert to contingency management at any time, and withhold resources until the child starts showing a reasonable responding. For example, if the child keeps overreacting when required to stop playing video games, and does not respond to reasonable discussions about the problem, the parent might prevent the child from playing until the child demonstrates cooperation with transitioning at other times. Given the intransigency of the child's behavior, the parent might not have any other viable way to handle the problem.

Of course, it is preferable for children to *agree* that certain consequences are necessary, but sometimes it might be necessary for parents to coerce *reparation.* For example, they might require a child to spend personal money to rectify damage that was the result of a tirade. In lieu of cash, parents might curtail takeout foods, buying new toys, going to the movies, and the like, until there is enough savings in the family budget to complete the repair or compensate others.

While these parental actions seem equivalent to punishments, parents are not trying to induce suffering to create compliance. The parental responses are attempts to find *logical* ways to *solve* problems and stop exploitations, as well as allow for natural consequences to play out, which will help the child learn. Promoting mutuality and personal responsibility is not weakening a parent's authority to govern the family, nor does it remove the typical consequences that occur when people behave with indiscretion. The objective is for children to learn the importance of limits and personal boundaries with the *least* amount of coercion

While this might be an admirable goal, it might not be an easy proposition, given the ways in which many people currently behave. Ideally, parents and other influential adults would have to learn to enact calm, compassionate, and rational patterns of behavior, and then help children learn to do the same. Adults would have to reduce the emphasis on *creating* happiness for their children, and at the same time, not shift to a pattern where children needlessly suffer, have no voice, or no opportunity for discretionary input. They would have to learn ways to create interdependency, mutual kindness, and shared responsibilities (i.e., inside ↔ outside).

Assuming these objectives, the initial problem is to help parents effectively extinguish the child's overreactions and refusals. This will entail figuring out what might be reinforcing those responses. For example, parents might be yielding to the child's demands as a quick and easy way to get the uncomfortable behaviors to stop. At other times, the child might glean revenge by disrupting the parent with statements that leave the parent feeling inadequate or disliked. Not surprisingly, captious tones of voice emanating from either the parent or child will likely disrupt a cooperative exchange.

Since dramatic behaviors are swaying, it is important for parents to maintain their integrity, composure, and the family's priorities despite the child's efforts to take over. It is important for children to learn to defer when the family agenda is not to their liking. It is in their best interest to learn to adapt to schedules, adjust to available options, enact routines, and meet obligations that they do not favor. We want them to recognize that nothing terrible will happen if they acclimate (i.e., inside → out).

When operating in this fashion, parents approach situations with poised, relaxed, and firm responding so that the child does not monopolize. While they might want to punish the child's disrespectful behavior, serenity is usually a better way to handle the problem so that the child's rudeness gleans no social power. After the child settles, the parent might ask the child to clarify objections, and encourage *talking about anger* instead of lashing out.

In this approach, it is important for parents to refrain from interacting until the child is ready to be congenial, as this will mitigate the reinforcement of histrionic responding. If a child starts to yell, parents might say, with open palms, *I can hear you better if you talk quietly*, or, *What if you tell me what you are angry about?* Parents do not escalate in response to the child's dramatizing, and the child has to deal with the parent's resolve to remain dispassionate. Overreactions have far less power within this method of socializing children.

As expected, this style works better when initiated as early as possible. For example, while toddlers test limits and show inquisitiveness, it remains important to establish safety. It is essential for parents to remain assertive, patient, and consistent when disciplining at these times. Often, it is advisable for parents to take action while saying as little as possible to avoid giving the behaviors more attention than necessary.

Parents may have to physically stop the child, or silently put the toddler in the desired space without saying a word when there is an overstepping of boundaries. If a toddler can dominate, what happens when the child develops more resources to overpower? Moreover, if parents are doing too much talking, yelling, and overreacting, the toddler (and child) might learn to disregard the parents' calmer efforts. The youngster might interpret situations as non-urgent until the parent is animated and harsh. In these instances, no one is learning to respond with tranquility.

In a similar vein, instead of pursuing the child who storms off, parents might linger until the child calmly re-engages. The important issue is that children learn the skill of calming down without the necessity for others to placate or assist. We want them to learn that disproportionate responding does not yield accommodating results. Parents can reinforce the development of emotional maturity by remarking in an admiring tone: "You handled that quite nicely."

However, and as noted with the emotion of hatred, overreactive responses often indicate that individuals have not adequately resolved problems that keep repeating. Surprisingly enough, explosiveness can frequently be resolved by helping children learn patterns of assertiveness during day-to-day interacting. Helping children feel comfortable saying their preferences and voicing objections at the time problems occur, often helps to avoid the buildup of resentments, which can eventually lead to the hyperemotional responding.

Parents will notice that these kinds of responses may occur in reaction to bedtime, school-related activities, visiting relatives, accepting new family members, joining organized groups, meeting strangers, touching animals, and eating particular foods. However, emotional intensities, tirades, distancing, and complaints may occur less often when parents make it easy for children to voice and resolve their concerns on a regular basis.

During these problem-solving encounters, it is vital for parents to investigate what is so terrible about the situation for the child to react with such magnitude. Often, parents will find that current situations are triggering unwanted memories. The reliving of unpleasant experience is difficult, and the excessive emotion can be an indication of fright and discomfort that the child anticipates and prefers to avoid. Addressing the child's concerns and unpacking what might be scaring or bothering the child is an alternative to bribing, coercing, or giving in to create temporary peace.

By identifying the reasons or the paired associations that are occurring in relation to the child's anxieties or hostilities, parents will obtain a better idea of what problems they are trying to resolve. Helping children identify the sources of their strong emotions may uncover an accumulation of many different unsettled issues, and this approach can help them understand themselves and others in refined ways.

The goal is to desensitize the child so that events are not so intimidating. Often, this entails reframing what is happening so that it is anodyne rather than oppressive. During this process, parents can assist children in clarifying their objections to current circumstances, help them discern the differences between previous events and what is currently happening, and help them identify calm and assertive behaviors that they could alternatively enact to resolve their dilemma. Children will like having a voice and increased agency, and they may respond positively when others care enough to consider their point of view as they struggle to adapt to the world (i.e., inside $\leftrightarrow$ outside).

Helping parents and children operate in this fashion may go a long way to reduce the hysteria that often occurs when people have competing interests. The hope is that these new family patterns will continue when children leave the family nest. While conflict resolution can be oppressive and unilateral, reciprocity and reason can also prevail when reinforced early in life. The behavioral enactments necessary for success in many different settings begins at home during family interactions, including when children observe their parents demonstrating reciprocity and mutual caring when they interact with each other.

CHAPTER SIX

THE IDENTITY REBELLION AND ITS AFTERMATH

American society seems to be at the precipice of a revolution—a shifting of power and ideation from one belief system to another. This transition for different societies may be abrupt or insidious, but it happens when there is sufficient discontentment to expel incumbent authorities and replace traditional patterns of behavior. Currently, there is an uprising that blames hardship and unhappiness on the status quo. This revolt, or "Identity Rebellion," is a quest to gain freedom from the oppressions caused by traditional expectations. As a way to advance their cause, they marshal a centralized force to take down what stands in their way. The following is a scenario of what might happen when this aggregate of the discontent accomplishes its imagined goal of equity.

Since there are two political camps, there are two different anticipated renditions of what could transpire as the rebellion unfolds. The accounts are fictitious, as it is unclear what will eventuate. However, the depictions might be predictive to some extent, and may provide some provocative insights. The first scenario is the Protector ideal, while the Promoter camp anticipates something different. The spirited and sometimes playful renditions are logical extensions of the previous chapters, and a review of many of the ideas presented in the text.

The Overthrow

The rebellion occurred in relation to those identifying with an outside → in conceptualization. That is, the first and primary way to lessen suffering is to change the outer world. Those struggling economically, or seeking to enhance self-liking, status, and social acceptance, anticipated that changing "others" would make it possible for them to *receive* the "good life." They believed that it would be curative to remove barriers caused by other people, as social forces were creating their lagging and suffering. They were not accountable for their struggles; impinging circumstances were victimizing them, and that needed to change. They knew they could feel whole if they killed the metaphorical white whale.

Historically, the youth typically shifted to an inside → outside worldview as the acquisition of resources and skills to adapt and succeed increased with age and experience. However, this was not happening. Graduates from college had inordinate debt that was making it difficult for them to flourish, and there were not enough jobs in the marketplace calling for the kinds of skills they had developed. They became disenchanted and blamed their failures on society, and maintained the outside → in dynamic, which bolstered the magnitude of the rebellion. Since they had already been indoctrinated into a Protector ideology in the academy, they simply persisted with those instilled beliefs.

With disenfranchisement occurring from numerous sources, such as drug abuse, growing categories of disabilities, exploding incidences of single parenthood, automation, artificial intelligence, and lack of skill development in a STEM-oriented economy, many were struggling within the current state of affairs, and in need of assistance. An overwhelming number began to contest the utility of conventional practice. They were looking for external changes; the traditional system based on personal responsibility was ripe to overturn. Sedition was close at hand, and people were eager to accept philosophies that would deconstruct it all.

With an increasing mass advocating an overthrow, the Protector group was gaining tremendous influence to take over all the structures of authority. Child-rearing, academic and journalistic proclivities, core curriculums in public schools, mega-organizations, numerous aggrieved sexual and racial minorities, and many striving females were all maintaining an outside → in mentality. All of these groups were reinforcing each other to foment the whirlwind that would displace those upholding the traditional culture and seats of power.

The feminist movement alone seemed sufficient to displace enough incumbents to change the complexion of numerous institutions, schools, family patterns, child-rearing, and businesses. Since they had up to half the population at their fingertips, and approximately half of the male population acquiescent with their views, vast throngs were ready to eat the forbidden fruit of rebellion. Little else seemed necessary to create a discharge of the old, and they could encapsulate themselves in an idealized world free from *patriarchal oppression*. Their only task was to overwhelm the others with an unrelenting push of emotion.

Many echoed the belief that the feminist movement was instrumental in promoting safety at all costs, and it helped to shift child-rearing and economic security from the family to governmental agencies. It led the charge to "believe all victims," which undermined the opportunity to disagree or implement *due process*. Even though concerns about racism formed the nucleus of the rebellion and was able to trump all other grievances, the feminist movement got the ball rolling fast.

When the anti-racists and feminists joined forces with other victimized identities, a vast majority of society now had the moral credibility to demand increased protection in the form of destroying the oppressors. Like nurturing a hungry family, this conglomerate of marginalized groups worked to redistribute assets to compensate for their deprivations and misfortunes caused by decades of heartless slave drivers.

The rebellion's cavalcade of ideas had been clandestinely brewing for decades within grade schools and university walls. Like a Trojan horse, there were now enough minions to seed prestigious jobs, bureaucracies, judicial appointments, media fact-checkers, and professorships. Since no one wanted to be on the incorrect side, people acquiesced, and the crumbling happened fast.

Since the entrenched leviathans were males with white skin, that group became the *hated other* who were responsible for all their suffering. They were the group that needed removal, and this new system of blame became the new *power-knowledge*. There was now an uplift of tribalism, which dissected society into a plethora of warring factions based on race, gender variations, and other marginalized identities. This growing contingent became the new civil rights movement, and they were now an overwhelming mob that could overthrow all that came before.

As the rebellion took hold, a vast array of power-hungry groups were now pursuing the jobs previously occupied by the now dehumanized White bigots. These collectives wanted a potent hammer to break the illicit glass ceiling. Anything that could obstruct their progress had to dissolve, and the demand for reparations hastened the process. Equal opportunity was not enough. They needed *affirmative action* to quell their grievances and make up for past wrongs and lost time.

Those longing for power highlighted the ways incumbents blocked their opportunities, while there was an absence of introspection that might identify ways to collaborate. More energy was expended, pointing out cheating, unfairness, brutality, and attempts to discriminate and exclude. External blame was preferable to self-examination, and they feverishly speculated about the criminal behaviors of their foes. They hoped that their schemes would increase abhorrence against the entrenched, and it worked better than expected.

Claims of being oppressed by the adversaries "immoral actions" became the cynosure means to obtain the social authority they desired. Spotlighting the illegitimacies and wrongdoings of the gammons in power became common methods to yield a rapid overthrow. Whether their misdeeds were negligible or extreme, all incumbents remained under the microscope. As long as misbehavior could be inferred, an exaggerated storm was unleashed to produce the desired effects of detestation and contempt. It was not that the opposition had different ideas; they were racists, coldhearted, and evil.

To maintain their riotous energy, they made sure never to forgive and never to resolve their complaints. Since the enemy might spring back in at a moment's notice, it was necessary to hold them down with these strategies and not relent. There was no bargaining, buyout, or apology acceptance; there had to be annihilation. To their delight, all of these tactics produced a bounty, as their devious character assassinations resulted in catapulting rebels into the positions of choice and authority before the old names could be scraped from the office doors.

With their loud voices, change flashed before everyone's eyes. The oppressed multitude coasted with the tsunami, and those without a rebel uniform went to lands unknown. Parochial beliefs had no place in this new world; the Overton window was only wide enough for rebel compliance to sneak through its opening.

The insurgents robotically controlled the new status quo. Vivid allegiance to the newfound order appeared in all "scientific" communications, which no one dared to depict as propaganda. Images showered adulation on their brethren, and depicted them as good-natured, competent, and likable chaps. They laughed at the benighted who were rubes, Neanderthals, and easily manipulated dolts.

Giant businesses promoting these ads did not want blowback for not being onboard. The largest companies were particularly interested in retaining their dominance, and playing ball with the new lawmakers was their only option. Only then would regulators favor their existence and squelch the others. At the snap of a finger, the strategy worked, as they took their place within the new structures of power.

Curiously, they were unconcerned about the long-term effects on their freedoms that had made them rich in the first place. Instead, those grifters among them cleverly stoked *online* resentments and redirected the populace from despising their opulence, to hating the conservatives who were unequivocally at fault. With the global stage in their sights, they pandered to the foreign elites, in tandem with their newly crowned leaders, and the machine never shut down.

Since their employees were unabashed "woke" college grads, there was additional pressure for them to promulgate equity ideals. Who would stay in their employment without that adherence? Workers were simpatico with the new social craze, and like obsessed suitors, they quested for their imagined society without identity harm. They now had the power to dictate the game, and they dispassionately gazed, while those clinging to traditional values watched their world collapse around them.

The tyrannis group contained three distinct factions. One flank included individuals experiencing relative safety and comfort throughout their lives. Their desires were gratified frequently by parental and societal accommodations. They wanted to continue their favored status, and an endowed government could be an idealized form of their effete elders, who never fully closed the oppression loopholes in society.

By becoming allies with the downtrodden, they justified their actions as morally superior to those who came before, and retained their privileged status by occupying positions in the mushrooming bureaucracies that would distribute equity fairness. They worked incessantly to create a world that blended with their fantasies, and their righteous banner let everyone know that they were *saving* lives.

A second bloc included individuals from a wide array of special interest groups. These distantly attached comrades were housing a hefty arsenal of endured privations, external harms, and frequent barring. Since their suffering was caused by the oppression of others, their remedy was the same—change the world and demand that the orthodox believers gift them a state of happiness.

Anyone not yielding to this proclamation would have their treasures forcefully removed. They had grown tired of the meager government entitlements, and they wanted more. Together, with the coddled, they proclaimed that the world *should* change to fill their needs, and a *cradle-to-grave* mentality accelerated with both blocs on deck.

Branching off, there was a third gathering that had special charm and charisma. These individuals, with self-endowed powers of intellect and prowess, advanced the idea that they had the knowledge and skill to release the well-being that the other two factions desired. They could shepherd everyone to the promised land of *identity actualization*, and expel all the confronted obstacles and impediments that would likely be encountered.

They were the gifted experts, visionaries, and idols who knew the *best* ways to direct others to produce the ideal of true *equity*; it was certainly wise to trust them, at all costs. They would annex exactly what the masses wanted, and unlike previous leaders, who only promoted their own egotistical desires, they would function as selfless deity incarnates. Within the traditions of sainthood and Jesus Christ, they would be the surrogate decision-makers who could make the world benign.

With great promise, the rebellion was in gear. Everyone looking to tear it all down for the *gift of enhancement,* and removal of what spoils, jumped on the train. Through millenarianism, believers in the status quo would vanish, and without the *bad*, there would only be the *good*.

The Protector's Prediction

Once the resurgence gained the upper hand, the linguistically persuasive moral pioneers drifted into the crowd. Their mission was accomplished, and their leadership was no longer a necessity. They were invaluable before, as only they could show the uniformed how life could be exemplary. But identity freedom was full sail ahead, and they could retreat without concern.

All along, the populace had the resources and inner strength to sublate a halcyon existence. The top-down control that some anticipated and feared was not what came to fruition. The expert class was important in the transition, but now *the people* were able to manage themselves. Yes, the specialists still existed, but they gave their recommendations only when requested.

The removal of the prim and proper released the unfettered drive of the populace that had been mercilessly restrained. The old strictures were abolished, and a tapestry of enlightenment surrounded everyone who had fallen prey to the false nobility. Those who had gained power through the deviousness of racism, and the oppression of identity variations, were no longer seen. Now, with those voices silenced, people could be true to themselves. They could finally be free.

The populace gained credentials at lightning speed. Proficiencies spread throughout the land, as the minted wisdom of the expert class was indelible, and it inked into their veins. The selfish were extirpated, and talent was liberated like never before. With the advent of self-actualization, and with the even spread of opportunity, no one fretted. Self-expression was not feared, nor was it controlled. And since hate was no longer experienced, hate was no longer expressed. The purity of humanity was no longer a mirage.

The righteous could now fulfill their capabilities and desires. No one would have the power to stop them, and there was no necessity for anyone to be in charge. Deference to what people initiated and enjoyed came naturally. Awareness of what others needed, and the unleashing of dormant aptitude, resulted in people bequeathing maximum productivity to their surroundings. The societal arrangement was the bacchanal of everyone's dreams.

With the removal of obstacles, full throttle was in force. A heightened commitment transfixed the group, and achievement propelled faster than ever before. Everyone had honor, and there was no one below. Yes, some excelled, but all attempts to achieve had the same value and admiration. Entertainers, architects, managers, inventors, and creators had no special standing. There were no proletariats, because everyone was a bourgeoisie.

If someone lagged or failed to contribute, people did not suspect wrongdoing. They assumed positive intent, and they knew that the problem must be *externally* caused. The blessed commandment was *from each according to his ability to each according to his needs*, and the echo of that unwavering gospel reverberated and soothed all distress. They held that mandate close to their heart, as it taught them to see goodness in everyone's souls.

From a bird's eye view, it was obvious that everyone was valued. Rarely did people hesitate when struggles were apparent. If someone asked, people assumed that it was for a worthy cause. With Quaker-like ease, whoever could discharge a need was quick to volunteer, while others eagerly waited for their turn to assist. And no one missed a beat.

All along, the culprit to economic well-being was the bane of private property, which presumed human negativity and the necessity to self-protect. But without that fear, everything was fine. Energy could be directed toward helping rather than armoring and blockade, and theft became a forgotten sin. People could finally relax and enjoy their affinities. They took care of others, so others took care of them. The elimination of criminality, intrusiveness, or insatiability meant that altruism had no downside, and narcissism no benefit.

They developed a heightened pleasure for gifting. Exchange of goods and services flowed between people without the necessity to count. Money was without utility except in special circumstances to deal with outsiders. The aroused family atmosphere soothed those who drank from the vessel, and everyone eagerly pledged to the hallowed fraternity.

It was at this point that borders were no longer necessary, as the love for humanity allowed everyone to enter. Assimilation was only a matter of getting the multiplicities immersed in the fervor of the times, and they knew that this goal would occur without a hitch. Those who entered would quickly join in, and their contributions would become a welcomed relief rather than a burden to drag.

They marched with the emblem, "*No police necessary in this Garden of Eden,*" and they realized that they no longer needed a God. They had accomplished the unfettering of every race and identity, light-years before anyone had expected. With awe in their eyes, the statues of Rousseau, Godwin, and Foucault stood majestically in the newly constructed courtyards for everyone to see.

The Forecast of the Promoters

Beneath it all, the new social order contained a mélange of bedfellows. They conjoined based on their quest to supplant authority, while their significant differences lingered in the shadows. The proverb, "The enemy of my enemy is my friend," said it quite well. Everything was fine as long as they were fighting the same dragon.

The rebels were content for a short period of time, and lived comfortably on the confiscated bounties from war. They created a society for the *benefit* of people, but they acquired their wealth at the *expense* of others. When the dust settled, and other people's money ran out, they slowly noticed their disparities and the lack of fuel to keep them in a comfortable state. But they had vanquished their oppressors, and they could not blame their demise on them anymore.

Once the formally weak gained control and removed those in authority, the defiant klatch now had to deal with their repressed differences and personal struggles. Without the distraction of a common enemy, there was a veiled haze exposing unwanted diversities of preferences, needs, and ideas. To their regret, the goal of maximum equity was better for some, but not for others. Infighting seeped into the novel social fabric, and some resented the new harnessing imposed upon them, just like the days of old.

Lying dormant was a growing contingent who did not agree with the proclamations of fairness exuding from the surrogate decision-makers. Since each person had a particular circumstance, blanket verdicts from afar did not always solve their problems. They thought social justice would be easy, but what did it actually mean when righteousness would come from a band of ruling elites who could not see the fine details of the problems at hand. Numerous people were experiencing substantial harm in the quest for their imagined equity ideal, and that moment of anagnorisis was chilling.

Adding to their discomfort, obsessions with equal results spoiled and infantilized the bunch. Everything had to be level, or someone would feel cheated and devoured in harm. Now, everyone had to receive a trophy, even if they did not try. While past generations required people to earn their well-being, now it was someone else who had to quell their complaints. But soon, the numbers of providers dwindled, as everyone wanted to be on the receiving side.

Contrary to predictions, the new societal arrangement created insatiability and resentment. Instead of satisfaction, there was relentless counting and comparing. In their desire to be equal, they liked each other less. After all, who would be grateful in a *garden of victimhood,* which feeds complaints even when mouths are full?

Rather than appreciate their gifts, they attended to what was missing, and defiled whoever blocked their wishes. They were entitled, and the *experts* told them that they would get their way. They clamored for privilege without responsibility, while those in charge hesitated to say no in order to evade imposing the horrors of exclusion.

Unfortunately, the only way out of this cauldron of grievance was for the "anointed" to increase coercion and force the displeased to work and show some inner strength. Now the sophisticates *had* to be mean-spirited, just like the authorities of old, to keep the boat afloat. While the populous tried to circumvent those efforts in a game of cat and mouse, the threat of starvation got them to comply.

It was then that a new rebellion began to sprout. However, this time they did not have the freedom or the resources to do anything about their dissatisfactions. They had given away their authority to those who knew best. Their bitterness became their only skill, and now they had to wait for permission to talk. They were hoist by their own petard, as their obsession to control the bad had led them to trade one oppressor for another.

A few were safe because they advanced the cause, but some went adrift to the digital gulag to prevent contamination of ideas. Since freedom of speech had long passed away, censorship reigned supreme to keep the line perfect. Now they were the ones smitten by the diversity and inclusion police, who they had so unabashedly supported prior to the war.

In this panopticon, any deviation from their newly stitched straight jacket would result in a loss of *social credit.* There would be an inability to access nourishment to survive, and they would be restricted from their pleasure-inducing substances if they dared to disagree. In their quest for diversity, they all had to be the same.

After all, the "experts knew best," and this motto was the ongoing tocsin in everyone's ears. The process made government comparable to a contingent of demigods, and any questioning or dissent was heretical. However, this reaction was not surprising, as it was conspicuous during the college years of many of the rebels, and in their places of employment.

Rarely did they have permission or encouragement to object to the raves and rants of their professors or human resource executives. In those days, questioning students or employees would suffer ridicule and expulsion. They would be defamed as bigots and spoilers of those spaces that were safe. They did not realize it, but they were learning obedience while criticizing the oppressive status quo that was stifling them.

They should have known better. Those same experts never voluntarily gave up their governmental positions, nor did they step down from their university sinecures for new scholars to have a seat. Why would they do it now? The leaders justified their standing by appealing to their esteemed knowledge that no one else could duplicate. It was ironic that the rebels were now required to endorse a meritocracy.

In this social caravel, all rising heads were pushed back with a mallet that just a few could wield. Only the foolish would dare to fight back against the veritable *Almighty*, and voices of dissention had to remain veiled and disguised, much like those who they conquered just a short time ago. They had rid themselves of the old White men, and now the people in charge had varied colors, but they did not feel any freer.

The experts had to be revered, and they flaunted and promoted their views as if they were reading from parchment scrolls. They inculcated the youth with their propaganda and "miraculous" thoughts, and now that was all the underlings knew, all they could say, and all they could understand. While the populace thought they were "progressive," the sad fact was that they were becoming progressively weaker, as the homogenizing churned the diversity away.

Constitutes would only know what they were permitted to know, and the ruling class had no culpability. They could not be wrong or held accountable, and they did not have to show how they had made life better. They simply announced that the struggle would have been worse without their command, blamed the underlings, and demanded more money and time rather than give up control. But since there were no alternatives, the subjects had to comply.

Yes, the servile could vote to change their plight, but that was not as easy as it sounded. Those in power protected each other like vigilant stone-faced praetorian guards. They controlled the election process, and all the "data" that was available to see. There were hundreds of channels, but there was only one show to watch.

The elites protested the "greedy capitalists," but they never used that thermometer to gauge their own voracity. While the masses below recycled their trash, gave up their guns, stayed in public schools, stood in line, and lived in cities without sanitation or safety, the ruling cleric-like sorts, and those sodden in charisma, traveled in jets, secured themselves with armament, and lived free of debris in their untouched estates. They declared that they needed protection and manicure, as only they could conjure the *magic of true equity*.

They had much work to do, as their sought-after result of "sameness" required constant monitoring, slicing, and dicing. Social justice was truly an enormous task. They had to push a little here and tug a little there to keep the picture perfect and fair. They were determined to make outcomes conform to their ideology. No matter the downside, if their calculations said it was equal, it was good.

Circumstances were quite regrettable, as those involved with the rebellion never wanted to be under the aegis of headstrong sources that could keep them confined. But the overarching bureaucratic umbrella only imparted fragility and a diminishment of competence. Feebleness and dependency infiltrated their collective, as the government rationed health care and access to anything else they might need. To achieve equal self-acceptance, they had to be enslaved. Yes, they could applaud and thank those doing the caretaking, but now that was all they *could* do, as their safety depended on keeping the umbilical cord between them flawless and intact.

The masses were totally reliant and unable to release their bonds, as their maître d' had metamorphosed into a warden. They were living in a *Brave New World*, with pleasures granted from those above. They were mascots, not players. And even if they wanted to leave their newfound home, it was perfectly clear that they could not. Their licensed cell phones had limited reception, and their medications were only available when they *earned* access to the pharmacy store. Their road to serfdom had reached its end. True equity was finally achieved, but they had to give up their personhood in the process.

The rebels advocated for central control to overtake the supremacists, but they did not foresee what would happen when they gave them the vestiges of private ownership they had possessed. While capitalistic societies allow many preferences to make its mechanisms tic, the newly born chieftains maintained all the artillery, and it was bolted to their thrones. The insurgents fought hard to create a dense core of power that would take them to the Promised Land, but there was now an iron fist pointed solely at them.

The goal was for everyone to *own* the means of production, but who had the reins? Preferences and options were still alive and well, but who had those freedoms? Only the Illuminati could be the maestros on stage. They were the overseers with plans galore, who provided the blueprints for the robots to follow. Their subjects could say that they owned the factory and everything else, but that was just on paper.

When standing back and looking from afar, "the people" had ownership of everything, with little chance to make a voluntary exchange, while the experts owned nothing except their right to dictate. In this New World Order, as long as their initiatives remained trapped in the elites' meticulously soldered cage, "the people" could be proprietors and free as birds to fly in that space. Often in jest, they called themselves "the owner puppets," but seldom did anyone laugh.

The hope was for some knowledgeable souls to come forward and expose the preposterous charade, but only experts who followed the party line qualified for admission into the citadel. Apostates offering nonconforming views were mercilessly denigrated and expunged. Unorthodox opinions, which might lead to meaningful changes, were rare indeed, while "science deniers" unceremoniously disappeared.

The new social order was in reality *a fait accompli democracy* run by equity-minded characters who tolerated only their disciples, sycophants, and those who agreed. They held all the cards and all the licenses to promulgate ideas; the system rose and fell in relation to their limited potencies and Achilles's heels. Vigor that often occurs from disagreement, power balance, and questioning was no longer available to steer the ship straight, and when the conductors were wrong, there was a flood that left everyone in its wake.

The group was edging closer to extinction. Productivity was vanishing, and as the older group members who knew how to contribute passed away, there was a scarcity of replacements. Since the government could only *give* as long as there was something to *take*, funds were running out quickly. Over time, with fewer people making donations that might feed the government goose, eggs were becoming harder to find. While the battle cry was that no one should feel deprived, many wondered who was left to fill those desires.

Those examining from afar might wonder if the populace simply traded one tormenter for another, and signed up for a program of self-diminishment rather than self-enhancement. The quest began with the hope of forging self-expression and an opportunity to excel. It was a pursuit to protect the castaways and the economically muted. But where did it go?

Disappointingly, without the power to forge their own lives, what power did they gain, and what self-actualization did they advance? They needed a fresh start, and they naively convinced themselves that *this time* they could get it right. They knew a new rebellion would eventually take place. It always does, as those below invariably fight for more. However, that possibility seemed distant, and it was probably beyond the purview of their lives.

POSTSCRIPT

Years later, many wondered why so many people were eager to give up their previous *liberties* and *rights* during the *Identity Rebellion*. While many insisted that they never had those freedoms, others claimed that those individuals could not bear the thought that they were contributing to their problems. It was then that a wise old person chimed in, "I think that was exactly what they were fighting about."

ABOUT THE AUTHOR

Craig B. Wiener is a licensed Clinical Psychologist based in Worcester, Massachusetts. He obtained his doctoral degree from Clark University in 1979. In addition to over forty years of private practice, he is an Assistant Professor in the Department of Family Medicine and Community Health at the University of Massachusetts Medical School. For over two decades, he was the Clinical Director of Mental Health Services at a community health center where he supervised a large staff of clinicians and graduate students.

Craig is the author of three books on Attention Deficit Hyperactivity Disorder, and he has presented his work at national and state conventions for Psychologists.

This current book, *Backyard Politics: Today's Divide and a Parenting Style to Bring Us Together* is a culmination of the author's clinical experience, which has helped him gain insight into the ways in which people resolve their difficulties.

Connect with and follow Craig:
www.craigwiener.com
Twitter: @CraigWiener4
Facebook: cbwiener
Instagram: craigwiener
Snapchat: craigwiener2021
Goodreads: Craig Wiener

REFERENCES

Academy of Achievement, "Milton Friedman, Academy Class of 1971, Full Interview," YouTube, February 9, 2017, www.youtube.com/watch?v=ujxLJx223-Y&t=2120s. Accessed March 3, 2021.

Alpha News, Heather Mac Donald: The Truth About Crime, Race, and Policing in America," YouTube, August 2, 2020, www.youtube.com/watch?v=l_daDil2M_c. Accessed April 10, 2021.

Amato, Paul R., and Frieda Fowler. "Parenting Practices, Child Adjustment, and Family Diversity." *Journal of Marriage and Family*, vol. 64, no. 3, pp. 703–716. August 2002. 10.1111/j.1741-3737.2002.00703.x.

Anderson, Ryan T. *When Harry Became Sally: Responding to the Transgender Moment.* New York and London: Encounter Books, 2018.

Applebaum, Barbara. *Being White, Being Good: White Complicity, White Moral Responsibility, and Social Justice Pedagogy.* Lanham, Maryland: Lexington Books, 2011.

"Thomas Sowell and Roger Ailes," YouTube, May 31, 2019, www.youtube.com/watch?v=k_2_J_X6Bqw. Accessed April 10, 2021.

Arcidiacono, Peter, et al. "What Happens after Enrollment? An Analysis of the Time Path of Racial Differences in GPA and Major Choice." *IZA Journal of Labor Economics*, vol. 1, no. 1, p. 5. 2012, public.econ.duke.edu/~psarcidi/grades_4.0.pdf, 10.1186/2193-8997-1-5. Accessed October 15, 2019.

Bailey, Motte, "Jordan Peterson Explains Why Males Are Increasingly Retreating into Videogames w/ Warren Farrell," YouTube, March 18, 2018, www.youtube.com/watch?v=ZBBPyCSJDE0&t=928s. Accessed March 29, 2021.

Ball, James, et al. "Race Variation in Jail Sentences, Study Suggests." *The Guardian*, November 26, 2011, www.theguardian.com/law/2011/nov/25/ethnic-variations-jail-sentences-study.

BasicEconomics. "Firing Line—Thomas Sowell w/ William F. Buckley Jr. (1981)." YouTube, May 25, 2012, www.youtube.com/watch?v=Yo21WAdUlW8&t=1194s. Accessed February 13, 2021.

"Milton Friedman @ 93 vs. the 'Anointed Rose' 2005 Interview on China, Inflation, the Federal Reserve," YouTube, July 21, 2021, www.youtube.com/watch?v=lzoBPst7DOE. Accessed 25 July 2021.

"Thomas Sowell—The Ethnic Flaw, 1984 1/2." YouTube, June 9, 2012, www.youtube.com/watch?v=lxH1pCZi4jw&t=604s. Accessed 5 Feb. 2021.

Big Think, "How Pharmaceutical Companies Game the Patent System | Tahir Amin | Big Think," YouTube, January 20, 2019, www.youtube.com/watch?v=5d6RT4lnlKQ&t=20s. Accessed September 19, 2020.

Bloggingheads.TV. "Discrimination at Harvard? | Glenn Loury & Peter Arcidiacono [The Glenn Show]." YouTube, September 10, 2020, www.youtube.com/watch?v=dnar1utivgk.

Bolotnyy, Valentin, et al. *Why Do Women Earn Less Than Men? Evidence from Bus and Train Operators.* 2018.

Boyce, Benjamin A. "How Critical Race Theory Is Wrong | with James Lindsay." YouTube, October 5, 2020, www.youtube.com/watch?v=6rWboyMld5l&t=5966s. Accessed December 5, 2020.

BrainyQuote, 2020, www.brainyquote.com/quotes/plato_162795.

Bränström, R, and J E Pachankis. "Reduction in Mental Health Treatment Utilization Among Transgender Individuals after Gender-Affirming Surgeries: A Total Population Study." *European Journal of Public Health*, vol. 29, no. 4. November 1, 2019, 10.1093/eurpub/ckz185.465. Accessed February 7, 2020.

brittle13. "Responsibility to the Poor," YouTube, July 20, 2009, www.youtube.com/watch?v=Rls8H6MktrA. Accessed January 11, 2020.

Brodkin, Karen. *How Jews Became White Folks: And What That Says about Race in America*. New Brunswick, NJ and London: Rutgers University Press, 2010.

Brooks, Arthur C. *Who Really Cares: The Surprising Truth about Compassionate Conservatism: America's Charity Divide—Who Gives, Who Doesn't, and Why It Matters*. New York: Basic Books, 2007.

Buckley Jr., W.F. "Amy Wax on 'What Is Happening to the Family, and Why?'" YouTube, October 26, 2017, www.youtube.com/watch?v=t-r7D7OtkgY. Accessed March 7, 2021.

"Firing Line with William F. Buckley Jr.: The Economic Crisis," YouTube, January 25, 2017, www.youtube.com/watch?v=Cjj-fCKGdts. Accessed February 18, 2021.

Darrel Burnette ll, "Student Outcomes: Does More Money Really Matter?—Education Week." Quality Counts, June 5, 2019, www.edweek.org/ew/articles/2019/06/05/student-outcomes-does-more-money-really-matter.html.

Centola, Damon. "The 25 Percent Tipping Point for Social Change | Psychology Today." *Psychology Today*, May 28, 2019, www.psychologytoday.com/us/blog/how-behavior-spreads/201905/the-25-percent-tipping-point-social-change. Accessed May 31, 2021.

Chalberg, John. "Prohibition and Women's Suffrage: A 100-Year Review." American Experiment, October 11, 2019, www.americanexperiment.org/2019/10/prohibition-and-womens-suffrage-a-100-year-review/. Accessed March 2, 2021.

"Charter Schools: Research and Report," National Conference of State Legislatures, www.ncsl.org/research/education/charter-schools-research-and-report.aspx. Accessed September 26, 2020.

Lauren Chen, "The Truth About White Privilege! | Debunking Racial Oppression," YouTube, March 8, 2018, www.youtube.com/watch?v=dlitKZhVr6g. Accessed September 23, 2020.

Churchill, Owen. "Yale Discriminates against Asian and White Applicants, US Justice Department Says." *South China Morning Post*, August 14, 2020, www.scmp.com/news/world/united-states-canada/article/3097311/yale-discriminates-against-asians-whites-its. Accessed August 29, 2020.

Condra, Elizabeth. "Over 50% of Liberal, White Women under 30 Have a Mental Health Issue. Are We Worried Yet?" *Evie Magazine*, April 15, 2021, www.eviemagazine.com/post/over-50-percent-white-liberal-women-under-30-mental-health-condition. Accessed April 23, 2021.

Cooper, Brittney C. *Eloquent Rage: A Black Feminist Discovers Her Superpower*. New York: Picador, 2019.

Crenshaw, Kimberlé. *On Intersectionality: Essential Writings*. New York: New Press, 2019.

"Critical Race Theory—Key Elements," LiquiSearch, www.liquisearch.com/critical_race_theory/key_elements. Accessed September 15, 2020.

Data Driven Conclusions, "Debunking White Privilege & Addressing Income Disparities in the U.S.," YouTube, September 13, 2020, www.youtube.com/watch?v=ODPcG_JNuqk. Accessed September 15, 2020.

"Pushing Back on the Narrative of Modern Systemic Racism & White Privilege by Casey Petersen." YouTube, August 25, 2020, www.youtube.com/watch?v=zyNW9nlFDBk&t=2573s. Accessed September 16, 2020.

Davidson, Jordan. "Smithsonian Pushes Racist Material Claiming, 'White Culture' Is 'Nuclear Family,' 'Self-Reliance,' Being 'Polite.'" *The Federalist*, July 15, 2020, thefederalist.com/2020/07/15/smithsonian-pushes-racist-material-claiming-white-culture-is-nuclear-family-self-reliance-being-polite/. Accessed February 21, 2021.

Dawkins, Richard. *The Blind Watchmaker: Why the Evidence of Evolution Reveals a Universe Without Design*. New York: W.W. Norton & Company, 2015.

Deary, Ian J. "The Stability of Intelligence From Childhood to Old Age." *Current Directions in Psychological Science*, vol. 23, no. 4, pp. 239–245. Aug. 2014. 10.1177/0963721414536905. Accessed August 29, 2020.

Merriam-Webster Dictionary, 2009, www.merriam-webster.com/dictionary/alt-right.

"Demographic Differences in Sentencing," United States Sentencing Commission, January 24, 2018, www.ussc.gov/research/research-reports/demographic-differences-sentencing.

DiAngelo, Robin J. *White Fragility: Why It's so Hard for White People to Talk about Racism*. Boston: Beacon Press, 2018.

Dishion, T. J., McCord, J., & Poulin, F. "When Interventions Harm." *American Psychologist,* vol. 54, no. 9 (1999): 755–64. 1999BC.

Downey Jr., Ken. "Preteens Experience 'Concerning' Level of Cyberbullying, Survey Finds." Healio, October 13, 2020, www.healio.com/news/primary-care/20201013/preteens-experience-concerning-level-of-cyberbullying-survey-finds?ecp%20=%20c3b42206-1c47-4982-a5dd-e161197dc009&M_BT=1841095321370. Accessed October 14, 2020.

Draganski, Bogdan, et al. "Changes in Grey Matter Induced by Training." *Nature*, vol. 427, no. 6972, pp. 311–312. January 2004, www.nature.com/articles/427311a, 10.1038/427311a. Accessed September 22, 2019.

Dinesh D'Souza, "The End of History," *Dinesh D'Souza Podcast,* ep. 119, YouTube, June 25, 2021, https://www.youtube.com/watch?v=dgnzGBa7NMI.

Dunkel, Curtis S., et al. "Polygenic Scores Mediate the Jewish Phenotypic Advantage in Educational Attainment and Cognitive Ability Compared with Catholics and Lutherans." *Evolutionary Behavioral Sciences*, vol. 13, no. 4, pp. 366–375. Oct. 2019. 10.1037/ebs0000158. Accessed March 15, 2021.

Eberstadt, Mary. *Primal Screams: How the Sexual Revolution Created Identity Politics*. West Conshohocken, PA: Templeton Press, 2021.

Economics in the Media, "Thomas Sowell: Economic vs Political Decision Making Complete," YouTube, June 10, 2015, www.youtube.com/watch?v=9TkKulS-5WQ&t=57s. Accessed February 6, 2021.

Elejalde-Ruiz, Alexia. "Hiring Bias Study: Resumes with Black, White, Hispanic Names Treated the Same," *Chicago Tribune*, May 4, 2016, www.chicagotribune.com/business/ct-bias-hiring-0504-biz-20160503-story.html. Accessed September 16, 2020.

Evans, David. "Rate of Domestic Violence Highest in Lesbian Relationships." The Wentworth Report, January 8, 2017, wentworthreport.com/2017/01/08/rate-of-domestic-violence-highest-in-lesbian-relationships/. Accessed February 28, 2021.

Will Flanders and Natalie Goodnow, "Feds in the Classroom: The Impact of the Obama Administration's Discipline Policy on Wisconsin's Public Schools," 2017.

Flynn, James R. "Massive IQ Gains in 14 Nations: What IQ Tests Really Measure." *Psychological Bulletin*, vol. 101, no. 2, pp. 171–191. March 1987. 10.1037/0033-2909.101.2.171. Accessed November 18, 2019.

"Searching for Justice: The Discovery of IQ Gains Over Time." *American Psychologist*, vol. 54, no. 1, 1999, pp. 5–20. 10.1037/0003-066x.54.1.5. Accessed October 21, 2019.

The Mean IQ of Americans: Massive Gains, 1932 to 1978." *Psychological Bulletin*, vol. 95, no. 1, 1984, pp. 29–51. 10.1037/0033-2909.95.1.29.

What Is Intelligence?: Beyond the Flynn Effect. Cambridge, UK and New York: Cambridge University Press, 2009.

Foucault, Michel, and Rabinow, Paul. *The Foucault Reader*. New York: Vintage Books, 2010.

Fox Business. "Heather Mac Donald on Race Relations under President Obama." YouTube, August 1, 2016, www.youtube.com/watch?v=ORMwjKxnl2s&t=14s. Accessed October 11, 2020.

Fox News. "Tucker: Did Dorsey Admit Twitter's Role in Capitol Riot?" YouTube, March 26, 2021, www.youtube.com/watch?v=D5NO-noe64w. Accessed Mar 29, 2021.

Frankl, Viktor E, et al. *Man's Search for Meaning*. Boston, Mass.: Beacon Press, 2015.

Frazier, E. Franklin. *Black Bourgeoisie*. New York: Free Press Paperbacks, 1997.

Freedom Speaks, "Ben Shapiro Dismantles Universal Healthcare," YouTube, Mar 19, 2017, www.youtube.com/watch?v=SznOanekygY. Accessed September 19, 2020.

Free To Choose Network, "Milton Friedman Speaks: Equality and Freedom in the Free Enterprise System (B1238)," YouTube, March 21, 2016, www.youtube.com/watch?v=ppGaozklGa4&t=2880s. Accessed February 14, 2021.

"Milton Friedman Speaks: What Is America? (B1225)," YouTube, March 21, 2016, www.youtube.com/watch?v=hoFdVuqrMZw. Accessed January 30, 2021.

"Testing Milton Friedman: Government Control." YouTube, December 30, 2015, www.youtube.com/watch?v=h5txloUG9vM.

"The Power of Choice: The Life and Ideas of Milton Friedman," YouTube, December 30, 2015, www.youtube.com/watch?v=BhfCrm74gGo&t=2815s. Accessed January 28, 2021.

Freud, Sigmund, and Strachey, James. *The Psychopathology of Everyday Life,* vol. 6. New York: Norton, 1965.

Friedman, Milton, and. *A Theory of the Consumption Function.* National Bureau Of Economic Research. Princeton, New Jersey: Martino Publishing, 2015.

Friedman, Milton, and Friedman, Rose D. *Capitalism and Freedom*. University Of Chicago Press. 1982.

Free to Choose. Houghton Mifflin Harcourt, 1990.

Fryer, Roland. "An Empirical Analysis of Racial Differences in Police Use of Force." *Journal of Political Economy*, vol. 127, no. 3, June 2019. law.yale.edu/system/files/area/workshop/leo/leo16_fryer.pdf, 10.1086/701423.

Gaser, Christian, and Gottfried Schlaug. "Brain Structures Differ between Musicians and Non-Musicians." *The Journal of Neuroscience*, vol. 23, no. 27, pp. 9240–9245. October 8, 2003. 10.1523/jneurosci.23-27-09240.2003.

Gibbons, Frederick X., et al. "The Impact of Early Racial Discrimination on Illegal Behavior, Arrest, and Incarceration among African Americans." *American Psychologist*, vol. 75, no. 7, pp. 952–968. October 17, 2020. 10.1037/amp0000533.

Giordano, S. "Lives in a Chiaroscuro. Should We Suspend the Puberty of Children with Gender Identity Disorder?" *Journal of Medical Ethics*, vol. 34, no. 8, pp. 580–584. August 1, 2008. 10.1136/jme.2007.021097. Accessed March 30, 2020.

Goodman, Michael, and Nash, Rebbeca. *Comparative Risks and Benefits of Gender Reassignment Therapies*. February 8, 2019. 10.25302/2.2019.ad.12114532. Accessed August 30, 2020.

Grabar, Mary. *FAKE HISTORY: How Howard Zinn's Lies Turned a Generation Against America*. Regnery Publishing, 2019.

Alexander Grace, "You Won't Believe What These Graphs Reveal About Women!" YouTube, December 10, 2020, www.youtube.com/watch?v=qeYts4AzRUo. Accessed January 10, 2021.

Gramsci, Antonio, et al. *Selections from the Prison Notebooks of Antonio Gramsci*. New York: International Publishers, 2014.

Greenstone, M., Looney, A. "Trends." *The Milken Review*, third quarter, 2011. https://www.brookings.edu/wp-content/uploads/2016/06/07_milken_greenstone_looney.pdf

Groth, A. N. "Sexual Trauma in the Life Histories of Rapists and Child Molesters." *Victimology*. vol. 4, issue 1. pp 10–16. 1979

Guest Editorial. "Blame the Welfare State, Not Racism, for Poor Blacks' Problems: Thomas Sowell." Penn Live, May 7, 2015, www.pennlive.com/opinion/2015/05/poor_blacks_looking_for_someon.html.

Hannah-Jones, Nikole. *The 1619 Project: A New Origin Story*. New York: One World, 2021.

Harvey, Philip D., and Conyers, Lisa. *The Human Cost of Welfare: How the System Hurts the People It's Supposed to Help*. Santa Barbara, California: Praeger, 2016.

Ron Haskins, "Three Simple Rules Poor Teens Should Follow to Join the Middle Class," Brookings, March 13, 2013, www.brookings.edu/opinions/three-simple-rules-poor-teens-should-follow-to-join-the-middle-class/.

Everette Hatcher III, "Milton Friedman and the Proper Functions of Government," *The Daily Hatch*, July 16, 2013, thedailyhatch.org/2013/07/16/milton-friedman-and-the-proper-functions-of-government/.

Hawley, Joshua David. *The Tyranny of Big Tech*. Washington, D.C.: Regnery Publishing, May 4, 2021.

Hayek, Friedrich A. *The Road to Serfdom.* 2015.

Hazlitt, Henry. *Economics in One Lesson : The Shortest & Surest Way to Understand Basic Economics*. New York: Three Rivers Press, 2014.

Heresy Financial, "Dismantling MMT | Book Review (and Thorough Rebuttal) of 'the Deficit Myth'—Modern Monetary Theory," YouTube, www.youtube.com/watch?v=AM7oKOOvZwA&t=1871. Accessed December 13, 2021.

Herrnstein, Richard J, and Murray, Charles A. *The Bell Curve: Intelligence and Class Structure in American Life*. New York: Free Press, 1994.

Hillsdale College, "Big Tech and Political Manipulation | Robert Epstein | CCA II: Big Tech," YouTube, November 10, 2020, www.youtube.com/watch?v=171-U6fY7Ol. Accessed November 11, 2020.

"The War on Poverty: A Report Card—Jason Riley," YouTube, October 22, 2015, www.youtube.com/watch?v=aEolgYSfP44&t=1681s. Accessed September 9, 2020.

Hines, Melissa. "Prenatal Endocrine Influences on Sexual Orientation and on Sexually Differentiated Childhood Behavior." *Frontiers in Neuroendocrinology*, vol. 32, no. 2, pp. 170–182. April 1, 2011, www.ncbi.nlm.nih.gov/pmc/articles/PMC3296090/, 10.1016/j.yfrne.2011.02.006.

Hofstadter, Albert. "Objective Teleology." *The Journal of Philosophy*, vol. 38, no. 2, p. 29. January 16, 1941. 10.2307/2018389. Accessed August 29, 2020.

Hoover Institution, "Discrimination and Disparities with Thomas Sowell," YouTube, May 3, 2018, www.youtube.com/watch?v=U7hmTRT8tb4&t=1643s. Accessed September 19, 2020.

"Heather Mac Donald: Double Standards on Discipline in Education Will Widen the Racial Divide," YouTube, October 11, 2018, www.youtube.com/watch?v=oKSNvkatj5E&t=378s. Accessed October 9, 2020.

"Jason Riley on 'False Black Power?'" YouTube, March 18, 2019, www.youtube.com/watch?v=bi2hqL5KkHc. Accessed September 9, 2020.

"Shelby Steele on 'How America's Past Sins Have Polarized Our Country,'" YouTube, February 8, 2018, www.youtube.com/watch?v=mMpQBWH-RwA&t=898s. Accessed September 7, 2020.

"Thomas Sowell on the Second Edition of Intellectuals and Society," YouTube, May 8, 2012, www.youtube.com/watch?v=JyufeHJlodE&t=1133s. Accessed October 6, 2020.

"Uncommon Knowledge with Thomas Sowell," YouTube, September 16, 2012, www.youtube.com/watch?v=YPEQMJow2ql. Accessed October 4, 2020.

"Wealth, Poverty, and Politics," YouTube, December 8, 2015, www.youtube.com/watch?v=sGYli7DiEwo&t=1555s. Accessed September 7, 2020.

Horowitz, David. *The Enemy Within: How a Totalitarian Movement Is Destroying America.* Washington, D.C.: Regnery Publishing, 2021.

Hruz, W., Mayer, L. S., McHugh, P. R. "Growing Pains: Problems with Puberty Suppression in Treating Gender Dysphoria." *The New Atlantis,* Spring 2017

Hunt, Melissa G., et al. "No More FOMO: Limiting Social Media Decreases Loneliness and Depression." *Journal of Social and Clinical Psychology*, vol. 37, no. 10, pp. 751–768. December 2018. 10.1521/jscp.2018.37.10.751.

Hutchens, Robert M. "Welfare, Remarriage, and Marital Search." *The American Economic Review*, vol. 69, no. 3, pp. 369–379. 1979, www.jstor.org/stable/1807371. Accessed August 29, 2020.

Independent Institute, "Shelby Steele | Is White Guilt Destroying the Promise of Civil Rights?" YouTube, November 25, 2014, www.youtube.com/watch?v=HF3VaJdConY. Accessed September 12, 2020.

Intercollegiate Studies Institute, "Cynical Theories: Living in a Woke World," YouTube, www.youtube.com/watch?v=2WbZLxnkHzg&t=1601s. Accessed December 19, 2020.

James, S. E., Herman, J. L., Rankin, S., Keisling, M., Mottet, L., & Anafi, M. "The Report of the 2015 U.S. Transgender Survey." Washington, DC: National Center for Transgender Equality, 2016.

"John Milton Quotes," BrainyQuote, www.brainyquote.com/quotes/john_milton_110201. Accessed January 10, 2021.

Joseph, Jay. *The Trouble with Twin Studies: A Reassessment of Twin Research in the Social and Behavioral Sciences*. New York: Routledge, Taylor & Francis Group, 2015.

Kang, Sonia K., et al. "Whitened Résumés." *Administrative Science Quarterly*, vol. 61, no. 3, pp. 469–502. July 8, 2016. 10.1177/0001839216639577.

Kendi, Ibram X. *How to Be An Antiracist*. New York: One World, August 13, 2019.

Helena Kerschner, "At What Cost? Trans Healthcare, Manipulated Data, and Self-Appointed Saviors," New Discourses, August 6, 2020, newdiscourses.com/2020/08/trans-healthcare-manipulated-data-self-appointed-saviors/. Accessed December 26, 2020.

Keynes, John Maynard. *A Tract on Monetary Reform*. BN publishing, January 23, 2009.

Koger, Larry. *Black Slaveowners: Free Black Slave Masters in South Carolina 1790–1860*. Jefferson, McFarland, 2012.

Kruta, Virginia. "Poll: Democrats Are More Concerned about Trump Supporters than White Supremacy, Systemic Racism." The Daily Caller, February 24, 2021, dailycaller.com/2021/02/24/poll-echelon-democreats-white-nationalism-supremacy-donald-trump-supporters/. Accessed February 27, 2021.

Larry Elder, "Denzel Washington: The Only Hollywood Star Telling the Truth about Race," YouTube, January 7, 2021, www.youtube.com/watch?v=Dofz9b86Th8.

Lepper, M. R., Greene, D., and Nisbett, R. E. "Undermining Children's Intrinsic Interest with Extrinsic Rewards: A Test of the Over-Justification Hypothesis." *Journal of Personality and Social Psychology* vol. 28 (1973): pp. 139–87.

Learn Liberty, "Economic Freedom by the Numbers," YouTube, October 30, 2017, www.youtube.com/watch?v=Q3EZiPyAVjk. Accessed 13 Sept. 2019.

LibertyPen, "Ayn Rand—Don't Confuse the Two Kinds of Capitalism," YouTube, March 18, 2020, www.youtube.com/watch?v=hKi8v2Vn8Ug. Accessed November 6, 2020.

"Milton Friedman—Solutions to Market Failures," YouTube, October 29, 2010, www.youtube.com/watch?v=BPnJHfiFWJw. Accessed January 24, 2021.

"Milton Friedman—The Robber Baron Myth," YouTube, March 15, 2010, www.youtube.com/watch?v=dmzZ8lCLhlk&t=314s. Accessed March 5, 2021.

Littman, Lisa. "Parent Reports of Adolescents and Young Adults Perceived to Show Signs of a Rapid Onset of Gender Dysphoria." *PLOS ONE*, vol. 13, no. 8, p. e0202330. August 16, 2018. journals.plos.org/plosone/article?id=10.1371/journal.pone.0202330, 10.1371/journal.pone.0202330. Accessed December 11, 2019.

Lukianoff, Greg, and Haidt, Jonathan. *The Coddling of the American Mind: How Good Intentions and Bad Ideas Are Setting up a Generation for Failure*. UK: Penguin Books, 2019.

Mac Donald, Heather. *Diversity Delusion: How Race and Gender Pandering Corrupt the University and Undermine Our Culture*. Griffin, 2019.

The War on Cops: How The New Attack on Law and Order Makes Everyone Less Safe. Encounter Books, September 19, 2017.

Maguire, E. A., et al. "Navigation-Related Structural Change in the Hippocampi of Taxi Drivers." *Proceedings of the National Academy of Sciences*, vol. 97, no. 8, pp. 4398–4403. March 14, 2000, www.ncbi.nlm.nih.gov/pmc/articles/PMC18253/, 10.1073/pnas.070039597.

Makary, Marty M D. *Price We Pay: What Broke American Health Care and How to Fix It*. Bloomsbury Publishing, June 2021.

Manhattan Institute, "Barriers to Black Progress: Structural, Cultural, or Both?" YouTube, February 11, 2019, www.youtube.com/watch?v=rzOApVTfT48&t=2936s. Accessed October 13, 2020.

"Man-in-the-House Rule," The Free Dictionary, legal-dictionary. thefreedictionary.com/Man-in-the-House+Rule. Accessed January 17, 2021.

Daniel Mitchell, "The Historical Lessons of Lower Tax Rates," The Heritage Foundation, 2019, www.heritage.org/taxes/report/ the-historical-lessons-lower-tax-rates.

Model, Suzanne. "The Secret of West Indian Success." *Society*, vol. 45, no. 6, pp. 544–548. September 16, 2008, people.umass.edu/ smodel/Society_45.pdf, 10.1007/s12115-008-9149-6. Accessed 29 Aug. 2020.

Moynihan, Daniel P. *The Negro Family: The Case for National Action*. Office of Policy Planning and Research, U.S. Department of Labor, Washington, DC, 1965.

Murray, Charles A. *Coming Apart: The State of White America, 1960– 2010*. New York: Crown Forum, 2012.

Human Diversity: The Biology of Gender, Race, and Class. New York: Twelve, 2020.

Murray, Douglas. *Madness of Crowds: Gender, Race, and Identity*. Continuum, 2020.

National Charter School Resource Center at Safal Partner. *Student Achievement in Charter Schools: What the Research Shows*. 2015.

"Neuroticism—an Overview | ScienceDirect Topics," Science Direct, www.sciencedirect.com/topics/neuroscience/neuroticism. Accessed September 21, 2020.

New Discourses, "Equity and the Unmaking of UT Austin," YouTube, May 3, 2021, www.youtube.com/ watch?v=pAoxKcENvmg&t=2396s. Accessed May 4, 2021.

"The Truth About Critical Methods | James Lindsay," YouTube, March 19, 2020, www.youtube.com/watch?v=rSHL-rSMlro. Accessed December 12, 2020.

Open Society Foundations, "How Patent Manipulation by Drug Companies Endangers Lives," YouTube, 2020, www.youtube. com/watch?v=pRwfpFqEL24. Accessed March 13, 2020.

"Opposition to Women's Suffrage," Nebraska Studies, www. nebraskastudies.org/en/1900-1924/votes-for-women/ opposition-to-womens-suffrage/. Accessed August 29, 2020.

Leonard Peikoff. "Health Care Is Not A Right," *Capitalism Magazine*," January 23, 1998, www.capitalismmagazine.com/1998/01/ health-care-is-not-a-right/. Accessed September 19, 2020.

Jordan Peterson. "Abigail Shrier," *The Jordan B. Peterson Podcast, season 4, ep. 11*," YouTube, March 22, 2021, www.youtube.com/ watch?v=fSKQfATa-1I&t=2017s. Accessed April 22, 2021.

Piketty, Thomas, and Goldhammer, Arthur. *Capital in the Twenty-First Century*. Cambridge Mass.: The Belknap Press Of Harvard University Press, 2014.

Dan Pink, "The Puzzle of Motivation," TED Talks, July 2009, www. ted.com/talks/dan_pink_the_puzzle_of_motivation.

Plomin, Robert, and von Stumm, Sophie. "The New Genetics of Intelligence." *Nature Reviews Genetics*, vol. 19, no. 3, pp. 148–159. January 8, 2018, www.nature.com/articles/nrg.2017.104, 10.1038/nrg.2017.104. Accessed March 1, 2019.

Pluckrose, Helen, and James Lindsay. *Cynical Theories: How Activist Scholarship Made Everything about Race, Gender, and Identity—and Why This Harms Everybody*. Durham, NC: Pitchstone Publishing, 2020.

Ponseti, Jorge, et al. "Original Research—Anatomy/Physiology: Assessment of Sexual Orientation Using the Hemodynamic Brain Response to Visual Sexual Stimuli." *The Journal of Sexual Medicine*, vol. 6, no. 6, pp. 1628–1634. June 2009. 10.1111/j.1743-6109.2009.01233.x. Accessed August 28, 2020.

PragerU, "Government Can't Fix Healthcare," YouTube, July 17, 2017, www.youtube.com/watch?v=qBfC1YG9wIs. Accessed September 19, 2020.

"Illegal Immigration: It's about Power," YouTube October 29, 2018, www.youtube.com/watch?v=qUU2iWxrH2M. Accessed February 7, 2020.

"Is Capitalism Moral?" YouTube, September 14, 2015, www.youtube.
com/watch?v=fJr2RO7g7jl. Accessed November 13, 2019.

"JFK: Democrat or Republican?" YouTube, June 26, 2017, www.
youtube.com/watch?v=H-Qg_4zqpDl. Accessed August 28,
2020.

"Myths, Lies, and Capitalism," YouTube, January 19, 2015, www.
youtube.com/watch?v=7_7Jv20h9s4&t=195s. Accessed October
14, 2020.

"Should Government Bail Out Big Banks?" YouTube, June 22, 2015,
www.youtube.com/watch?v=GTiWqlkg9es.

The Candace Owens Show, "Carol Swain," YouTube, February
21, 2021, www.youtube.com/watch?v=IF8quaC53ic&t=1379s.
Accessed February21, 2021.

"The Inconvenient Truth about the Democratic Party," YouTube,
May 22, 2017, www.youtube.com/watch?v=g_a7dQXilCo.
Accessed December 9, 2019.

"The War on Work," YouTube, July 21, 2014, www.youtube.com/
watch?v=1nNiHqAps4Y. Accessed November 12, 2019.

"What Are Your Kids Learning in School?" YouTube, February 22,
2021, www.youtube.com/watch?v=0ycazbeFTcc. Accessed
February 22, 2021.

"What Is Critical Race Theory?" YouTube, April 26, 2021, www.
youtube.com/watch?v=8Zy6DQoRYQw. Accessed April 26,
2021.

"What Is Crony Capitalism?" YouTube, February 22, 2016, www.
youtube.com/watch?v=4DxXHh-p-O4. Accessed November 13,
2019.

"What's Wrong with the 1619 Project?" YouTube, November 30,
2020, www.youtube.com/watch?v=OrqFbyTABmQ. Accessed
May 31, 2021.

"Why Is Healthcare So Expensive?" YouTube, June 23, 2017, www.youtube.com/watch?v=gBxROPwxtwE. Accessed November 22, 2019.

"Preamble," 2020, www.democrats.org/where-we-stand/party-platform/preamble-2/. Accessed October 5, 2020.

Amanda Prestigiacomo, "Yes, Biden's HHS Pick Advocates Puberty Blockers, Medical Transition of Minors," The Daily Wire, February 23, 2021, www.dailywire.com/news/yes-bidens-hhs-pick-advocates-puberty-blockers-medical-transition-of-minors. Accessed February 27, 2021.

Program on Constitutional Government at Harvard, "Heather Mac Donald on the Diversity Delusion," YouTube, December 21, 2018, www.youtube.com/watch?v=io9818pkxw8&t=4230s. Accessed January 31, 2021.

Ramaswamy, Vivek. *Woke, Inc.: Inside Corporate America's Social Justice Scam*. New York: Center Street, August 17, 2021.

Ramsden, Sue, et al. "Addendum: Verbal and Non-Verbal Intelligence Changes in the Teenage Brain." *Nature*, vol. 485, no. 7400, pp. 666–666. May 2012. 10.1038/nature11113.

Rawls, J. *A Theory of Justice.* The Belknap Press Of Harvard University Press, 1999.

Luis Razo Bravo, "Amy Wax on Pursuing Diversity in the Workplace," YouTube, December 8, 2020, www.youtube.com/watch?v=jUnF62_W9Ck. Accessed March 12, 2021.

Rehavi, M. Marit, and Sonja B. Starr. "Racial Disparity in Federal Criminal Charging and its Sentencing Consequences." *SSRN Electronic Journal*, 2012, 10.2139/ssrn.1985377. Accessed April 11, 2019.

Riley, Jason L. *False Black Power?* Templeton Press, 2017.

Please Stop Helping Us: How Liberals Make it Harder for Blacks to Succeed. New York: Encounter Books, 2016.

Ian Rowe, "The Power of the Two-Parent Home is Not a Myth," The Thomas B. Fordham Institute, January 8, 2020, fordhaminstitute.org/national/commentary/power-two-parent-home-not-myth.

Rubenfeld, Jed, "Privatization, State Action, and Title IX: Do Campus Sexual Assault Hearings Violate Due Process?" *SSRN Electronic Journal*, vol. 96, no. 15. 2016. 10.2139/ssrn.2857153.

Rushton, J. P., & A. R., Jensen. Thirty Years of Research on Race Differences in Cognitive Ability. *Psychology, Public Policy, and Law*, vol. 11, no, 2, pp. 235–294. 2005, https://doi.org/10.1037/1076-8971.11.2.235.

Saint Vincent College, CPET, Amy Wax, "On the Margin: Out of the Mainstream in Liberal Societies," YouTube, April 18, 2019, www.youtube.com/watch?v=lY8Hv8R8Xx4. Accessed March 15, 2021.

Sander, Richard, and Taylor, Stuart. *Mismatch: How Affirmative Action Hurts Students It's Intended to Help, and Why Universities Won't Admit It*. New York: Basic Books, 2012.

Greg Scorzo, Interview with Karen Straughan, pt. 1, Culture on the Offensive, May 4, 2015, www.cultureontheoffensive.com/gender-politics-on-the-offensive-karen-straughan-part-1/.

Scotty, "Free Market Healthcare vs. Universal Health Care—Healthcare Costs in America," YouTube, October 12, 2018, www.youtube.com/watch?v=bGJ_gzRTOGs. Accessed September 19, 2020.

Williams, Stacey L. and Frieze, Irene Hanson. "Patterns of Violent Relationships, Psychological Distress, and Marital Satisfaction in a National Sample of Men and Women." *Sex Roles*, vol. 52, nos. 11/12. June 2005. DOI: 10.1007/s11199-005-4198-4.

Ben Shapiro, "The Authoritarian Left is Out of Control," YouTube, February 23, 2021, www.youtube.com/watch?v=_wnmkrGyeik&t=605s. Accessed March 8, 2021.

Shrier, Abigail. *Irreversible Damage: The Transgender Craze Seducing Our Daughters*. Washington, DC: Regnery Publishing, 2020.

Simons, Ronald L., et al. "Social Environment, Genes, and Aggression." *American Sociological Review*, vol. 76, no. 6, pp. 883–912. Dec. 2011. 10.1177/0003122411427580. Accessed October 21, 2020.

Skinner, B. F. *About Behaviorism*. New York: Vintage Books, 1976.

Soh, Debra. *The End of Gender: Debunking the Myths about Sex and Identity in Our Society*. New York: Threshold Editions, 2020.

John Stossel, "Abolish the FDA?" YouTube, www.youtube.com/watch?v=Kyg9liQE5nU. Accessed December 15, 2021.

Sowell, Thomas. *A Conflict of Visions: Ideological Origins of Political Struggles*. New York: Basic Books, 2007.

Affirmative Action Around the World: An Empirical Study. New Haven, Conn. and London: Yale University Press, 2005.

Applied Economics: Thinking Beyond Stage One. Basic Books, 2008.

Basic Economics. New York: Basic Books, 2015.

Black Rednecks and White Liberals. New York: Encounter Books, 2006.

Charter Schools and Their Enemies. New York: Basic Books, 2020.

Discrimination and Disparities. New York: Basic Books, March 2019.

Economic Facts and Fallacies. New York: Basic Books, 2011.

Intellectuals and Race. New York: Basic Books, 2013.

Intellectuals and Society. New York: Basic Books, 2012.

Knowledge and Decisions. New York: Basic Books, 1996.

Race and Culture: A World View. New York: Basic Books, 1994.

The Vision of the Anointed : Self-Congratulation as a Basis for Social Policy. New York, Basic Books, 1995.

"Thomas Sowell on Black History MYTHS Promoted by the Left," YouTube, February 7, 2021, www.youtube.com/watch?v=CDltQlrU5nE. Accessed February 10, 2021.

"Thomas Sowell, "The Education of Minority Children," 2019, www.tsowell.com/speducat.html. Accessed December 16, 2019.

Wealth, Poverty and Politics. The Perseus Books Group, 2016.

Steele, Shelby, *White Guilt: How Blacks and Whites Together Destroyed the Promise of the Civil Rights Era.* New York: HarperCollins Publishers, 2006.

Steensma, Thomas D., et al. "Factors Associated With Desistence and Persistence of Childhood Gender Dysphoria: A Quantitative Follow-Up Study." *Journal of the American Academy of Child & Adolescent Psychiatry*, vol. 52, no. 6, pp. 582–590. June 2013, www.transgendertrend.com/wp-content/uploads/2017/10/Steensma-2013_desistance-rates.pdf, 10.1016/j.jaac.2013.03.016. Accessed August 28, 2019.

Stefancic, Jean, and Delgado, Richard. *Critical Race Theory: An Introduction.* New York University Press, 2017.

Patrick Steinkuhl, "Chomsky vs. Buckley," YouTube, February 10, 2006, www.youtube.com/watch?v=Dt-GUAxmxdk&t=329s. Accessed September 16,. 2020.

Karen Straughan, YouTube, www.youtube.com/user/girlwriteswhat/videos. Accessed August 30, 2020.

"Men Not Marrying? How Deep Does 'the Problem' Go?" YouTube, March 12, 2012, www.youtube.com/watch?v=rlvMAS_20K4&t=1252s. Accessed March 22, 2021.

The Sun, "'Woke Utopia,' the End of the West & A New Cult," James Lindsay Interview—BQ #33, YouTube, October 2, 2020, www.youtube.com/watch?v=dE8p-mcFdNg&t=2070s. Accessed January 24, 2021.

"Support the GOP's Principles for American Renewal," GOP, 2020, www.gop.com/principles-for-american-renewal.

Taleb, Nassim Nicholas. *Skin in the Game: Hidden Asymmetries in Daily Life.* New York: RandomHouse, January 7, 2020.

Michael Tanner, "Relationship Between the Welfare State and Crime," Cato Institute, June 7, 1995, www.cato.org/publications/congressional-testimony/relationship-between-welfare-state-crime-0.

Taylor Gatto, John. *Dumbing Us Down: The Hidden Curriculum of Compulsory Schooling.* New Society Publishers, Ltd., 2017.

Taylor, Maureen P., and Bloom, Allan. "The Closing of the American Mind: How Higher Education Has Failed Democracy and Impoverished the Souls of Today's Students." *Michigan Law Review*, vol. 86, no. 6, p. 1135. May 1988. 10.2307/1289159. Accessed June 29, 2019.

Templer, Donald I., and Tangen, Kimberly. "Jewish Population Percentage in the United States: An Index of Opportunity." *Comprehensive Psychology*, vol. 3, p. 17. Jan. 2014. 49.CP.3.8, 10.2466/17.49.cp.3.8.

The Archangle911. "Viciously Powerful Predictor of Long Term Life Success," Jordan Peterson, YouTube, September 11, 2017, www.youtube.com/watch?v=MoqbCto g7Mw.

"The Benefits of Socioeconomically and Racially Integrated Schools and Classrooms." The Century Foundation, April 29, 2019, tcf.org/content/facts/the-benefits-of-socioeconomically-and-racially-integrated-schools-and-classrooms/?agreed=1.

The Federalist Editors, "Here's What Amy Wax Really Said About Immigration," *The Federalist*, July 26, 2019, thefederalist.com/2019/07/26/heres-amy-wax-really-said-immigration/. Accessed August 30, 2020.

The Heritage Foundation, "Shelby Steele—Modern Liberalism and America's Racial Divide," YouTube, November 3, 2017, www.youtube.com/watch?v=UXqBsn94-eA&t=1569s. Accessed September 11, 2020.

"The National Study of Millionaires," Ramsey Solutions Research, January 7, 2019, www.daveramsey.com/research/the-national-study-of-millionaires. Accessed September 16, 2020.

The Rubin Report, "Discrimination and Disparities | Thomas Sowell | POLITICS | Rubin Report," YouTube, April 18, 2018, www.youtube.com/watch?v=5lvf9jrXGAY&t=9s. Accessed February 11, 2021.

"Slavery: The Details They Don't Teach You in School, pt. 3 | Candace Owens | POLITICS | Rubin Report," YouTube, September 18, 2020, www.youtube.com/watch?v=gzoh_39-LVl. Accessed September 18, 2020.

The School of Life, "Political Theory—Adam Smith," YouTube, December 26, 2014,

www.youtube.com/watch?v=ejJRhn53X2M.

The Thomas Sowell Channel, "Thomas Sowell: 'Diversity' Is a Magical Word." YouTube, February 24, 2021, www.youtube.com/watch?v=egKxl1ciMN8. Accessed March 17, 2021.

Triggernometry, "Our Report Found No Evidence of Widespread Institutional Racism," Mercy Muroki, YouTube, April 11, 2021, www.youtube.com/watch?v=AYGfNVtZvzA&t=1563s.

"Benjamin Boyce, "The Rise of Social Justice Is a Wake-Up Call." YouTube, July 22, 2020, www.youtube.com/watch?v=LPkO3Dbb4ac. Accessed January 17, 2021.

Trueman, Carl R., and Dreher, Rod. *The Rise and Triumph of the Modern Self: Cultural Amnesia, Expressive Individualism, and the Road to Sexual Revolution*. Wheaton, Illinois: Crossway, 2020.

"Understanding the Three-Fifths Compromise," Constitutional Accountability Center, 2012, www.theusconstitution.org/news/understanding-the-three-fifths-compromise/.

Andre Van Mol,, et al. "Correction: Transgender Surgery Provides No Mental Health Benefit," Public Discourse, September 13, 2020, www.thepublicdiscourse.com/2020/09/71296/.

Andre Van Mol, "UK Government to Investigate as Rates of Children Requesting Transition Skyrockets by 4,000%," The Bridgehead, September 20, 2018, https://Thebridgehead.ca/2018/09/20/Uk-Government-to-Investigate-as-Rates-of-Children-Requesting-Transition-Skyrockets-by-4000/. Accessed August 25, 2020.

Voltaire. *Candide*. Millenium Publications, 2014.

A. Wax and L. Alexander, "Paying the Price for the Breakdown of the Country's Bourgeois Culture," *The Philadelphia Inquirer*, August 9, 2017.

Wiener, Craig. *Parenting Your Child with ADHD: A No-Nonsense Guide for Nurturing Self-Reliance and Cooperation*. Oakland, CA: New Harbinger Publications, 2012.

Wikipedia Contributors, "Chevrolet Corvair," Wikipedia, December 30, 2018, en.wikipedia.org/wiki/chevroletcorvair.

Wikipedia Contributors, "Neuroticism," Wikipedia, July 29, 2019, en.wikipedia.org/wiki/neuroticism.

Cristan Williams, "Fact Check: Study Shows Transition Makes Trans People Suicidal," TransAdvocate, November 2, 2015, www.transadvocate.com/fact-check-study-shows-transition-makes-trans-people-suicidal_n_15483.htm. Accessed November 13, 2019.

Rob Wipond, "Did the No Child Left Behind Act Boost ADHD Diagnosing?" Mad In America, October 11, 2014, www.madinamerica.com/2014/10/child-left-behind-act-boost-adhd-diagnosing/. Accessed September 22, 2020.

Wolff, Robert P., Moore, Barrington Jr., and Marcuse, Herbert. *"Repressive Tolerance" in a Critique of Pure Tolerance*. Boston: Beacon Press, 1970.

Yglesias, Matthew. *One Billion Americans: The Case for Thinking Bigger*. New York: Portfolio, 2020.

Yu, Qiuping, et al, "Research: When a Higher Minimum Wage Leads
    to Lower Compensation," *Harvard Business Review*, June 10,
    2021, hbr.org/2021/06/research-when-a-higher-minimum-
    wage-leads-to-lower-compensation. Accessed June 11, 2021.

ZeroFox Given, "Thomas Sowell— 3 Questions for the
    Left," YouTube, April 21, 2017, www.youtube.com/
    watch?v=Do6wp9Vydys. Accessed December 26, 2020.

Zinn, Howard. *A People's History of the United States*. New York:
    Harper, 2017.

CPSIA information can be obtained
at www.ICGtesting.com
Printed in the USA
BVHW031438050422
633412BV00003B/418

9 781611 534542